36559520

7/79

D1207158

MANAGING THE SOCIALLY RESPONSIBLE CORPORATION

MANAGING THE SOCIALLY RESPONSIBLE CORPORATION

The 1972–1973 Paul Garrett Lectures

Studies of the Modern Corporation
Columbia University
Graduate School of Business

Edited with Commentaries by

Melvin Anshen

Paul Garrett Professor of Public Policy
and Business Responsibility

The Graduate School of Business
Columbia University

AN ARKVILLE PRESS BOOK

MACMILLAN PUBLISHING CO., INC.
New York

COLLIER MACMILLAN PUBLISHERS
London

Copyright © 1974 by Trustees of Columbia University
in the City of New York

All rights reserved. No part of this book may be reproduced
or transmitted in any form or by any means, electronic or
mechanical, including photocopying, recording, or by any
information storage and retrieval system, without permission
in writing from the Publisher.

Macmillan Publishing Co., Inc.
866 Third Avenue, New York, N.Y. 10022

Collier–Macmillan Canada Ltd.

Library of Congress Catalog Card Number: 73-13364

Printed in the United States of America

printing number
1   2   3   4   5   6   7   8   9   10

110886

Studies of the Modern Corporation

Columbia University Graduate School of Business

The Program for Studies of the Modern Corporation is devoted to the advancement and dissemination of knowledge about the corporation. Its publications are designed to stimulate inquiry, research, criticism, and reflection. They fall into three categories: works by outstanding businessmen, scholars, and professional men from a variety of backgrounds and academic disciplines; annotated and edited selections of business literature; and business classics that merit republication. The studies are supported by outside grants from private business, professional, and philanthropic institutions interested in the program's objectives.

RICHARD EELLS
Editor of the Studies

CONTENTS

PREFACE

THE INITIATIVE that resulted in this book was Mr. Paul Garrett's generous and imaginative gift to Columbia University in 1971. His perceptive understanding of the need for clarification of the role of business in
contemporary society induced him to endow a professorship in Public
Policy and Business Responsibility in the Graduate School of Business.
The gift reflected Mr. Garrett's deep concern with the complex problems
at the interface of business and society which grew from his experiences
during the twenty-five years he served as Vice President – Public Relations
of the General Motors Corporation and the following years of extraordinarily active "retirement" in which he continued to be involved in diversified business affairs.

As he pondered the implications of changes in our society's structure,
values, and needs, his conviction strengthened that business must undergo
related changes. Since business draws its ultimate operating franchise
from the society of which it is a part, it must be responsive to society's expectations for business performance and behavior. But responsiveness
alone, in Paul Garrett's view, was not enough—indeed was no more than
the minimum necessary to assure business survival on terms laid down by
the society. Beyond that minimum he saw a business responsibility to take
initiatives in anticipating and adapting to emerging social needs, and in
contributing to constructive relationships with social institutions and groups.

He believed no greater mistake could be made by leaders of business
organizations, with all their dynamic potential for enriching human lives
through accomplishments and rewards, than to take up positions opposed
to the social will. He believed that business leaders have the knowledge
and skill required to help society draw from business organizations contributions that will aid in accomplishing social goals, and that they owe it to
society as well as to the business system to make these contributions in a
creative and forthright manner.

His objective in endowing the Paul Garrett Professorship in Public
Policy and Business Responsibility was to stimulate educational and research programs the results of which would influence the ideas and actions
of business students and practicing managers. One of the activities funded
by his grant was the series of public Garrett Lectures on Managing the
Socially Responsible Corporation, delivered by a group of distinguished

business and professional leaders at Columbia's Graduate School of Business in the fall and winter of 1972–73. The edited lecture papers together with commentaries stimulated by the lectures and the post-lecture discussions are incorporated in this book.

Mr. Garrett was keenly interested in the ideas expressed by the lecturers and often discussed them with me. From these conversations I gained valuable insights that are reflected in the commentaries. I am happy to have this opportunity to acknowledge an intellectual indebtedness that transcends the thanks due a donor of financial support.

I am also indebted to Dr. Courtney C. Brown, Dean Emeritus of the Graduate School of Business and the first Garrett Professor. Dr. Brown recognized at the outset of his occupancy of the Garrett Chair the importance of a central focus of attention on management problems associated with implementing corporate social responsibility, the focus reflected in this book. He has been an unfailing source of counsel and encouragement in the organization of the lecture series and in planning the diversified educational and research programs that are now developing from the seed of Paul Garrett's gift.

MELVIN ANSHEN

CHAPTER **I**

The Socially Responsible Corporation: From Concept to Implementation

Melvin Anshen

The recent growth in the scope and number of society's expectations and demands for corporate performance can be viewed in broad perspective as the incremental drafting of a new social contract for business. What is at stake is more than a requirement for changed attitudes of business leaders and changed behavior of corporations. Acceptance of the concept of corporate social responsibility leads inescapably to a number of new and complex management problems which must be resolved if that concept is to be implemented effectively and efficiently.

This introductory chapter surveys the principal issues involved in the concept of corporate social responsibility and the principal management problems that will be examined in detail in the rest of the book.

This chapter and the commentaries following each chapter except the last are by Melvin Anshen, Paul Garrett Professor of Public Policy and Business Responsibility in the Graduate School of Business, Columbia University.–EDITOR

A N ANCIENT Chinese curse proposes for a favorite enemy: "May you live in interesting times." The wish suggests that "interesting times" are periods of turbulence and change in which established institutions and individuals are brought under pressures which threaten to overthrow them. Such a malediction may now be operating against American business and its leaders, because they are surely experiencing interesting times, although few chief executives would use this phrase to describe what they are going through.

We are in the opening phase of a revolution that will, if it runs its apparent course, radically change the character and performance of business institutions in our society. The forces generating this revolution appear to be fundamental and so powerful that they seem likely to overwhelm any opposition. If this judgment is correct, the significant question facing managers is not how to prevent the change (because this will be self-destructive and probably impossible), but rather how to understand it, accommodate to it, and bring constructive influences to bear upon it. Those in opposition may find themselves repeating in the 1970s and 1980s the familiar history of the nineteenth-century Neanderthal types of whom some wit observed that they had to be dragged kicking and screaming into the twentieth century.

THE SOCIALLY RESPONSIBLE CORPORATION

Observers of the business scene often use the term "socially responsible corporation" to identify the company whose top management has decided that it should be or must be responsive in some way to the new demands placed upon business by the society in which it operates. The concept of social responsibility has been a debated notion. But more interesting and more important are issues that follow understanding and acceptance of the concept: what management problems confront the chief executive officer who has decided that his organization will behave in a socially responsible manner? In the familiar context of corporate strategic planning, the big questions are: what to do and how to do it—what specific socially responsible policies and programs to adopt, and how to implement them effectively and efficiently. Later chapters in this book will examine in detail important operating issues in the socially responsible corporation, and the management tools and methods that may be useful for successful administration. This introductory chapter describes the issues in broad perspective.

The proposition that society is challenging business organizations and their managers with demands that can fairly be described as revolutionary seems obvious beyond debate. Consider some of these demands widely publicized in recent years:

> Refrain from or lessen price increases which would cover rising costs (or even to take advantage of strong market demand—after all, pricing decisions used to be regarded as quintessentially a right of private management);
> Invest in nonproductive equipment to minimize environmental contamination by eliminating, controlling, or cleaning industrial process discharges into air and water;
> Provide special training and jobs for the hardcore unemployed;
> Assure equitable progress into and through management ranks for members of minority groups (including that most recently discovered minority: women); in more extreme form, create instant equality;
> Contribute generously to the support of charitable, educational, and artistic organizations and activities;
> Avoid or dispose of investments in countries whose racial, political, or social policies and practices offend groups of our citizens;
> Provide for public interest, minority, and consumer representation on boards of directors;
> Make executives available to serve without compensation on a variety of nonbusiness assignments.

The common element in all these pressures (and more, because the list could easily be extended) is their departure from, even contradiction of, the economic criteria that have long been regarded as appropriate for determining how to allocate and use privately owned resources. In one way or another they challenge Adam Smith's classic thesis that decisions taken with a view to maximizing private profit also maximize public benefits.

A NEW SOCIAL CONTRACT FOR BUSINESS

One way of looking at this whole development is to see it as an expression of an implicit movement to change the unwritten social contract that has existed for almost two hundred years between private enterprise and the American society. We are all familiar with the historic terms of that contract. Economic growth—which we now appraise by the grand measure of gross national product—was viewed as the source of all progress, social as well as economic. The engine of economic growth was identified as the drive for profits by competitive private enterprise. Natural and human resources were bought in an open market and administered in the interest of profit maximization. Constraints, applied only at the margin, were imposed either to assure the continuity of the system (as in the anti-trust area), or to protect those who could not protect themselves in market transactions (as in legislation prohibiting child labor, assuring labor's right to organize, or safeguarding consumers against deliberate injury or deception). The implicit social contract stipulated that business *could* operate freely within these and similar rules of the game—and *should* do so in the common interest.

Under this contract serious questions were rarely raised about the costs thrown out upon society. The external costs of private industry (unemployment, unpensioned retirement, environmental contamination, prejudicial treatment of minority groups, etc.) were not even recognized as costs. Certainly they were not measured and accounted for. Even beyond the notion of the external costs of private enterprise, the social contract implicitly stipulated that business bore no responsibility for the general conditions of life in the nation or for the specific conditions in local communities.

The most dramatic element in the newly emerging social contract for private business is a shift in the balance between economic progress and social progress—in the popular phrase, between the quantity of life and the quality of life. This shift is leading to the identification of some of the unpleasant or wounding byproducts of economic growth. We are beginning to speak of economic and social costs not recorded in the accounts of private companies, nor reflected in their costs and prices. We are beginning to identify and question the need for the persistence of a poor nation within an affluent nation, the growth of boneyards of urban and rural decay that blight lives and the process of living, the personally and socially destructive constraints imposed on minorities who are members of our society without sharing equitably in its benefits and opportunities. More important for business institutions and their managers, the questions and skepticism and criticism are framing the terms of a new social contract for business that demands the internalization of social costs by corporations, positive contributions to removing or minimizing environmental contamination, affirmative actions to open up jobs and careers to equal access by all, private as well as public programs to counter and remove urban and rural blight.

As Daniel Bell described it recently, the justification of the business corporation no longer is found solely in the natural rights of private property or in its performance in providing more goods to more people. Now its legitimacy is challenged on the grounds that business is making our society ugly, dirty, polluted, dangerous; that business is acting as a powerful social instrument for perpetuating economic inequities. Rather than functioning as Adam Smith's "invisible hand" to maximize public benefits, profit-oriented private decisions are now often seen as antisocial.

That some of these judgments are inaccurate or unbalanced or biased is irrelevant. Right or wrong, they exist and they are helping to formulate a new standard for corporate behavior. They find expression in the force of public opinion, and also in the specific mechanics of legislation and public administration.

SOCIAL RESPONSIBILITY PRO AND CON

Business leaders have begun to acknowledge a certain social responsibility. Some are surely genuinely committed to a new code of business behavior. Others undoubtedly believe that the times demand at least a new public relations posture. In either case, the idea of the socially responsible corporation is part of the national dialogue on ends and means. Not all business leaders are prepared to accept it as a sound or even feasible idea; not all intellectuals are either. Economist Milton Friedman has taken the highest ground, the most uncompromising position, in the debate. He argues that the concept of social responsibility embodies a fundamental contradiction, and will, if implemented, erode the foundations of the enterprise system and grossly diminish its ability to contribute to economic growth.

In an interview published in *Business and Society Review,* the matter was put to him in these terms:[1]

> In recent years there has been a great deal of discussion about the social responsibilities of the business corporation. Many corporate executives have made speeches about how big business should contribute to the solution of the nation's social ills. Candidates for office have reiterated the theme. What do you feel are the responsibilities of business, if any, above and beyond maximizing profits for their shareholders?

Professor Friedman replied:

> Most of the talk has been utter hogwash. In the first place, the only entities who can have responsibilities are individuals; a business cannot have responsibilities. So the question is, do corporate executives, provided they stay within the law, have responsibilities in their business activities other than to make as much money for their stockholders as possible? My answer to that is, no, they do not. Take the corporate executive who says "I have responsibilities over and above that of making profits." If he feels he has such responsibilities, he is going to spend money

[1] "A Business and Society Review," *Business and Society Review,* 1 (Spring 1972).

in a way that is not in the interest of the shareholders. Where does he get that money? Perhaps from the company's employees. If he can pay his employees lower wages than otherwise, he'll have some extra money to spend. It may have to come from the company's customers, if he can charge them more than they would otherwise pay. Or it may come from the company's stockholders. The crucial question is: What right does the executive have to spend his stockholders' money? Who gave him the right to decide how their money should be spent? If "socially responsive" business executives would stop and think, they would recognize that in effect they are acting irresponsibly.

Professor Friedman is such a sharp debater that one welcomes the opportunity to respond to him in his absence. He is so thoroughly committed to the assumption that he is right that he fails to give adequate recognition to the possibility that society may change the rules of the game. If this should occur, Professor Friedman, conceptually right or wrong, will have confused what *should* happen with what *will* happen—a common confusion and an unprofitable one. Later in that same interview, he comes much closer to stating the root of reality. He was asked: "Do you draw a distinction between corporate sponsorship of a program which has some direct effect on its own profit and loss statement and a similar type of corporate program which is only a contribution to goodwill?" He replied:

> Of course. There is a big distinction. Most of the time when corporate executives talk about exercising their social responsibility, all they are doing is engaging in window dressing. This is why, in fact, there is very little actual social responsibility in a meaningful sense. Take the major business in a community. It's hiring workers in that community. It's producing products in that community. It may very well be in the self-interest of that corporation to spend money on improving conditions in that community. That may be the cheapest way it can improve the quality of the labor it attracts. The crucial question for a corporation is not whether some action is in the interest of the corporation, but whether it is enough in its interest to justify the money spent.

Continuing the unfair but pleasant game of scoring points in the absence of rebuttal opportunity for Professor Friedman, one may observe that the operational meaning of the new social contract is precisely that it *is* in the monetary interest of the corporation to behave in a socially responsible manner when the rules of the game are in the process of being changed to encourage and even command such behavior. Only if enough corporations behave in this way are we likely to continue to enjoy the benefits of a competitive enterprise system. The alternative will be some form of socialism in which both freedom and living standards are susceptible to attrition. On this point it is worth noting that even such a well-known critic of many aspects of the performance of competitive enterprise as Robert Heilbroner observed in his concluding chapter of that recent book of corporate horror stories, *In the Name of Profit,* that he was coming around to the belief that nationalization of giant organizations probably would not improve either their economic or their social performance.[2] This would seem to mean that the necessary or desired changes must be brought about within the existing system—somehow. Unfortunately, Professor Heilbroner stops short of suggesting how this is to be accomplished.

Important operational constraints stand between concept and performance. First, a profitable return for some kinds of socially responsible behavior may be realized only in the long run—and Keynes gave us the final word on that dimension. Second, in some areas, such as local environmental contamination, action by a single firm may make only a negligible contribution to solving the basic problem, while at the same time creating a substantial competitive cost disadvantage for the responsible innovator. Third, other interest groups in our society may establish positions of power in the social responsibility decision process. Stockholders, consumers, community groups, employees, to cite some obvious possibilities, may reach out to participate in defining preferred socially responsible policies and programs. In sum, the fundamental decisions on what to do and how to do it are not likely to be management prerogatives uniquely. Indeed, some who hold skeptical views about the general ability of managers to make reasonable decisions in an area where they lack both training and experience have already announced their opposition to allowing managers to exercise their personal judgment. They prefer to use the legislative process to specify in detail what shall be done, by whom, how, and when.

Some business leaders appear to share this view. They want to be told by governmental authority, rather than determine for themselves, what should be the character and method of their firm's social performance. They cite two reasons for this position: (1) to avoid criticism for unpopular decisions; (2) to maintain competitive equality in investment and operating costs and risks. The position has its dangers, but it is easy to be sympathetic with the concerns of those managers who favor it. A response is not easily made to the stockholder who asks management: "What are you doing with my money? I didn't invest in your company for philanthropic, humanitarian, or social objectives. I invested for profits. I'll make my own decisions about other uses of my money." For some managers, apparently, a superficially attractive reply would be: "We have to do it. It's the law."

[2] Robert Heilbroner, *In the Name of Profit* (Garden City, N.Y.: Doubleday, 1972).

One version of this business view takes a somewhat different expression. It was stated with some precision by Mr. John Diebold in an address on the social responsibility of business delivered in Paris in June, 1972, before an international conference on "An Economic Society for Man."

> The dynamics of the market and feedback control through profit—not corporate form or management techniques—make private business the most effective innovator and resource allocator man has ever invented. For society to benefit from this much needed ability to fulfill human needs, it is the social responsibility of business to pursue profit. The task of government is to establish incentives and restraints in such a way that profit is made doing what society most needs done, in a manner society finds acceptable. Good corporate citizenship is not enough.

The first part of Mr. Diebold's statement presents no problem. However, the notion that business should look to government to establish incentives and restraints that will lead business to pursue profit in directed ways is troubling, for two reasons. First, experienced, successful managers have valuable contributions to make to the design of a complex system of incentives and restraints. Managers understand technological feasibilities, administrative systems, and organizational behavior. The absence of this understanding can lead to a misdirection of effort and gross waste of resources. Many examples of precisely this outcome have been visible recently: in the provision of health services to the aged, in efforts to legislate product safety, in some of the legislation and public administration affecting environmental contamination, in some of the programs to protect uninformed or unsophisticated consumers in their market transactions.

Second, the emerging new social contract for business both compels and creates opportunities for business to undertake initiatives on its own, without the sanctions of public power. Given this positive environment, it will be valuable for business to respond with vigor and imagination. If the only alternative to a failure of business organizations to act on their own were a system of governmental incentives and constraints, concern might be minimal. But this is not the only alternative. Another possibility is a broad movement toward nationalizing large segments of the private business sector. The price for such a development, in terms of lost economic, social, and intellectual freedom, would be unattractive.

PRACTICAL MANAGEMENT PROBLEMS

Whatever the constraints may be, the tidal movement in our society is strongly toward a new social contract for business. The critical issues are not found in the debate about philosophy and concept. Rather, they appear in the practical management considerations of what to do and how to do it. How can a management group that is sensitive to the changing business environment decide what socially responsible policies and programs are feasible for their corporation to adopt? And, whatever policies and programs may be adopted, how can managers assure their effective and efficient implementation?

A number of management problems are readily identified with these operational questions. Some of these problems are no more than familiar administrative issues in a new setting; others are genuinely new, uniquely related to the special characteristics of social benefit goals, rather than traditional economic goals. One interesting cluster of three problems focuses on the design and behavior of corporate organization structures. The first of these is sighted when social performance considerations appear on the agenda of boards of directors. The second is related to the placement of responsibility for formulating and implementing socially responsive policies and programs within the executive hierarchy. The third is related to ways and means for motivating middle-level managers to participate seriously and thoroughly in carrying out policies and programs adopted by top management. Administrative difficulties can occur in each of these areas.

A chief executive officer who develops on his own initiative an intellectual posture favoring socially responsible performance by his company needs positive support from his board for both the general concept and specific policies and programs. Alternatively, of course, the initiative may come from within the board. Either way, the emerging social pressure favors some kind of representation on the board that might be described as a trusteeship for the public interest. We see a growing number of corporate directors whose responsibilities appear to be related to interests other than those of shareholders. We also see directors apparently chosen because they are members of one minority or another. General Motors added its first black director in 1971, the Reverend Leon H. Sullivan, a leader in stimulating both black enterprise and training of black workers for employment opportunities. In 1972 the same corporation announced the addition to its board of Miss Catherine Cleary, President of First Wisconsin Trust Co. of Milwaukee and already a director of American Telephone and Telegraph, Kraftco, Wisconsin Telephone, and a trustee of Northwestern Mutual Life Insurance Co. Whether such "minority" directors are in any sense also "public interest" directors is not always clear. Dr. Sullivan issued a statement, on the occasion of his joining the General Motors board, asserting his paramount interest in assuring equal opportunities for blacks in initial employment, advancement through management ranks, and among independently owned General Motors franchised dealerships. On the other hand, Miss Cleary has observed: "I share the concern about the position of women, but I don't regard this as my responsibility or believe that I'm on the board to speak for women. I have a strong feeling that I don't represent any constituency."

These statements suggest interesting questions about how issues of support for equitable treatment of minorities at the hiring gate and throughout employee and management ranks, of support for consumer interests (product quality, safety, service, etc.), and of the morality of corporate behavior (as, for example, through investment in South Africa) come together within the focus of a concept of social responsibility. In addition, we have practical management questions about the opportunities and limitations that may be encountered by any public or minority interest director. What weight can one, two, or even three such individuals impose on a board's thinking and therefore on corporate performance? Bearing in mind the traditionally rather passive behavior of directors, is it reasonable to anticipate an active role for this new class of directors? In the crassest terms, is their role cosmetic or functional?

One can be confident that every individual selected for a public interest directorship would strongly defend the operational vitality of his role, as he sees it. Further, a determined board member possesses a substantial clout if he wants to use it: threat of resignation with a public statement of criticism of corporate performance. We can be sure, for example, that General Motors would not want Dr. Sullivan to resign and issue a statement condemning the corporation's treatment of blacks. However, former Supreme Court Justice Arthur Goldberg recently resigned from the board of Trans World Airlines and issued a statement that he (and by implication his fellow nonmanagement directors) could not serve as an effective trustee of the interests of either the public or TWA stockholders unless the outside directors had staff support responsible only to them and met from time to time by themselves.

A different question emerges as we shift attention from the very broad policy-oriented work of the board of directors to the top-executive level where specific policies and programs are formulated, resources and action commitments are made, and organizational performance is supervised and appraised. Here the critical question is: where should administrative responsibility for social performance be placed, within the top-management layer? Recently reported business practice offers examples of at least three different answers: (1) in the chief executive officer, who then delegates specific segments of the total responsibility to individual associates, in accordance with their interest and competence; (2) in a newly created management position, identified as some variant of "Vice President for Social Responsibility"; (3) in a top-management committee on which major functions and divisions of the business are represented.

Any student of organization behavior—and equally any experienced manager who has lived and learned in large-scale organizations—will quickly recognize advantages and difficulties in all three schemes. The authority and prestige of the chief executive officer will signal the importance attached to social performance throughout the organization. On the other hand, effective coordination of delegated sub-responsibilities can be a serious drain on his valuable time. If he resorts to the familiar device of creating a special assistantship to "bird-dog" the total program for him, the energy of the thrust may be weakened and political maneuvering among staff and line officers may be encouraged. If examples of this kind of administrative arrangement for other types of chief executive functions can be taken as useful predictors, one might conclude that the performance record will depend on the status and maneuvering skills of the special assistant who is likely to find himself working in an environment of skepticism.

Creation of a vice-presidency for socially responsible performance would offer the obvious advantage of full-time specialization in the function. The extensive literature of staff-line relationships makes clear, however, that success is not routinely determined by job description. The effective staff officer needs a unique combination of status, credibility, functional expertise, sensitivity to line prerogatives, and skill in handling interpersonal relationships. At least one cautionary observation is in order, therefore. This would probably not be a good assignment for the twilight years of a line manager drawn from within the organization, or for a newcomer to the organization, hired for the position on the basis of his professional competence in one or several of the social program areas.

The third option, a top-management committee with broad representation across the operational range of a business, probably needs little comment. The advantages of committees for ventilating contrasting viewpoints and educating their members are well known. So, too, are the special circumstances (some critics would say the rare circumstances) in which committees can function effectively in implementing policies and programs.

Those who have worked in or studied the performance of large, complex organizations know that the support of middle-level managers is essential for the successful implementation of policies and programs determined at the top of the hierarchy. Middle managers concentrate their attention and skill on the accomplishment of performance objectives for which they know they are going to be held responsible by their superiors. They assess responsibility in terms of two familiar criteria. The first is what is measured, and the second is what is rewarded. The strongest performance occurs when the organization is perceived consistently to reward outstanding achievers along a measured activity vector.

A familiar example of this proposition is found in management behavior connected with the use of budgets. If a budget focuses on cost control, if actual costs during the budget period are regularly compared with budget targets, and if visible rewards and penalties are handed out on the basis of performance against budget, managers will concentrate their best efforts on meeting or beating budget objectives. Similar results will follow when budgets are developed around sales targets for marketing managers, or around profit targets for profit center managers. In systems of this type, failures occur when targets are unattainable, when unanticipated disruptions intervene, or when managers lack competence. They never occur because of management disinterest, inattention, or disbelief in the seriousness with which higher management considers the budget goals.

Since most budgets are designed for relatively short time periods (rarely exceeding one year), this behavior pattern is inevitably skewed toward short-run results. This is the source of a common difficulty in getting middle-level managers to devote adequate attention to investments and activities that have negative impact on short-run performance and positive impact on long-run performance, such as funding research and development, or committing time and energy to the training of subordinates in aspects of their performance that do not generate prompt returns in quantity or quality of output.

This suggests an important observation for chief executive officers who want socially responsible policies and programs to be implemented as planned throughout their organizations, and not to be treated as high-level announcements aimed at impressing a naive public while remaining empty of operational content. The corporate president who wants his organization to hire and promote members of minority groups must do more than announce this policy and order its execution. He must see to it that specific action programs with identified time-phased targets for accomplishment are laid down for every manager with employment and supervisory responsibilities. He must establish procedures for measuring every manager's performance against these targets. And he must visibly reward those managers who succeed and punish those who fail. The same course must be followed for every other socially responsible policy and program. Anything less rigorous will result in top-level commitments that will be viewed by subordinate managers as empty gestures intended for the outside public but not to be taken seriously by internal management.

MEASUREMENT AND CONTROL SYSTEMS

Passing from issues related to organization structure to those related to measurement and control, we come to a truly novel complex of management problems. Existing cost and financial control systems have not been designed to illuminate most of the resource management problems that are associated with socially responsible policies and programs. For example, little is known, and quantitative instruments to increase knowledge are lacking, about measuring the social cost throw-offs of environmental contamination caused by operations in steel-making, chemical-processing, power-generation, and a multitude of other manufacturing activities. Equally serious, knowledge and instruments are lacking for measuring the social gains (social revenues, in the accounting vocabulary) that follow productive efforts to reduce contamination—or, indeed, to contribute to solving or easing problems in any other area in which elements of the society are demanding business response. Without this knowledge, expressed in some kind of quantitative terms, however crude, that can be meshed with the output of traditional accounting techniques and financial control systems, business will be a long way from rationality in allocating resources to social programs or appraising their contribution as quasi-revenue gains to offset against investment and expenses.

Private business need not delay social responses until the kind of quantitative instruments just described become available. There are many examples of affirmative actions by corporations in the last few years taken without precise knowledge of costs and benefits: in reducing environmental contamination, in opening up job and career paths for members of disadvantaged minority groups, in ghetto investments, to name only a few. However, broad affirmative responses to the requirements of our changing society by a large number of companies will not be forthcoming until corporate executives can take reasonable sightings on costs and pay-backs. This will be essential not only to establish a confidence base for internal decisions about the allocation of important money and personnel resources, but also to build a record for reporting in meaningful terms to the financial community, to shareholders, to customers, and to employees.

Three approaches to measurement and control deserve detailed study. The first involves the discipline of managerial economics; the second, the discipline of cost-benefit analysis; the last, the discipline of accounting. These three approaches should be viewed as complementary, rather than alternative or competitive.

Managerial economics and cost-benefit techniques provide concepts and analytical tools that help to answer two key questions in rational decision making: what to measure and how to measure it. From the accounting discipline, the principal contribution is a system for recording revenues and costs in financial terms. Imaginatively combined, these disciplines provide a strong potential for expressing in familiar accounting terms and displays (balance sheets and operating statements) cost and revenue concepts that include both internal and external, or social, elements. A descriptive phrase has already been coined for the end product of this combination: the "social audit."

The specific potential input of managerial economics to the social audit or, more broadly expressed, the social accounting component of a total accounting system, can be described as the inclusion in intra-firm resource decisions of the result of applying profit, revenue, and cost concepts to economic externalities. Starting with profits, costs, and revenues, managerial economics moves into the construction of analytical designs for appraising relationships that can be quantified by some mixture of accounting measures, statistical measures, and judgment.

The cost-benefit, or, as it is sometimes called, the cost-effectiveness, technique is a principal tool of the broader field of systems analysis—a way of looking at complex problems of choice, usually under conditions of uncertainty. The potential contribution to the social audit process of this relatively new discipline is its powerful thrust toward the logical organization of inputs and outputs in resource allocation situations that (1) are inherently disorderly in composition and (2) contain elements not quantified in data banks. Examples can be cited from recent applications of cost-benefit analysis in such areas as water resources development, surface and air transportation networks, educational programs, and space exploration programs. The technique can be applied in either of two modes: (1) for a specified level of effectiveness, find the minimum-cost alternative; (2) for a specified level of cost, find the alternative that maximizes effectiveness.

The resemblance of managerial economics and cost-benefit approaches to the intellectual processes involved in determining costs and benefits in the social responsibility arena are at least interesting. The optimistically inclined may also find them constructive. What they lack for managerial decision use is the practice of recording inputs and outputs in a common, numerical language with a uniform grammar. The accountant has such a language. He calls it double-entry bookkeeping. From its building blocks he assembles information for management decisions. Managers understand the language. The visible need, therefore, is to develop techniques for introducing into the familiar vocabulary and grammar of accounting the relevant output of managerial economics and cost-benefit analysis.

Those who have examined the initial efforts to use this procedure in the social audit process have observed that rough judgments often have to be made in translating qualitative into quantitative measures. This should alarm no one who understands accounting. Only those who don't speak this numerical language tend to regard it as an instrument of precision.

The professionals know that accountancy is rather more of an art than a science. Its art component does not in any way reduce its value in organizing information for decision making. It exhibits many of the characteristics of a well-developed and long-practiced art: formal principles of design, professional standards of composition and performance, potential for adapting to new requirements, and, probably above all, respectability. These are all valuable characteristics for contributing to the formulation and implementation of socially responsible policies and programs.

THE ROLE OF BUSINESS IN PUBLIC POLICY FORMULATION

The most important and challenging issue of all, however, is the role of business in the formulation of public policy. The roots of the discontent with the performance of our society that is generating a new social contract for private business are strong and deeply embedded. They include profound concern about visible poverty in the midst of visible affluence, nonparticipation by minorities in institutional processes for improving their economic and social positions, urban and rural decay, environmental destruction and contamination, consumers' vulnerability to product and information risks, and others of somewhat less dramatic character. The growing demand for dealing with these problems positively and visibly shows no sign of abating. Forces of this intensity will compel legislative response unless private organizations act promptly to remove or ameliorate the objectionable conditions. Initial political responses have already appeared in many areas identified above and more are visibly in preparation. There can no longer be serious debate about the question of new rules for business behavior. But there is dramatic need for hard thinking about the nature of the new rules.

Business leaders therefore have three good reasons for being concerned about how they relate to and participate in the formulation of public policy that bears on the social performance of business institutions. The first is their recognition that the familiar forms of private business may not survive in a society bereft of stability and confidence. Henry Ford II made probably the sharpest statement of this judgment when, observing the flames of riot-torn Detroit a few years ago, he said that there could be no place for private business in a society bent on self-destruction. The second reason is business leaders' recognition that their actions and their predecessors' actions have been directly responsible for some of the causes of the general discontent. And the third reason is their knowledge that, in the absence of participation by managers, critical clauses in the new social contract are likely to be drafted by those who take up their work in ignorance, or even contempt, of the operations of the enterprise system.

The alternatives are not attractive. The likeliest possibility is the wholesale substitution of public for private goals, strategies, and actions— what President Eisenhower once described as the effort to achieve the level of security known only by the inmates of a penitentiary. In such a transformation would disappear not only the dynamism of private business initiatives and of consumer dominance in the marketplace, but also many of our political liberties and personal freedoms. Short of this grim extreme, we can visualize large transfers of economic activities from the private to the public sector, and the accompanying development of bureaucracies likely to inhibit experimentation and risk assumption.

To retain the advantages and values of the enterprise system we need a flexible modification of those elements in the system that have either contributed to extreme public disaffection and social injury, or failed to generate positive responses to the human and physical decay of our times. This adaptation is more likely to be effective and efficient if those who understand and value the enterprise system are willing to share in its redesign and are skilled in implementing their desire to participate. Unless today's and tomorrow's business leaders accept this responsibility we are all going to be in trouble. There can be no greater economic and social danger than in permitting the terms of the new contract to be formulated by either the small group of critics armed only with malevolence toward the enterprise system, or the much larger group genuinely motivated by concern for curing social ills, but grossly handicapped by and indifferent to their ignorance of how to bring the resources and skills of the enterprise system to bear on creating viable solutions.

Implementation of this assignment will compel business managers to become much more knowledgeable about social and political processes than most of them have hitherto demonstrated themselves to be. To influence social and political change one has to understand how that change occurs. One has to understand the structure and behavior of social and political institutions. One has to be perceptive about the formal and informal channels through which influence and persuasion move, and about the opportunities and constraints that confront those who want to influence and persuade. The issues are not those commonly associated with the support of political candidates, and the moving force is not commonly money.

Interests, knowledge, and skills of this kind are not often found among business leaders. There is a simple explanation for this situation. Business leaders have not depended on these talents in building successful careers, have not had occasion for acquiring valuable educational experiences in these areas, and have not been selected because of their possession of these assets. In the emerging business environment, however, requirements for effective performance of public leadership roles will be among the most visible areas in which dramatic changes can be anticipated. As top managers spend a larger share of their time working with problems at the interface between their companies and the external environment—and this is increasingly the character of their lives today, and almost certainly will be still more so tomorrow—they will be compelled to recognize the value of the relevant knowledge and skill. This recognition will influence future selection of managers for top-level assignments, and will bring into the selection process a new criterion: skill in interrelating with and influencing social and political institutions and processes.

The incentive for business management to enroll in the ranks of those who are exploring ways and means for removing cancerous growths in the society is classically selfish. Recognition is spreading that a continuance of these growths will be intolerable. Somehow, these growths will be removed; some effort to create an ameliorating response is inevitable in a democracy. Some of the proposed or predicted solutions may be destructive of other valued constituent elements in our society, including the private enterprise system itself. Managers as a class are equipped to contribute rational analysis, technical competence, and imaginative innovations. Their interest in continuing the enterprise system coincides here with the interest of other social groups.

These and comparable innovations imply for private managers a willingness to think about new economic roles and social relationships that many will see as dangerous cracks in the wall of tradition. However, we are considering nothing more adventurous than the explorations and commitments that managers have long been accustomed to undertake in administering resources in the interest of profit maximization. The only significant difference may be that the stakes are higher. In place of the limited calculus of profit and loss, what may be involved is the preservation of the social and economic system that has created a wealth and power without parallel through history.

EDITOR'S COMMENTARY

Corporate managers considering socially responsible programs will find it helpful to distinguish among three alternative strategies: (1) unilateral action by one company; (2) cooperative or coordinated action (a) by all or leading companies in a single industry, or (b) by all or leading companies in a single geographic area; and (3) initiatives by one company, several companies, or an industry association aimed at securing or influencing legislative or administrative action by some level of government.

Each of the three strategies is uniquely related to an identifiable set of conditions which define the limits of feasibility for corporate action. Determining these limits is an essential first step for executives concerned about moving social responsibility from concept to performance.

In general, circumstances favoring unilateral action by a single company have two characteristics. First, a program of socially responsible action can be executed that will generate meaningful results—and the results can be described, measured (at least roughly), and reported, if desired, to outside audiences. Second, the program has an interesting probability of being profitable, "in the long run" if not sooner, or, as a rock-bottom constraint, of not creating economic losses that would adversely affect the sponsoring company's competitive position or financial posture.

Minority hiring and promotion programs that are equitable, or even discriminatory in reverse, often (but not always) possess these characteristics. Often (but again not always), these characteristics are present in programs for investing in enterprises owned or managed by members of minority groups, aiding and using minority suppliers, and directing funds toward investment and use in ghetto areas. In some circumstances, probably more often than is presently recognized, single-company programs for limiting or removing environmental contamination can be implemented within a profit context. (See Chapter 3.)

A number of programs that represent significant contributions to socially responsible business behavior apply to ongoing business operations. In many instances, the changes have direct profit payoffs. Removing specific policies or unofficial practices that block progression through management ranks of talented members of minority groups (including women) will enrich the total management resources of a company and contribute to more effective operating performance. Improvements in product design that simplify or reduce maintenance, remove hazards, or increase safety in use are positive social contributions that can also strengthen market position. Upgraded working conditions can be related to productivity gains, advantageous employment results in tight labor markets, and improved employee morale. Good community citizenship can yield a variety of short- and long-term benefits, both tangible and intangible.

Unilateral action by a single company is not feasible or productive in many circumstances, however. Some type of cooperative or coordinated strategy is indicated in either of the following situations: (1) when a socially responsible program undertaken by one company would result in substantial cost (or other) disadvantage relative to competitors, without compensating gains; (2) when a single-company program would make no significant contribution (even by example) to the solution or amelioration of a local or regional problem.

The issue of competitive disadvantage emphasizes the potential for conflict between the profit-making responsibilities of corporate managers, on one side, and their intellectual and emotional response to social needs and demands, on the other. Unless publicly owned corporations earn profits at a level satisfactory to their shareholders—and for any company shareholder "satisfaction" can be roughly defined for this purpose as the profit performance relative to that of other publicly owned companies in the same industry—chief executives will be brought under severe pressure to bring earnings to competitive levels. The simplest and most effective short-run strategy to increase earnings is cost cutting. The costs most vulnerable to cutting are those associated with activities not essential to current operations. Confronting this irrefutable economic logic, corporate executives should and must avoid commitments to social programs that will be competitively disadvantageous.

This reasoning does not deny the reality, for many such programs, of social gains equal to or exceeding the single-company investment in their support. It simply says that these programs will not be funded by single companies operating in a competitive, profit-seeking environment. A manufacturer will not invest in costly equipment to minimize environmental pollution if his principal competitors do not take comparable action. A financial institution will not commit substantial funds to high-risk loans (for example, in urban ghetto districts) if competing financial institutions do not take parallel action.

A similar situation exists when single-company action to improve an undesirable social condition will not lead to removal of or visible improvement in this condition. If ten companies operate plants situated along the banks of a river into which they discharge effluent that degrades the stream for drinking or recreational use, investment by one firm in an expensive effluent-treatment process will not meaningfully improve the cleanliness of the river. Cleansing the contaminating discharge into the atmosphere from one plant's smokestacks is an insignificant action if a dozen neighbor stacks continue to foul the community's air.

The intensity of society's demands for responsible business performance will not, of course, be reduced because of the impracticality of single-company action in these circumstances. As we know from many recent examples in such areas as environmental contamination, product safety, urban decay, and inequitable employment practices, organized groups, often with large unorganized popular support, insist on ameliorative action. They search out and exert pressure through many channels of influence:

publicity, corporate shareholder procedures, consumer purchase decisions, the common-law activities of the courts, and the legislative and administrative powers of government at all levels from local to federal. Sooner or later, they are effective in getting some kind of response. Whether the response will produce constructive results is another matter. And so is the question of whether the results achieved, even if constructive, are accomplished efficiently in terms of the ratio of economic and social inputs to economic and social outputs. Many recent examples document the negative potential in both of these questions.

A chief executive officer, therefore, should continue to have a critical interest in organizing constructive responses to social needs and demands even in circumstances in which remedial action by his organization operating independently would clearly be either economically disadvantageous or socially meaningless. His choice should be viewed not as one of objective, but rather of strategy. The strategic decision lies between initiating efforts to organize a cooperative or coordinated socially responsible program (to meet a specific social need) and moving, alone or with others, to solicit some kind of government action.

Important long-range social and political considerations are involved in this strategic choice. There are legal considerations, as well, since many types of cooperative or coordinated actions run afoul of or move dangerously close to antitrust prohibitions. Putting legal constraints to one side, we can note some social and political issues about which business leaders will find it profitable to develop sophisticated understanding.

The most compelling reason for trying to mount some form of coordinated program is that its scope, technical character, and scale of investment can be determined in the context of management considerations in which cost-benefit relationships are paramount. Whether the program in view is one of importance to a single industry (as in automobile safety or tailpipe emission control) or to all companies in a single geographic area (as in air or water contamination), engineering and economic information and standards familiar in general management practice can be derived and applied and trade-offs between incremental inputs and incremental outputs can be appraised. The general prognosis is positive for such intra- or inter-industry undertakings, if seriously pursued and not adopted for cosmetic purposes.

There is an important second reason for pursuing this strategy. The long-run interests of business in an open society are better served when business organizations take an aggressive attitude toward social betterment. Managers who understand how the American democracy works at curing social ills, and who know that social problems not solved by private means will be attacked by public means, recognize that the stereotype of the business leader as the defender of established systems and practices is a dangerous weapon in the hands of critics of private business institutions. If the enterprise system is abandoned in the United States, it will not be for its economic inadequacies, but because it did not vividly demonstrate an interest in contributing to a qualitatively superior society. There is imperative need for business leadership to take a forward position among those who want to make the lives of our citizens safer, cleaner, quieter, healthier, fairer.

In many industry and regional business environments, unfortunately, enlightened and imaginative executives are not successful in encouraging their peers to join in cooperative initiatives for greater social responsibility. In these circumstances it is desirable for business leaders to move at an early stage to solicit and influence governmental action. This strategy is distasteful to many executives whose philosophic commitment is to minimum government, less government rather than more, and generally to governmental rather than private determination of the "rules of the game." This attitude has always assured a losing game for business, and it will continue to have this result in the future. It is a particularly dangerous attitude if the recent trend toward greater government intervention continues—a standard current forecast along economic, political, and social parameters.

The institutions of government at every level of a democratic society must be responsive, sooner or later, to the needs of its citizens. Since these needs are not uniform for all citizen groups, there will be a complex interplay of conflicting interests through the political process (including advances and retreats, experiments and abandonments). But the underlying trend is clear in our recorded history and there is every reason to predict its continuance.

The business leader who accepts this judgment will quickly recognize that the procedure of government action is more important for both business and society than its politics, because the political outcome is inevitable while the procedural outcome is not. There are many ways to bring about a cleaner environment. Some are better than others, cheaper, more effective, developed in a more advantageous, cost-benefit balance. Similarly, there are many ways to make the automobile a safer means of transportation, many ways to provide more and better health services to all people, many ways to restrain the excesses of advertising. In all these situations, rational choice for both business and the whole society requires an understanding of technological potentials and constraints, cost inputs related to benefit outputs, administrative feasibilities and impediments. With rare exceptions, politicians lack expertise in these matters, and so do most of the leaders of pressure groups who combine enthusiastic interest in social results with meager competence in designing the optimal machinery for attaining them.

Business managers can make important technological and administrative contributions to government programs. To create an environment in which their credibility as contributors will be respected and their advice heeded, however, they must recognize the necessary conditions. The first is an understanding of the political process and how to interact with it. The second is early participation. The record of most business efforts to influence government actions on social issues is poor on both counts. Questions of technology and administrative procedure are not effectively approached by way of contributions to political campaign funds, contrary to the apparent belief of many executives. Advice is not welcomed from individuals or organizations whose strategy is to oppose government action up to the point when action becomes clearly inevitable, and then rush forward with offers to help draft legislation or administrative orders. The history of business-government interaction in environmental contamination, product safety, packaging, advertising, and other areas is dramatic evidence of the inadequacy of late-hour conversion from opposition to affirmative support.

CHAPTER 2

Organizing for Socially Responsible Management

Courtney C. Brown

Whether a business accepts the idea of corporate social responsibility as a central management concept, and how it relates that concept to operating policies and practices, will be determined at the top of the organization structure through interaction among the board of directors, the chief executive officer, and that officer's close administrative associates. Effective implementation of approved socially responsible strategies and programs will also require top-level leadership in ideas and actions.

Both conceptualization and implementation will place new demands on and create new problems for this level of corporate management. This chapter examines the principal problems and ways of coping with them.

The author of this chapter, Courtney C. Brown, is Dean Emeritus of the Graduate School of Business, Columbia University, and was, in 1971–1972, the first Garrett Professor of Public Policy and Business Responsibility.—EDITOR

BIOLOGISTS tell us that those forms of animal life that best adapt to their environment survive and prosper. Sociologists make a similar observation about human institutions and organizations. It is interesting, therefore, to speculate about the patterns of corporate organization that may develop as companies respond to the expanded and new responsibilities laid on business by a rapidly changing society.

The character of all organizations, including business organizations, is, in a sense, a response to their internal and external environments. The environment defines the tasks to be performed. The organization, whether business, political, or other, must conform to the environment that sanctions its existence, and both the facts and the organizational structures are going to be different in the decades to come.

FUNCTION AND STRUCTURE IN BUSINESS ORGANIZATIONS

The several unique characteristics associated with the traditional business function of producing goods and services efficiently are reflected in the familiar corporate organization structure. The development of widely accepted accounting principles and procedures has provided a record of activities and results. Moreover, production and distribution operations have been reasonably stable, modified only over predictable periods of time by changing technology and administrative knowledge. Still another significant feature is the essentially competitive character of producing and selling. The most effective producer and marketer has received the greatest rewards and has been the most secure.

These characteristics of the traditional role of business have in combination resulted in the typical pattern of business organization that is well known to all. The basic form is the pyramid that describes a hierarchy of authority and responsibility. Within the total organization pyramid are numerous sub-pyramids called groups, departments, and divisions. The major pyramid is headed by the chief executive officer and the substructures by group vice presidents, department heads, and other officers. The departmental structure is elaborated into line departments of purchasing, manufacturing, transportation, and marketing, and into staff departments of accounting, finance, personnel, public relations, and law. This structural design is typical of all manufacturing corporations. Such differences as occur in financial and public utility organizations represent comparable adaptations to their respective environments.

Efforts to strengthen incentives and stimulate initiative have decentralized authority and responsibility in varying degrees. The so-called profit center has been designed to make these efforts more effective. Profit centers may be organized around functions, homogeneous products, or integrated businesses in the case of conglomerates.

This basic structure has evolved over many years by trial and error. It has been effective in maximizing efficiency in routine, repetitive kinds of operations. In an environment that is competitive above all, it is a stable and predictable arrangement. It contains a significant negative element: certain control and incentive systems tend to inhibit rather than encourage change and imaginative initiative.

This is the kind of structure that dominates our thinking about business organizations and against which we are prone to measure most proposals for change. Yet unless supplemented or modified, the measures and procedures of this pyramidal organization will be inadequate to cope with the expanded range of activities that are beginning to fall within the functional range of the business corporation.

NEW FUNCTIONS IN THE
SOCIALLY RESPONSIBLE CORPORATION

Since the nature of organizational structure is a logical function of the tasks to be accomplished, a closer look is in order for some of the newly emerging policies and activities of business. The implications for corporate organization may be more profound than is generally realized.

There is one area of business activity where change may be minimal. The growing public concerns that are subsumed under the consumerism movement will intensify demands for integrity of products and honesty of advertising, but these do not involve new activities for business. The appeal to consumer interest has long been a primary means of achieving business success and does not necessarily require organizational changes to make it more effective.

A good place to start a recitation of new activities that will require organizational changes is with the human side of business. Employment and personnel policies are undoubtedly going through a process of change. Most labor and personnel legislation, administrative rulings, and in-house policies are based on the assumption of an inherent conflict of interest. The validity of the assumption of industrial conflict is debatable. More significant to the issue here is the question of whether conflict is a good foundation for improving the quality of life in general.

The collective bargaining process provides a good case in point. The myth is that management, representing capital, sits on one side of the table, with labor leaders, representing organized workers, on the other. Since the respective interests are alleged to be contradictory, public policy has long been directed to equalizing the bargaining strength of the respective parties. If successful, it was expected the result of the collective bargaining process would best serve the interest of the public as a whole.

But what has happened? Collective bargaining is now regarded by many as at best a charade, at worst, as near collapse. Instead of assuring appropriate shares of the national product for those at the bargaining table, the process has diverted national product from those unrepresented and unorganized to a degree that may be approaching the limits of the bearable. The punishment extends further to the community at large, including those at the table, as can be seen clearly in the generation of inflationary pressures, and, currently, in the imposition of direct wage and price controls.

In its own interest, as well as in the interest of the community at large, business must find new patterns of employment and personnel practice that minimize the exercise of comparative muscle and coercion, patterns that recognize the values of incentives, and, most important, of mutual effort and interest. These patterns are not without precedent. Until recently, the Japanese have succeeded brilliantly in applying a sense of mutual interest in their labor relations. Life-time career employment with reciprocal loyalties has been the common practice, rather than the hire-fire cycle characteristic of the West.

Business must continue to take leadership in finding more civilized employment and personnel practices. Current experiments include assigning a totality of tasks to a worker or a group of workers, worker participation in organizing and scheduling the work-day, even setting their own hours within a stipulated total. But the modifications must go beyond more enlightened minority hiring, training, and promotion, and beyond job enrichment. Enlargement of the proportion of the total work force under salary, in contrast to wages, must be explored. And programs must be devised to occupy constructively the time of those made surplus in slack periods.

These tasks of "human engineering" can be done only by business, probably with collaboration among firms in different industries, if they are to be accomplished effectively. What are the implications of these or other modifications for organizational structure dealing with personnel policy and practice? A variety of experience here and elsewhere in the world is available, ranging from the quasi-paternalism of Japan to the participatory co-determination practices of West Germany and the emergence of workers' councils in the U.S. and elsewhere. What kind of amalgamation of the developments will occur with the best features of our other traditions? The results cannot now be foreseen, but the patterns that emerge must contribute to an escape from the consequences of the basic assumption of industrial conflict if the quality of life is to be improved. Any of the means of escape will necessarily mean a change in the manner in which personnel and employment practices are organized and administered within the corporation.

Another task ahead is a revision of business-government relations and of regulation is general. Some observers have begun to feel that the societal tasks ahead are so great that their alleviation will prove to be intractable unless ways can be found, and attitudes modified, that will promote joint efforts by governmental and private organizations.

The inherited view that government is the regulator and business the regulated is no longer useful. The pace of change has become too rapid, both sociologically and technologically, to permit traditional governmental regulatory practices to be effective. There is urgent need for careful reappraisal of the opportunities of self-regulation, accompanied by appropriate checks and balances. Business is not now organized, either within business organizations or externally in business associations, to manage or live with such modifications in its interface with government. Nor are most government officials prepared to modify imaginatively the semifrozen concepts inherited from past practices and attitudes.

Business must clarify its relationship to the political process as well as to government procedures. This is true of a corporation limited to operations within a single nation; it is even more true of a corporation with multinational production and marketing operations. It is difficult for a businessman to divest himself of political alignments as an individual, nor should he, but it is highly questionable practice to exercise political pressure in the context of the business organization. Political activism has no place in the spectrum of corporate activities even though labor unions may have been less circumspect in their behavior. Political alignment with specific politicians will not serve either the political interest or the business interest in the long run. But an apolitical posture does not deny the need and the opportunity to make known the relevant facts. A greater ambiguity arises, however, when the purely business interests of the multinational organization are incompatible with the political policies, particularly foreign policies, of either its home or its host governments. That is an issue that will take some time to resolve.

There is an urgent need for the clarification of the political posture of business organizations, in contrast to the political posture of businessmen as individuals, as a preface to expanding their participation in societal tasks. Where in the contemporary business organization should we look for a clarification? Our legal talent is usually better at telling us about the relationships between business and government in the past than at illuminating what these relationships may be, or should be, as participation in societal affairs develops.

It has long been recognized that business can achieve its objectives most effectively in a congenial environment. The characteristics of environmental congeniality are not simple, however. Business conditions the environment even more than the environment conditions business. The public is now fully aware that the environment is conditioned profoundly by ecological balance and conservation practices, or the lack of those practices. The environment is also influenced by the amenities and stresses of life in urban centers; by the availability of schools and churches, recreation and museum facilities, and adequate mass transportation; and by enforcement of law and order. Certainly business should not and cannot take the lead in all of these matters. It can formulate and execute a positive posture to all of them, however. In some matters, such as pollution-retarding programs to help restore ecological balance and conservation, business has both the interest and competence to take a leading role.

The adjustments in attitudes and incentives to cope effectively with pollution and other ecological and conservational problems will require philosophic understanding as well as economic interpretation. The adjustments will not be easy. They will be costly. They will cut deeply into the motivations and the incentives of business. To understand the adjustments, business will need thoughtful and wise participation in the decision-making process. Many solutions to environmental problems, for instance, will require that competition be commingled with collaboration within and among business organizations, as well as between business and governmental agencies. Where shall these newly emerging responsibilities for environmentally responsible actions be assigned in the typical pyramidal organization structure, which has tied its motivations and incentives to the results of profit centers? There does not seem to be a comfortable fit. The obvious answer is that new organizational devices must be developed, devices that go beyond the traditional staff functions of recording, counseling, communicating, and financial negotiating.

A further complexity must be added to the organizational requirements of many socially responsible corporations. In the quarter century since World War II, business organizations have developed globally. They have cut across political boundaries and have woven a world network of channels of communication that will in the course of time tend to harmonize business practices and attitudes wherever they occur. The arena of business has become the planet earth and the full repercussions are yet to be adequately appraised.

Nationalistic resistance to this global development in the structure of business is growing in intensity: on the part of home governments worried about the export of capital and the balance of payments; on the part of host governments worried about foreign influence on their domestic economies; and on the part of labor, in both home and host countries, worried respectively about the export of jobs and about foreigners taking domestic jobs. Moreover, the attitudes of governments differ with regard to the degree of competitiveness expected in business practices. All host governments resent the efforts of home governments to control the behavior of affiliates operating in foreign jurisdictions, a conspicuous practice of the United States government.

The rules are yet to be written to govern business in its global spread, and, indeed, to govern governments in their attitudes toward multinational business activities. Business must participate in writing these rules if the penalties of excessive nationalism are to be avoided. To what extent should business organizations be concerned with and adjust their activities to foreign policies of home governments, or incompatible or contradictory policies of home and host governments, or the human impulse to contribute to closing the gaps between the haves and the have-nots by changing competitive relationships among nations, such as by moving a part of their first-processing or component-manufacturing operations to low-cost, lesser-developed countries?

These are complex problems even in business terms. They become still more complex if the business organization permits itself to become involved in politics beyond making the facts of its activities known.

To what extent, for example, should a business organization yield to pressures by stockholders, church groups, or others to use its influence to change political policies at home or to apply extraterritorial political influence abroad? Pressure to withdraw from South Africa and Angola provide recent examples. One might ask about the propriety of political pressures applied by self-appointed groups through business organizations rather than directly through the government. But pressures have been applied, which leads to a secondary organizational question. Is the present arrangement for handling stockholder relations in a rather formal manner by the corporate secretary's office likely to be effective?

Changes that loom ahead in these several areas in the human relations of business, in business-government relations, in participation by business in alleviation of environmental problems, in the complex relationships of multinational businesses with their home government and with the numerous host governments of their foreign affiliates—all provide a catalogue of complexity for which no precise guidelines are now available. The catalogue also provides convincing evidence that traditional organizational patterns of business must be supplemented and modified if the challenging opportunities presented to business at the outset of the 1970's are to be successfully met.

SOCIAL RISKS AND ILLS

Before examining some of the specific organizational changes that may be required, a brief look at the more general characteristics of the tasks ahead may be helpful. First, it should be recognized that the ills of society have a very long time dimension. They are not going to be cured quickly, with or without business participation. Disappointments and frustrations are inevitable. Good intentions will be misinterpreted. Indeed, the results of action based on good intentions can often be perverse and counter-productive, hence, discouraging and frustrating.

Yet the leaders of business must learn to accept and live with social risks as they have accepted business risks. Ways must be found to speak out frankly and perceptively about the interests of the public in the conviction that ultimately those interests will coincide with the interests of business. This does not mean simply a defensive response to accusations of inaction or of unperceptive conduct; rather, it means a positive initiative in expressing opinions about the community interest despite the risks involved. Business has too long been muted by the conviction that public issues not immediately related to its specific activities are none of its business. That practice must be changed.

Social ills have been with us as long as recorded history, which means that if business is to succeed in its social purposes, constancy and consistency of program must be accepted. Awareness of responsibility to the community is not a one-time or part-time thing. It is not something that becomes a part of the operating agenda only in response to intermittent public protest. It is not something to indulge in prosperity and abandon in depression. The commitment of both purpose and financial resources must be firm and continuous, or the commitment should not be undertaken at all.

The principle of continuity must be recognized in a still more important way. The classical economist concentrated on the laws of supply and demand as they affected single transactions. But business is a continuous flow of transactions and of enduring contacts and associations. If the element of mutual benefit in the marketplace is missing, the flow will soon cease and the relationship will terminate. Likewise, business practices that fail to recognize a mutuality of human interests are simply not good business; particularly, failure to recognize that the interests of labor and of the community and the public at large are harmonious with those of business is not good business.

In other words, the conviction must be unqualified that over extended periods of time the private interest and the public interest are synonymous. Practices of business organizations that fail to serve all of their publics will not long endure regardless of their legal authorities, for they will eventually lose public sanction. Managers who succeed in identifying the true public interest and adapt their actions and organizations to that interest, will, in the long run, be most assured of enduring success in all of its aspects.

A second general characteristic of the tasks ahead is that cooperation and collaboration will inevitably play a larger role in business policy and practice relative to competition. New forms of collaboration between government and business must be found, additional to the many that have already been designed. In spite of the antitrust laws, government, in turn, must find ways to facilitate forms of collaboration *among* business organizations, thus avoiding the disincentive of competitive disadvantage incurred in activities undertaken independently. The functions of trade and industry associations will no doubt be greatly enlarged. The "devil-take-the-hindmost" society has gone.

In all of this, one characteristic of business must be preserved. Business must operate at a profit, or it will not operate at all. There is no point in discussing the participation of the business community in alleviating social ills if it becomes unprofitable in its normal business activities. Accountancy is a harsh disciplinarian. That is a major source of strength, for it has served as a continuous spur to effectiveness. In their newly evolving posture in society, businessmen must never lose their awareness of the realities that underpin their past accomplishments and that have made business the recipient of the public sanction it now enjoys. Nor should they for one moment modify the high value they have placed on individual initiative and self-reliance. Their emerging role is not one of coddler; rather, it must be one of facilitator of self-reliance.

One of the implications that must be explored, for instance, is whether acceptance by business organizations of an extension of their functions may not require additional safeguards to avoid impairment of the effectiveness with which they fulfill their traditional role of producing and distributing goods and services. It is important to everyone that this task be done in an efficient and beneficial manner to assure an appropriate allocation of national resources. The effectiveness of the market economy depends on the maintenance of a degree of external competition that must not be lost. Economists coined a phrase for it several decades ago: "workable competition," contrasted with monopoly, on the one hand, and to so-called perfect competition, on the other.

These are some of the general characteristics to which business must adjust to cope with the expanded tasks that lie ahead. They involve subtleties and nuances, even contradictions, that lie outside the characteristics of past business experience. One is tempted to ask: why should business involve itself at all? One obvious answer is that business has no choice. It must do so in the interest of its own long-range survival.

ALTERNATIVE ORGANIZATION STRUCTURES

This recitation of some of the tasks ahead, together with some of their ambiguities, suggests, without fully identifying them, the nature of the organizational changes that will be required. At least minimally, it provides a measure of the adequacy of some of the initial organizational changes that have already been reported.

Some companies have established a special committee of the board of directors, charged with reviewing external and internal relations of a societal nature. Regularly scheduled meetings of such a board committee, with prepared agenda of specific issues, with participation in discussions by line and staff officers, identify for the organization the importance of social responsibility in the decision process. The success of this device has been limited, however. Directors are likely to differ in defining and limiting concepts of corporate social responsibility; proposals that involve increased costs unaccompanied by visible, near-term pay-backs, are seldom embraced with enthusiasm by line officers. Since the conclusions of such a special committee are subject to review and disposition by the full board, there is opportunity for further dilution of policy and program proposals. A variation of the board committee is a committee composed of line and staff officers as regular members, with perhaps several members of the board as minority members. This arrangement has the additional flexibility of permitting inclusion of outside public members from community groups or academic faculties. The difficulty is that such a group is more than likely to be consultative rather than operational in nature; it would be hard to give it the effective authority to assure that its recommendations become part of the ongoing decision-making process of a large business organization.

Concern with societal matters has led some business organizations to accept the idea of special interest representation on the board of directors: representation of blacks, of women, of consumers, of geographic regions, and, in the case of the multinational corporation, of nationalities. Positive psychological values can be visualized in this structure, but it is of doubtful value in changing the basic orientation and policies of the total organization. To the extent it might be effective, the result is as likely to be a destructive divisiveness as it is a constructive shift of policy and practice. This is particularly true if the special interest representative is provided with a staff, in which event the subtle line between board policy and administrative responsibility and practice can become quickly confused. The most effective way to get a constructive shift of policy is for the chief executive officer to want it that way. It is one of the verities of corporation life that attitudes throughout the organization reflect to a high degree those of the chief executive officer.

A more promising variant of board reorganization is suggested by the growing movement toward early retirement from their daily responsibilities of senior corporate officers who may or may not have reached board membership in their career progress. An example is provided by the recently announced program by a major corporation to give an option to the six or seven top men at age sixty to relinquish line or staff duties until age sixty-five, and to accept a reduced schedule and comparatively reduced salary. Such men would typically have the respect and loyalty of operating officers and could provide an effective bridge to communicate public thinking and attitudes to the organization. In most cases, revised organizational patterns within the company would be needed to make this arrangement effective. How they would be integrated into the decision process of the organization would depend upon company traditions, the personalities involved, and the degree to which existing structures could be used. Time released from company affairs would become available for association and interchange with leaders of political, academic, and journalistic thought, at which they could work quite as hard as when they were in full company harness.

While no one organizational device will assure effectiveness in discharging social responsibilities, one of the most logical internal structural changes is to build upon the present public relations function. For the most part, public relations officers are now charged simply with "telling the story." Seldom are they in a position to influence decisively the important decisions of business policy and practice. Usually their task focuses on favorable interpretation after the decision is made. It may be feasible, by elevating the authority of the public relations function, perhaps by assigning it to a senior officer of board of directors status, to make certain that the social responsibility aspect of all decision making is an input equal in importance to the legal, technological, and competitive marketing aspects of the problems under discussion. Another possibility would be to attach the semi-retired senior officers just described to the public relations function. The interpretation of the consequences of decisions made can then be carried to the public with total conviction by the communicators, representing decisions and actions in which they have participated fully from the outset.

Another organizational change could, and probably will, contribute to managing the socially responsible corporation, especially in its programs that involve action outside the normal operations of the company. Indeed, it may prove the most effective of all organizational devices to achieve business participation in community rehabilitation, ending pollution, and maintaining the ecological balance, even though, as previously noted, no single device is likely to be adequate alone. New and distinctive corporation abilities will be needed. Means must be found for new initiatives, as well as ways to make funds available, such as through "anti-pollution bonds" or other comparable devices. The number of special projects that must be dealt with promises to multiply. Better abilities and analytical methods must be developed to anticipate problems before they become critical. Flexibility is probably the key concept. If the corporation is to be effective in extending its activities into this new and strange world of social responsibility, tasks must be assigned in ways that are now novel and unfamiliar. Certainly, traditional corporate units are not equipped by experience to cope with the tasks. The tasks that loom ahead are too complicated for one man to grasp, or even for the professional competence of a single department. A possible device is the so-called task force, which may be action-oriented or simply assigned to study and report. The action group is the most significant option.

The task force as a collaboration of expert professionals who represent a diverse set of skills, assigned to project-oriented problems, is not new to business. In some organizations it has been used for many years for special projects, typically, although not necessarily, on a basis of temporary assignment. Personnel may be drawn from both line and staff and may also include individuals from outside the company.

The question of who will pay the bill for action programs has not yet been clearly faced. There are several alternatives. If the assignment is to action groups within the company, organized for a specific task closely related to the company's operation, they would operate either for the account of the corporation, which is the most likely, or perhaps as agents for the government on a commission, or possibly on a joint account with the government. But regardless of the account for which they would operate, in most cases they would be action groups to accomplish specific assignments. They would be study or research groups only when limited to those functions.

Business has a history of creating operating units to collaborate with governmental bodies. The activity of NASA in its successful space program was subcontracted over a wide spectrum of businesses. The earlier Manhattan Project, which developed the nuclear bomb, provided another dramatic example. But even before that, this kind of structure was used. Starting early in World War II, the Commodity Credit Corporation bought over a billion dollars worth of foods and fibers abroad for the Allied effort, using designated groups in business organizations as agents. The Defense Supplies Corporation did about as much business in other products, using business organizations as agents.

What is implied by these arrangements is a second bifurcation in the nature of the corporation, separating its talents from its investments. In 1934, Adolph Berle and Gardiner Means wrote a book on the corporation that identified the bifurcation of beneficial ownership by stockholders from control by professional managers as a result of proxy voting. At that time they thought it was pernicious. Surprisingly, it has been one of the most constructive business developments of the century, because it has encouraged management to focus on long-range benefits in contrast to short-term profits. The second bifurcation takes the form of the separation of talent groups from the normal business of the corporation to work on projects not directly related to the company's own investments. They are provided with their own budgets, are novel in their nature, and usually involve an extension of personal experience.

This does not mean that business organizations will dissolve existing departments. Rather, growing up alongside the traditional departments will be new structures. No doubt it will become increasingly important to appoint a small group in the company with assigned responsibility to make continuous study of these structural matters, to supervise how new or modified groups relate to existing groups, how individuals are assigned to and removed from task groups, what happens to them in the process of carrying out their assignments, and determining when they have outlived their usefulness. Probably such a small "overview" group would operate most effectively under the immediate supervision of the president's office.

Such an arrangement could be uncomfortable and disturbing to stable management habits. Managers like to have things precise, orderly, carefully developed, and settled. But it is unlikely to be that way. Numerous new societal problems, both internal and external, will appear in continuous procession and they must be resolved.

To what extent does this ambiguous organizational structure of the future involve an attitude of cooperation in contrast to the traditional competition among personnel for position? How will individuals react when removed from what has heretofore been regarded as the line of progression in their career development? We should bear in mind that the present structure was designed to be most effective in a competitive situation, but units concerned with societal matters must develop an attitude of collaboration and cooperation not only among the men assigned to them, but with respect to the total company performance. Profits are not the necessary measure of their individual performance. But what means are available to measure the performance of individuals on these assignments? Can incentives and rewards be calibrated so as to be mutually understood? Even the success of the group itself can in many cases be measured only over an extended period of time.

These are significant but not insurmountable difficulties. They may be small relative to the advantages of the added flexibility, adaptability, and initiative that innovative organizational structures can generate.

While the situation will be rough on past management practices, it may be more conducive to attracting to business some of the brightest young people graduating from the colleges and universities. There will be opportunities for individuals to express themselves much earlier than is now the case in the traditional pattern of taking an assignment in a department and in the course of time moving up as superiors advance or retire. With this prospective flexibility, the best talent, the genuine talent, should bubble up to visibility much faster.

The many changes ahead in organizational structure reflect the fact that the firm is a creature of its environment, and that environment and the tasks associated with it are changing rapidly. The changes cannot all be seen now, but those that are beginning to make their appearance point to exciting developments ahead. One thing is clear: the last word has not been heard on management practices, and on organization theory and patterns, as they apply to the socially responsible corporation.

Editor's Commentary

The central issue in top management organization for corporate social responsibility was expressed simply and dramatically in a recent publication of the Chamber of Commerce of the United States: ". . . If business corporations are to adjust to continually changing demands for social as well as economic performance, they must do something more fundamental than respond to the proposals of others. Business must restructure its objectives so that social goals are put on a par with economic goals."[1]

Until the performance of its social responsibilities becomes as much a part of a corporation's business as its production and distribution of goods and services, the analysis of alternative options for organizing the social responsibility function will remain a sterile exercise. When social responsibility is peripheral, decisions on how to organize its administration will be both difficult and trivial: difficult because rational criteria are lacking for choosing among alternatives; trivial because the choice is unimportant. With full incorporation of social responsibility, decisions about organizational placement of the function will resemble decisions related to other problems of organization design. They will not be simple, but familiar criteria will be available for selecting among alternative possibilities, and all managers will recognize the importance of the choice.

The design of top-level management arrangements for socially responsible performance must begin with recognition of one characteristic of human behavior within organization structures. The placement of responsibility for a selected business function near the top of the organization chart fulfills two general operating roles that are matched by two motivational needs of the people who work at all organizational levels. One of

[1] *The Corporation in Transition: Redefining Its Social Charter.* (Washington, D.C.: Chamber of Commerce of the United States, 1973), p. 23.

these roles (and related needs) is functional: it defines an identified activity and describes its formal relationships with other designated activities. The second role is symbolic: it conveys a message about the relative importance of the designated activity.

The two roles are mutually reinforcing. They are also continually tested by operating performance and over time are strengthened or weakened by the record of that performance as it influences how managers throughout the organization assess shifting emphases and balances. Such assessments lead managers at lower levels to identify the fundamental thrust of a business. Thus, one hears managers describe their companies as "production-oriented," or "marketing-oriented," or "control-oriented," or "research-oriented." These descriptions in different companies are all based on top-level placement of functions and the reinforcing or contradicting clues developed through operating performance. For example, the relative importance of the marketing function in a corporation is diminished in the perception of middle-level managers if they observe that most critical product and pricing decisions are shaped by production considerations. Both production and marketing functions are almost certain to be downgraded in the thinking of middle managers in the company in which top management continually stresses short-term financial results.

Such perceptions have significance far beyond descriptive labels. They provide clues to managers throughout a business about the principal concerns of the chief executive officer and his immediate associates. The clues in turn influence the efforts of middle managers and their subordinates who are inclined, for the most natural and obvious of reasons, to emphasize in their own activities what they judge their superiors want emphasized. The clues may be misleading or misunderstood, of course, and may result in erroneous perceptions that lead to inconsistencies between the real interests of top management and the evoked operating interests at lower administrative levels. In an ongoing business, all of this behavior is generated under conditions of dynamic tension in which organization goals and personal goals interact continually, new signals are transmitted and interpreted through time, and established behavior is reinforced or modified accordingly.

In corporations which operate for extended periods of time with unchanged organization structures and routine top leadership succession of known individuals promoted from within in familiar pattern, the functional and symbolic roles are continually reinforced by clues drawn from operating performance. There are no significant discontinuities, no challenges to the status quo. Top management intent and lower management perception achieve and easily maintain a stable accommodation.

This behavior pattern explains the great shock, with accompanying uncertainties and even dysfunctional performance, that follows such a common business event as the appointment of a new chief executive officer from outside the organization. Even greater disturbance is created if dramatic changes are then made in the organization structure, such as shifting from centralized to decentralized decision making or the reverse. All existing perceptions are immediately obsolete. A new set of perceptions must be formulated, based on official pronouncements tested against clues from operating performance. Considerable time is likely to pass before stability is again established. During this period the intent of top management is tested repeatedly by evidence drawn from daily operations, tentative judgments (often later proved erroneous) are formulated, rumors circulate, and the total economic performance may be erratic.

The foregoing observations have particular bite when applied to the introduction in a corporation of an interest or activity that most managers view as a radical innovation. The concept of social responsibility certainly qualifies for this description. If taken seriously, it cannot fail to introduce new considerations in decision making and substantially modify the way the business is conducted. It poses direct challenges to long-established criteria of business performance. It may intrude into and require changes in familiar patterns of hiring and promoting. It may disturb union relationships. It may compel the introduction of new work arrangements and new standards of job performance. It may affect familiar cost structures. It may threaten disturbing shifts in competitive position within an industry, or even across industry boundaries. It may pose previously unknown problems in human relationships between supervisors and subordinates and among employees at every level. These issues are surely the ingredients of radical innovation.

In this setting, the importance of thinking carefully through the problem of the organizational placement of the social responsibility function is clearly identified. Introduction of the concept of social responsibility in a profit-oriented enterprise will disturb and confuse many managers. Some, as a result of earlier education and experience, will view it with distaste, if not outright hostility. Many will make a preliminary assessment that the concept has been introduced by the chief executive officer for cosmetic purposes, or simply as the kind of high-minded but essentially meaningless gesture expected of a corporate leader in a time of noisy criticism of the business system. What the concept will ultimately mean in any business organization will be worked out in the perceptions of managers through their identification of the clues they have learned to value as significant indicators of top management intent.

The operating experience of any business always develops certain unique elements not shared with other firms. As a result, no single prescription for organizational placement and handling of the social responsibility function can be offered as a packaged program equally useful for all corporations. However, bearing in mind the dual roles of organization design—functional and symbolic—we can cite the characteristics that should be expressed in any company's treatment of the concept, in a way consistent with its unique experience and the patterns of organization structure that are familiar to its managers.

First, and surely the most obvious for a new and strange area, responsibility for the definition and performance of a corporation's social responsibility should be lodged in a position of high visibility close to the chief executive officer and reporting directly to him. It should be a new position specifically identified with the activity, not an enlargement in scope of an existing position (for example, not added to the duties of the top public relations officer), and not an enlargement in scope of all corporate officers' duties. The object in view is to establish social responsibility as a new element in management, an element that commands the importance and stature of its own position near the top of the organization and under the personal jurisdiction of the chief executive. At a later stage, when years of experience have made the accomplishment of social responsibility objectives unmistakably part of a corporation's way of life, the special position might be abolished. At the beginning, however, such a radical and challenging innovation requires its own identity and the status that comes from immediate access to the organization's power center. This placement will not guarantee effective implementation, of course, but it is an essential foundation for all related development.

The second requirement is that the position be filled by an individual whose previous achievements command the respect of all managers, whose appointment to this job cannot be interpreted as either disguised early retirement or an operationally empty public relations gesture, and who possesses a deep interest in and concern for corporate social responsibility. Because the introduction of an outsider near the top of the chart creates special perturbations unrelated to the specific content of his announced assignment, it is generally preferable to make this appointment from within if the right individual is available. If an outsider has to be selected, his credentials should be strong and easily recognized throughout the business.

A third general requirement is that the chief executive officer demonstrate to his entire management corps that he is determined that his announced commitment to socially responsible performance be translated into operating reality. He can do this by taking two related actions. One is to incorporate social responsibility considerations into long-range plans as they are developed throughout the organization. The other is to factor them in specific terms into short-range budgets and middle-management job responsibilities, and to police their fulfillment as thoroughly as traditional budget commitments are reviewed. Until managers see these two lines of action actually working, they are likely to be skeptical about the seriousness of top-level policy statements and hortatory communications.

An effective way to reinforce the total program at the apex of the organization structure is to appoint a special committee of the board of directors to focus on defining and reviewing the company's socially responsible performance. The committee should be dominated by, if not entirely composed of, outside directors who share the chief executive officer's concern about the company's interface with its social environment. (Obviously, if directors of this disposition do not sit on the board it will be necessary to find them and bring them into the organization.) The board committee should have two primary tasks. First, to give guidance to the corporate leadership in identifying specific socially responsible programs that are appraised as feasible undertakings for the company acting on its own, as well as programs that can be implemented only through cooperation with other corporations or through some type of governmental action; second, to review corporate social performance through the medium of periodic formal implementation reports.

Finally, the chief executive officer should make a personal commitment to report annually in specific terms, with maximum quantification, to owners and managers on the corporation's social objectives and their accomplishment in performance.

CHAPTER 3

Creating a Management Environment for Socially Responsible Performance

Carl A. Gerstacker

Some of the most critical problems in translating corporate social re-sponsibility from policy to practice are found in the company engine room for operations—the ranks of middle line management. Lack of identity of corporate and individual objectives, skepticism about top management's sincerity, perceived impediments to career advancement, novel and diffi-cult administrative problems, hostile attitudes to social expectations and demands—all combine to create a setting in which, lacking imaginative and thorough planning and follow-through from the top, socially respon-sible policies and programs are likely to falter and fail.

The following chapter examines the roots of these problems and pro-poses ways to cope with them.

Carl A. Gerstacker, Chairman of the Board, The Dow Chemical Company, is the author of this chapter.—EDITOR

WHEN Henry Kissinger is interviewed by the press, he is occasionally asked to repeat or rephrase a statement, or to put it in simpler lan-guage. Dr. Kissinger's standard answer to this kind of request is: "I'm sorry, but that's as simple as I ever get."

When a businessman is asked to appear in an academic setting, especially when he is asked to deliver a lecture, I think there is a great temptation to move away from simplicity and in the direction of obfuscation. I intend to resist this temptation. I promise to stick by and large to simple declarative sentences and I hope that they will be clear and simple.

BUSINESS INSTITUTIONS AND SOCIAL EXPECTATIONS

Implicit in the title of this paper is the assumption that management does indeed want to create a climate of social responsibility in the corporation. Rather than blithely accept this assumption, I'd like to inspect it, at least sketchily, because it backs us right up into the hidden question: what *is* the social responsibility of the corporation? Let's consider that first.

A great deal has been said and written on this subject in recent years. The opinions expressed on it range from the conviction, as Milton Friedman has put it, that the responsibility of a business enterprise is simply to make a profit, to the just as radical other extreme that the function of business is to serve the needs of society, and that business should be controlled by the government or some other institution, to make certain that it does have this as its primary goal.

I am something of a moderate on this subject, in the sense that I see no conflict between profit, on the one hand, and social responsibility, on the other, and I am tired of the argument over which comes first. This is a modern-day version of the old chicken-and-egg question. You cannot have a corporation if it does not make a profit, and you cannot have a profit if the corporation does not fulfill a social need.

The fabric of our complex society is woven by many institutions. The corporation is our basic economic institution. Its function is to provide the goods and services that the society wants and needs, and profit is the measure of its success in performing this function. We don't usually or primarily judge our spiritual institutions, or our educational institutions, on how well they perform economically, although they have economic aspects, but some of us have recently insisted upon judging the corporations, not simply upon their economic performance, but upon their social performance as well.

I point this out not as a protest, but to indicate one of the anomalies of modern corporate existence. It emphasizes two aspects of the modern-day corporation: first, that the corporation is changing (and is being required by society to change) more swiftly than most other institutions; and second, that this is taking place because of the very success of the corporation as an economic instrument.

Of all our institutions, it is the corporation that has been most successful in fulfilling its promise. That promise was to provide material abundance for the citizens of this country. This it has done on a scale well beyond the most grandiose dreams of our grandfathers. Our affluence continues to grow more swiftly than anywhere else in the world, and this growth is generated primarily by the resounding success of our economic engines, the corporations.

It is because of this unique success that society is asking the U.S. corporation to take on additional tasks—often, tasks which other institutions failed to perform; often, tasks unrelated to the corporation's basic skills and knowledge.

George Romney, former Secretary of Housing and Urban Development, recently suggested that the federal government ought to get out of the housing business. That does not mean that housing has become any less of a problem, but it does seem to mean that government efforts have not succeeded very well in this area—and it does seem to mean that a different approach to the problem is needed. The federal government has taken steps to get out of the postal service, and put it on a business basis. Perhaps the same approach is needed for housing.

We are asking more of all our institutions today, possibly because our more complex society generates greater demands across the whole institutional range. Some institutions, like the government, have been asked to do more than they can perform efficiently. Others, like business corporations, are being asked not only to do more than heretofore, but also to invent new ways of doing both old and new tasks.

THE PROFIT MOTIVE

Almost a century ago, Samuel Gompers, the father of the AFL, was asked what this new thing called a labor union really wanted. "More," he said.

"And when your members have been granted more, Mr. Gompers, what will you ask for then?" the reporter asked.

"More," said Samuel Gompers.

We ought to build a statue to Mr. Gompers. He set the tone for our demands on all our institutions, and we are still following his lead.

Profit making is the most important function of business because all the other accomplishments of business are impossible without it. I have heard labor leaders say, "No, profit making is only the second most important thing a corporation does. The most important thing it does is to provide jobs for people." The fact of the matter, of course, is that profits make jobs. When profits decline, jobs decline; when profits climb, jobs climb. Profits finance research, open up new markets, provide capital, and attract capital. They make possible the expansion that creates new jobs, and without profits a company eventually will provide no jobs.

In the five-year period from 1966 to 1971, for example, the profits of manufacturers dropped 17 percent, and employment in the manufacturing industries dropped 3 percent. In the same five-year period, profits in the service industries, on the other hand, rose 18 percent, and employment in the service industries also rose 18 percent. The service industries generated 5.4 million new jobs in that period while the manufacturing industries lost about 600,000. The key factor in this job-generating phenomenon was profits. It is simply a fact of life that most businesses hire more people when their profits are up, and don't hire (or even let people go) when profits are down.

We tend to overemphasize the importance of the number of unemployed, which expresses a negative fact; it is the number who do *not* have jobs. We ought to emphasize the positive factor, which is the generation of jobs, and do all we can to encourage the generation of profits, which are what generates jobs and the ability to pay taxes.

When I compare the number of jobs in the country today with the number that we will need in years to come, I see most clearly what the responsibility of business should be, from the viewpoint of the man who says, "The most important thing a corporation does is to provide jobs for people."

By 1980 the United States will have a population of about 230 million people and a labor force of about 100 million. From now to 1980 the labor force will grow at a rate of 1.9 percent annually. Thus we will need to generate, in round numbers, 1.7 million jobs every year, or a total of 13.5 million jobs, by 1980.

Is this possible? I believe it is, if we work hard at it. We averaged 1.3 million new jobs per year in the 1960s, and only 700,000 in the 1950s. The estimates are that we added 1.9 million new jobs in 1972, an exceptional year. About 8.6 million new jobs have been added since 1965. In the light of these numbers, I think my point is clear: we can only produce these 13.5 million new jobs if we have a sustained period of the high profits that stimulate the generation of jobs, from now until 1980.

If business can fulfill this function, it will have fulfilled a major part of its responsibility to society, but obviously not all of it. The generation of jobs, important as it is, cannot be our do-all and end-all.

I don't have a very high opinion of the corporation that functions simply as a do-gooder. However unstylish it may be to say so, the corporation is not a welfare or a charitable institution. It should leave these activities to organizations specializing in them and stick to what it does best: providing goods and services. With some of the profits it earns, it may (and should) support noneconomic activities, but it can never itself become an eleemosynary institution.

To put it another way, the activities of the corporation should never be separated from the profit motive. Part of the problem of the business community today is not that we have been too devoted to the profit motive, but that we have somehow lost some of our faith in it. Too many business leaders have tried to respond to social demands by giving away money. Reproached for not fulfilling their social responsibilities, they tend to respond by giving more money to more social organizations. If the lines on the charts are moving up for both the number of organizations business gives money to and for the amount of money involved, businessmen seem to think they have incontrovertible proof that they are fulfilling their social responsibilities. And if a company receives three awards from socially oriented organizations this year and had another one last year, then it is viewed as a leader of industry, living proof that a company can really be socially responsible.

I think that road doesn't go anywhere. The high road for the company is still the profit road. What we really should be trying to do is to hitch up the profit motive to the social need or social problem.

RELATING PROFITS TO SOCIAL PERFORMANCE

We forget that every company was established in response to some social need, by some person who saw a way to make money out of serving that social need. That is true whether the company is in automobiles, or banking, or lemon cream pies, or lipsticks. If successful, it makes money and stays in business only by filling some need of society.

We should really be trying to figure out how to fill the needs of society by use of the profit motive. This is the core of my message. When we can do this, we usually have a winning strategy.

Where a product is involved, or a service, this is easy to understand. We can all recognize the social value of, say, a measles vaccine. But when a social problem is involved, this is more difficult to see.

Consider, as an example, industrial safety. At one time industrial injuries were fairly commonplace. As time passed, however, people began to see these accidents as events that should not be allowed to happen.

Highly sophisticated programs were developed for preventing industrial accidents and injuries. In the process, however, business discovered that accident prevention was not only humanitarian, it was good business. The money spent on preventing injuries actually paid off in increased production and earnings.

The real growth of safety programs in industry has occurred in the years since the discovery that safety was profitable. Preaching safety, long and hard and cleverly, was not effective until safety was tied to self-interest in the form of profits. The brute fact is that in most of us the profit motive is stronger than the humanitarian motive.

The profit motive is not as popular today as it once was. It is treated in many places, including a great many campuses, with scorn and derision. It is seen as an outmoded concept, an obsolete instrument of motivation, even as a capitalistic invention of the robber barons.

Those who treat it with such scorn simply do not realize how the concept of profit has changed in most American corporations in the last seventy-five years. The corporation has evolved in the last century from one-man satrapies and family ownership to control by boards of directors and ownership by thousands, even millions, of shareholders.

One facet of this evolution has been virtually ignored, namely, the change it has caused in the treatment and use of profits. There was a time when the profits of an enterprise were treated much as the owner wished. He might use them to expand the business, or he might simply put them in his own bank account. That is how many of the great family fortunes were accrued in this country a couple of generations ago. Under such a system there were bound to be social abuses.

Today, profits are treated entirely differently. The profits belong to the corporations, not to any individual, or (with increasingly rare exceptions) to any family. They are devoted to a great variety of *beneficial* uses, such as the expansion of the business, the payment of a reasonable reward to shareholders, investment in research, and the payment of taxes. Profits are not used primarily to fatten the coffers of the "boss," but to fulfill the material needs of society and to generate jobs.

In spite of this evolution in the use and treatment of profits we persist in thinking of them as tainted and undesirable, as in the old phrases "filthy lucre" and "ill-gotten gains." The old stereotype of profit as evil or ill-gotten gains has been nurtured by a variety of people: those who don't understand the free enterprise system or who are unaware of the changes that have taken place in it—which, unfortunately, includes many in the academic community; those who covet money for their own purposes, such as government administrators who see profits only as a source of taxes to further their own programs and objectives; and those who represent special interests, such as organized labor, consumer organizations, and conservation groups, who would like to see corporate profits used exclusively for *their* purposes, which are to raise wages and fringe benefits, or to reduce costs to the consumer, or to clean up our environment. Everyone wants the whole profit melon, and if not the whole melon, then as big a slice as he can get. But not many are willing to help grow a bigger melon, and few see the corporation—the farmer who grows the melons—as having very much to say about what happens to it.

The management of a company is no longer anointed with absolute power. Rather, it holds its power in trusteeship, and it can exercise this power only so long as it does so in a socially acceptable way. This means that the company must operate so that it balances the interests of the entire collectivity that it represents: employees, stockholders, customers, and suppliers, as well as the governments to which it is subject and the general public to which it is eventually accountable for its total performance. The board of directors of the corporation must operate in this collective interest, and only if the board operates in the interest of all is it genuinely discharging its social responsibilities.

CREATING THE SOCIALLY RESPONSIVE ENVIRONMENT

I have discussed the relationship of the profit motive and social responsibility at length because they are as closely related as the chicken and the egg. This brings me to the point where I can lay down critical postulates for creating a socially responsible management environment within a corporation.

Postulate No. 1: Social responsibility must be a firm, deep-seated belief of the management. It must be soundly and deeply a part of the ongoing goals and strategy of the corporation. Unless there is a genuine commitment on the part of the management this is not going to happen.

A social responsibility program is not something that can be hung on somewhere, like a bumper sticker. If it is, it will not last long, and it will not be successful. If social responsibility is treated as an expense item that is increased or reduced according to the economic performance of the business, there will not be a viable program. If the board of directors discusses how much it is going to devote to "social responsibility projects" in the coming year, you can be sure that the company is not really committed to responsibility and is not apt to be very highly rated as a socially responsible company by the general public, or by people outside the company who evaluate its responsiveness to social problems, or even by its own employees who know it best.

Perhaps the most noxious is the company that spends a few dollars for a few showcase social responsibility projects, and a great number of dollars in an advertising campaign to tell people how socially responsible it is. This kind of hypocrisy is eventually found out, and it reflects on all business. Advertising that you're socially responsible doesn't make you socially responsible any more than going into a garage makes you an automobile.

Postulate No. 2: Management must be consistent in its support of social responsibility. Consistency is the cornerstone when you are trying to build an environment, whether the objective is an environment for social responsibility or for growth or quality or any other management goal. If directions are changed frequently, people will simply turn off their hearing aids. If a company, for example, has a research program that is cut to the bone one year and souped up for a crash effort the next, it probably has a research program that is worthless. Social responsibility programs cannot be turned on and off. If they are, employees will quickly find out and credibility will be zero. The quickest way for management to persuade its employees that it does not believe in any program is to allocate lots of money for it in good years and chop the budget in bad years.

This consistency must extend throughout the organization. If local management is saying one thing and the people back at headquarters are saying another, the signals are bound to be confusing and the program will stutter and sputter. Social responsibility can't be like a weather vane, turning with every wind.

Postulate No. 3: Management commitment must be long-term. This seems to be self-evident, but it is vitally important. No major management commitment, whether it is social responsibility or anything else, can be directed toward only short-term goals if it is to be successful. If management enters upon an Equal Employment Opportunity program, for example, with short-term goals, or decides to launch a program to upgrade use of women's talents, and does not establish long-term goals, it is not really committed to these programs. If earnings decline and management announces, "Well, we can't do these things this year, business is down," it will be seen, and seen correctly, that there is no substantial long-term commitment.

Building a sense of social responsibility in a given area of activity requires a long period of time during which management demonstrates, consistently, its interest and its seriousness. In my experience this usually takes ten years or more before a company can move from a management commitment to a deeply ingrained facet of the corporate personality, shared in, believed in, and acted upon at every personnel level throughout the organization.

In essence, these postulates state that to establish an organizational climate for social responsibility (or for anything else, for that matter) one must start with a management commitment; that the commitment to these new goals must be made an integral part of the corporation's ongoing life; that strategy and communications related to these goals must be faithful and consistent; and that there must be a steadfast commitment in good times and bad.

These postulates are foundation stones only. Every company and every program will require its own individual blueprint for social responsibility, but these will be fundamental principles common to all such efforts.

Pollution Control in Dow Chemical

It may be useful to trace the applications of these principles to an actual case history in the company I know best, Dow Chemical. How we went about establishing a climate for socially responsible performance in the field of environmental affairs makes a good case history for two reasons: first, because it fits all the major parameters I have laid down; and, second, because, frankly, it's a success story. Dow recently was awarded the 1972 *Business Week* magazine Public Service Award for its excellent performance in this field.

As everyone knows, chemical companies have serious pollution problems. Dow makes some 1,100 different products, many of them highly hazardous, and in making and marketing some $2.25 billion worth of these products annually some are bound to spill and some to spoil, creating pollution problems of a major magnitude. At our plant in Midland, Michigan, the waste disposal area is larger than the manufacturing facility. The silver lining in this is that because we have so many problems we also know more than most about handling pollution.

We established a separate and distinct pollution control function back in 1934. Over the years we developed many innovations in pollution control: instruments for measuring it, processes for handling it, and products for treating it. By 1958 we were ready to set up a separate business (which we did) to intensify our research and development in pollution control and to market this know-how and the related products. Our background in environmental matters, in short, was soundly based and solidly established by the time environmental contamination became a front-page topic about ten years ago.

Because of this background, there was no difficulty in arriving at a complete commitment by management to environmental cleanup; we had been committed to that for many years. In fact, we believed this was an area where we could, to a considerable degree, exercise leadership, and the board of directors adopted a policy that Dow would stand for "excellence and leadership in environmental improvement."

Getting this message to all employees, and getting them genuinely to believe it and act upon it, too, required considerably more planning and doing. At an early date, the board of directors determined that the plans for any new plant for which capital funds were appropriated must incorporate specific provisions for handling the wastes generated. No appropriation request would be considered by the board without such provisions. In relation to the environmental impact of our products, we were in relatively good shape; in 1933 we had established one of industry's first toxicology laboratories, whose job has always been to determine and safeguard the safety of our products.

However, as time went on, we felt we needed something more, something that would dramatize management's belief in "environmental excellence" and provide a vehicle for consistency of communication and action at all levels and in every geographical area of the company's operations. In response to this need we established what we call our Ecology Council. This is an eleven-member Council, formed principally of top-management personnel (including the president and the chairman of the board), whose job is to guide and expand the company's work in environmental improvement. It also serves as a communications network throughout the company. All of our manufacturing locations and product departments have their own Ecology Sub-Councils, as do our geographic regions. We have an Ecology Council in Latin America, for example, and in Europe, and elsewhere, just as there is one at major plants in Louisiana, Texas, and California.

We also now require that every research report include a discussion of the environmental effects of the product or project. We have put rather more emphasis on waste prevention than on waste disposal, in line with the profit concepts that I have already discussed. Preventing waste is our primary goal because if you prevent waste you will have more product to sell and earnings will increase. Concentrating on waste disposal and building waste disposal facilities creates a drain on earnings and is entirely the wrong way to go about it. Therefore we have shifted a great deal of our research emphasis to increased yields, recycling, better waste treatment procedures, and the like.

This has been a long-term commitment. While our Ecology Council was formally set up only three years ago, management's position on environmental improvement has been clear and consistent for at least the last twelve or fourteen years, going back to about the time we set up our Environmental Control Systems department as a separate business. Looking back on it, I estimate that we kept up a sustained board-level interest in the subject for about ten years before we could be confident that our employees at large, at every level, were aware of, interested in, and supportive of the concept. It was highly significant to me that during the years 1969 and 1970, which were rather sour years in a business sense, Dow people neither suggested any cutbacks in our environmental improvement projects nor made any move to institute any such cutbacks on their own. This signified to me that the program was finally totally integrated into the warp and woof of company life and had become part of our thinking.

Parenthetically, let me say that I'm not sure whether to give credit for this devotion to (a) the fine caliber of employees we have at Dow Chemical, or (b) the thoroughness with which management instilled in employees the advantages of such a policy. Probably some of both were at work, although (a) may have been more important than (b). The most powerful effect surely comes from the combination of (a) and (b).

This program continues to expand and to bear new fruit. We have now established what we call "global guidelines" for our environmental controls. I believe we are the first company to establish guidelines for air pollution control, water pollution control, and the like, for manufacturing plants around the world. We direct our plant managers to comply with local regulations or Dow regulations on environmental matters, whichever are more stringent; in many countries, of course, government regulations simply do not exist.

With respect to our employees, we have undertaken a variety of communications projects which are examples of the kind of essential supporting actions needed to establish a climate for social responsibility. We produced a film for employee use, detailing their responsibilities in environmental improvement and setting forth the company's position on this subject. We conducted a school for employee volunteers who wanted to know more about environmental subjects, with several members of our board, including myself, on the faculty. The school was operated by our Environmental Testing Advisory Board, a group of company scientists who counseled on testing procedures in many areas. We awarded the company's first (and to date only) Public Service Award to a young, waste control engineer who in his spare time devised a series of environmental lesson plans for classroom use in elementary and high schools. Those lesson plans are now being used by teachers in schools across the nation.

Much of our current effort is being devoted to what we call "product stewardship." This is an important aspect of social responsibility. As we define the concept, it means that we have a responsibility for a product every step of the way, in manufacture, in shipping and distribution, in its use, and on to its final disposal.

Our marketing people work with our customers so that safe handling, safe use, and safe disposal are hallmarks of our activities, and so that our products are not used in ways not intended or tested for. Our manufacturing people are concerned not only with meeting our pollution control standards but with safety in the packaging and movement of goods. Our research and development personnel emphasize safe products, environmentally sound products, and part of their responsibility is to develop information for safe handling, use, and disposal of our products.

In brief, we now have virtually complete integration of activity in this area throughout the company. I would even like to think that we have come reasonably close to "excellence and leadership" in this area, as we early expressed our goal—even though I will be the first to admit that we still have a long way to go.

The Profit Approach to Social Action

I am firmly convinced by this experience that it is possible to establish an environment for socially responsible performance, given the ingredients that I have mentioned, and to do so successfully. Let me suggest two examples of more esoteric social problems and suggest ways of getting at them. The first of these problems is how to eradicate the various diseases which we are medically and technologically now in a position to eradicate. We have low-cost vaccines for the prevention of measles, polio, diphtheria, tetanus, whooping cough, rubella, and mumps. But we have not sufficiently organized our resources to stamp out these diseases. The annual reported number of cases of measles, for example, dropped from 200,000 in 1966 to only 22,000 in 1968, but the immunization effort was transitory and the number moved back up to 75,000 cases in 1971.

Plainly, we ought to mount a great national campaign to stamp out these diseases once and for all. We have not done it. The campaign ought to be carried on by government agencies, in concert with the manufacturers of the vaccines, in such a way that everyone profits from the effort. If we make it profitable to everyone, it will get done.

As a start in this direction, Dow has been instrumental in the establishment of an organization called the "Action Committee for Childhood Immunizations." This is a nonprofit agency whose mission is "to develop a plan for the national financing and coordinated local administration of an immunization program to reduce the number of susceptibles to such a perennial level as to achieve the objective of permanent national eradication" of the seven childhood diseases I have mentioned.

Three possible areas of profit potential can be identified: first, from the vaccine manufacturers, straight commissions to the Action Committee on gross vaccine sales; second, fees to the Committee for acting as central administrator of, and vaccine purchasing and distribution agent for, the national eradication program; and third, fees from the Committee to outside consultants for research and planning.

This is, in a sense, simply an innovation in marketing. In a larger sense, it is clearly a vehicle for linking up the profit motive and the solution to a real social problem.

The second problem is the economic status of the American Indian. Much publicity has recently been given to the deprivations suffered by this group of people. An Indian's life expectancy is only forty-four years; he suffers more than 50 percent unemployment; his suicide and alcoholism rates are many times the national averages. We tend to merely wring our hands about such a problem, and, at best, to appropriate more government funds to their solution this year than we did last year.

My contention is that we need to approach this kind of problem by asking ourselves again how we can tie in the profit motive. I suggest (and I emphasize that this is simply a suggestion) that we need to establish Indian business groups as profit centers for the Indians themselves, and, on their initiative, to develop job opportunities in the reservation setting. Another profit-making possibility lies in recruitment of Indians for specialized business training and education at secondary, college, and graduate levels for these Indian-operated companies, by a reasonable commitment of funds to underwrite this education, with government, foundation, and religious organization funds as the main sources.

Postulate No. 4: The business executive must never underestimate the power of nonverbal communication. A business leader cannot preach one thing and do another; it must be, "Do as I do," not, "Do as I say." In establishing a climate for social responsibility he ignores this rule at his peril.

In the case study I have described, the establishment of our Ecology Council was effective in the Dow company primarily because it involved the top managers of the company directly in the effort to do something about a problem. It said in a nonverbal way, "Do as I do." If we had merely appointed a group of people to do this for us, I don't think very much would have happened.

Let me go back to the safety example. For many years at Dow we preached at people about "safety first" and the prevention of accidents and told them how concerned we were about safety. But we didn't seem to get through. In retrospect, what was happening was that people noticed that the supervisors and managers who did best, and who most frequently were promoted, were still those who got the production out or got their job done, whatever it was, regardless of their safety records. They didn't believe management when it said "safety first" because our actions were proving otherwise.

Eventually, we assigned a member of our board of directors to be directly, 100 percent responsible for safety. The first thing on the agenda at each board meeting was safety. The board determined that no project would be approved without provision for its safety aspects. Our president began personally to hand out safety awards and to show great interest in safety, and we all encouraged interest and participation in safety contests and dinners and related activities.

These kinds of actions were several ways better than anything communicated on the subject of safety previously, because they said, "Do as I do," not, "Do as I say."

Postulate No. 5: The carrot is a more effective motivator than the stick.

If the company is to be established as socially responsible, it will not be productive to announce that every employee who shows signs of being socially irresponsible will be horsewhipped or given early retirement, at his option. Coercion is not the route to anywhere anymore. Does that mean bonuses should be paid to socially responsible employees? Perhaps in isolated cases—and Dow does. But I have a different type of carrot in mind, and that carrot is the self-interest of the employee and the identification of his self-interest with that of the company.

Let me give you an example. We are presently undertaking a major effort to revise our views of the role of women in chemical companies (it has not been very large, traditionally). We are moving as rapidly as we can to improve the status of women in the company, and this again has a top management commitment behind it. We have promoted two of our most capable women to be assistant secretaries of the company, we have established a group of "ombuds-women" to push the advancement of women, and we are doing a variety of other things related to this objective.

In this kind of effort, the most difficult thing to accomplish is not the actual promotions or appointments or other related matters; far more difficult is to change the social context of the workplace. In this case, what a woman employee does and how she feels about herself are determined to a great degree by what people around her expect her to do and be, and by what the situation in which she finds herself implies she should do and be. (Here is nonverbal communication at work again.)

How do you change this social context? Well, there are a great many things you can do, and I have discussed several of them, but I think basically what you have to do is to hold out a carrot to the people who need to change—the carrot that shows them how it is to their advantage to change.

Our management commitment to the advancement of women is simply based on self-interest and the profit motive. We believe we can increase our earnings as well as our corporate effectiveness by increasing our utilization of women's talents. We believe the under-utilized reserve of women's talents is the greatest reservoir of ability presently open to us. It would be shortsighted as well as uneconomic to ignore this. What we have to do is to communicate to our people that changes here are in the best interests of Dow and of Dow profits, and, therefore, in their own best interests.

People will head toward business goals, and do so enthusiastically, if the goals are stated simply and understandably and if they are credible and acceptable. Goals become credible and acceptable when management shows an interest in them, participates in them, supports them, follows through on them, and rewards those who contribute most to their achievement. It will, of course, help considerably if employees have a natural liking for the goals to begin with.

This is true whether the goal has to do with the advancement of women, safety, environmental improvement, or any other aspect of social responsibility. And motivating social responsibility with a carrot rather than a stick will strongly contribute to successful results.

The five postulates or principles that I have discussed are necessary to the establishment of a favorable management climate in any organization that is going to exhibit socially responsible performance. You must have a deep management commitment to social responsibility; it must be an integral part of the business, and the management must be consistent in its communications about the subject, and willing to stick with its commitment through thick and thin. Further, the management must avoid doing one thing and saying another, and it must tie rewards to success.

But these rules, important as they are, must always be subordinate to the most important principle of all. The corporation's first responsibility is long-term profit growth. All its efforts to solve social problems will fail, or be only shallowly successful, if they are not integrated into the primary objective of long-term profit growth, and understood in this fashion by management and all other employees. In other words, solving social problems must be good business as well as good citizenship.

EDITOR'S COMMENTARY

As every experienced executive knows, determining policy is one thing, executing determined policy effectively and efficiently is another. And between the policy determination and execution there can be, and often is, a gap. There are many reasons for the existence of the gap, but probably the principal one is discrepancy between the goals of top management, the policy makers, and the goals of middle and junior management, the policy implementers. There is nothing unusual about this discrepancy. It is only one example out of many that document the contrast between corporate objectives and personal objectives. Even at the level of the chief executive officer, personal objectives may not be fully consistent with optimal goals for the business as an entity, although in most cases there is greater likelihood of such consistency here than at lower levels in the organization—and, indeed, in practice top management objectives become corporate objectives. At lower management levels motivations associated with career building may create gross differences between what is good for a company and what is perceived by individual managers as good for themselves.

Much of the machinery of administration represents an effort to bring the objectives of middle management into line with corporate objectives, as determined by top management. Organization structure, job descriptions, budgets and other targets for accomplishment, performance measurement systems, reward and punishment devices—all serve this end. Operating realities often create dissonance, however, between the target of administrative machinery and management behavior. A common difficulty in many corporations, for example, is the discrepancy between top management's concern with strategic planning and lower management's interest in short-run performance generated by pressures to meet budget and similar short-term targets. When managers perceive the reward system offering high personal career payoffs for meeting short-term operating targets, their interest in planning and making commitments for a more distant future declines sharply. The only effective prescription for handling this common problem is to build contributions to corporate objectives into the specific job responsibilities of each operating manager, set targets for accomplishment, measure performance, and use the reward system to reinforce behavior.

These observations apply with even greater force to the execution throughout a business of socially responsible policies and programs determined by the top-management group. The key element in converting these decisions into operating reality is middle management. Directives and exhortations are not likely to be effective in getting the results top management has in view. In addition to the normal dissonance, described above, special difficulties can be anticipated. Some middle managers are likely, at least in the early stages, to be skeptical of the sincerity of top management's interest in socially responsible performance. Some will conclude that expressions of concern by the chief executive about responding to social demands on business are part of the public relations posture required at that visible apex of the business. Even more important, however, will be the specific fact that implementing socially responsible policies and programs will be perceived as handicapping operating managers' ability to accomplish established revenue, cost, and profit performance objectives. Introducing members of minority groups and women into a work force in which they have not been represented previously creates personnel administration problems and may have a negative effect on short-term costs and productivity. Controlling environmental contamination disrupts normal operating systems and may also add to expenses without compensating short-term revenue benefits. Investment in pollution control technology may be seen as limiting funds available for normal operations. Directing procurement to inexperienced and untested minority suppliers is likely to create product quality and delivery schedule problems. Many other rather obvious examples could be added to this list.

If top management is serious in its commitment to corporate social responsibility, it will have to confront this issue of dissonant objectives. As far as informed observers of corporate performance are concerned, the real test of top management's commitment in any company will be action to redefine operating management job responsibilities by adding specific goals related to specific programs, establishing procedures for measuring management performance in each responsibility area, and making it clear that each manager's record of accomplishment with respect to these new responsibilities will be considered along with the rest of his operating record in the distribution of rewards and punishments. In short, socially responsible performance needs to be supported by the same array of motivational devices required for every other aspect of management performance.

Some who are skeptical about the feasibility of substantial improvements in corporate performance in areas where response to new social pressures appears to run head on into rooted racial and sexual attitudes have suggested that even the motivational structure described here will be ineffective. They point out that managers who don't want these programs to succeed can find ways to render them ineffective without damage to their standard operations, and that others who don't expect them to succeed (because of ingrained stereotypic beliefs about the limited capabilities of unfamiliar groups of workers or managers) will not apply their imagination and energy to achieve positive results.

There is some basis for these concerns and it is useful to have them openly identified. They are related to the general class of problem associated with innovation in ongoing organization systems, with its familiar syndrome of opposition to change by those who see change as a threat to their position and prospects, or at least as a source of insecurity. And there is a potential for even more sharply focused negativism because the particular innovations involved in some socially responsible programs touch attitudes with deep emotional implications, developed from and sustained by influences and experiences outside the work-place.

There is an operational response to these skeptics, grounded in a body of research in social and industrial psychology and practical work experience. It is certainly true that deeply rooted racial and sexual attitudes are not easily or quickly modified, although they are likely to be adaptively responsive over time to new experiences that challenge the validity of the ingrained attitudes. But attitude is not the only determinant of behavior. Other motivational influences can be brought to bear on behavior and can be so structured as to override the influence of attitude. The operating manager who says (or feels, even if he hesitates to say), "I have never worked for a woman [or a black, or an Indian, or . . .] and I certainly won't ask any of my people to," can be influenced to behave contrary to his expressed or implicit attitude. He has a larger interest than the self-gratification of implementing his own prejudices, and that is maintaining his position and advancing his career. If clearly stated corporate policy, reinforced by superior management exposition, built into specific job responsibility, tested by periodic measurement of performance, with achievement of goals rewarded and failures punished all combine to influence behavior along desired lines, they will prevail over cherished attitudes, at least in the workplace. In the longer term, positive experiences on the job are likely to be additionally supportive and, for most people, an erosion effect on attitudes can be predicted. Whether or not this occurs, however, although perhaps important for the individual manager's ultimate peace of mind, is not important for his job performance.

CHAPTER 4

Business Responsibility and Economic Behavior

William J. Baumol

The economist considers corporate social responsibility from a different viewpoint than the business executive. He is more concerned than the individual executive is likely to be about the total performance of the system and about relationships among firms that affect their decisions in allocating and using resources. Looking through the economist's assessment, we can gain insights into management problems and ways of responding to them that can be related, in turn, to the aggregate economic response of the business system to the society in which it functions.

The following chapter presents an economist's view of the changing character of social expectations and demands for business performance, and of patterns of response and their implications for economic results.

*The author of this chapter is William J. Baumol, Joseph Douglas Green '95 Professor of Economics, Princeton University.–*EDITOR

UNDER pressure from many sides, corporate managements have been quick to assert their agreement in principle to the proposition that the firm should concern itself with the ills of society, particularly as those ills have begun to seem increasingly threatening. After all, the modern firm has shown itself to be one of the most efficient economic instruments in history. Since the beginning of the industrial revolution it has increased real per capita incomes perhaps twenty-fold, incredible though that may seem. It has doubled and redoubled and redoubled again the energy placed at the service of mankind, and has achieved an increasing productivity of human labor which is astonishing both in its magnitude and its persistence. With such a record, what other institution can be better adapted to deal with the difficult economic problems that underlie so many of our social issues?

I will argue that this line of reasoning is fundamentally valid, but not if interpreted and implemented in the obvious manner which generally seems to be proposed by both business and its critics. The proposal seems to be that industry should exhibit a massive outburst of altruism, modifying its goals to include in addition to the earning of profits, improvement of the environment, the training of the unskilled, and much more. As John Diebold has put the matter in a recent address: "[There is the danger that] . . . business as 'good corporate citizen' [will] start to view itself, or be viewed by others, as an all-purpose institution that should right all social wrongs. (If you added together the rhetoric in this field you wouldn't fall far short of business being called upon to do just this!)."[1]

I will argue that any such undertaking is undesirable even if it were achievable. Moreover I will give reasons why it cannot be expected to work—why the task undertaken on such a basis is likely to be managed badly. Tokenism is the natural product of such a process. Indeed, not only is business likely to prove inefficient as a voluntary healer of the ills of society, but the attempt to play such a role may well have adverse effects on its efficiency in the fields where it now operates and in which its abilities have been demonstrated so strikingly.

I will argue that the primary job of business is to make money for its stockholders. This does not mean that the best way to do everything is as it is done now. On the contrary, society has every reason to ask business to be much more careful in its use of the environment, to do much more to protect the interests of consumers, etc. But we neither should nor can rely on "voluntarism" for the purpose.

If we want business to behave differently from the way it does today we must change the rules of the game so that the behavior we desire becomes more profitable than the activity patterns we want to modify. If pollution is made expensive enough, we will be treated quickly to a spectacular display of business efficiency in reducing emission rates. If the production of unsafe products is made sufficiently costly, one can be confi-

---

[1] "The Social Responsibility of Business," Address at the conference on "An Economic Society for Man," June 21, 1972.

dent of a remarkable acceleration in the flow of innovations making for greater safety. Business will then do the things it knows how to do best and society will be the beneficiary.

Under the terms of such an approach, is there no role for "business responsibility"? Is the firm simply to pursue profits and no more? That is not quite enough. Responsibility on the part of business, from this viewpoint, has two requirements: (1) when appropriate changes in the rules are proposed by the duly constituted representatives of the community, responsible management must refrain from efforts to sabotage this undertaking; (2) business should cooperate in the design of these rules to assure their effectiveness in achieving their purpose and to make certain that their provisions interfere as little as possible with the efficient working of the economy. But, by and large, these are just the things businessmen have, in effect, refused to do.

DANGERS OF VOLUNTEER "SOCIAL RESPONSIBILITY"

The notion that firms should by themselves pursue the objectives of society is, in fact, a rather frightening proposition. Corporate management holds in its hands enormous financial resources. Voluntarism suggests, or rather demands, that management use these resources to influence the social and political course of events. But who is to determine in what way these events ought to be influenced? Who is to select these goals? If it is management itself, the power of interference with our lives and the lives of others that management is asked to assume is surely intolerable. The threat to effective democracy should be clear enough.

The point is made most clearly by recent demands that business firms exercise responsibility in their investments abroad, meaning specifically that firms should abstain from investment in countries whose governments draw the disapproval of the person who happens to advocate such a course. The firm may be asked to eschew investment in countries that repress or persecute particular ethnic groups, or whose governments trample civil liberties, or are aggressive militarily, or simply oppose United States foreign policy with sufficient vigor. I do not want to argue here either the efficacy or the desirability of boycotts. Nor do I wish to defend the countries which have been attacked by critics of corporate policies on overseas investment. I, too, am repelled by some of their governments. In sum, I am not arguing for isolation or for the ignoring of oppression. Rather, I deplore the notion that American business should attempt to arrogate to itself the determination of our foreign policy.

It may or may not make sense to boycott some particular foreign government. But I do not want a business management to decide what government should be boycotted. And certainly I do not want management to use the capital I have entrusted to it to impose its notions of international morality upon the world.

Again, in Diebold's words,

I personally believe [the choice of social goals] is the job of the politician working in a democratic political process. The businessman as businessman should not be making essentially social decisions. The businessman should be the tool who responds to market demand by making what society shows it wants. Do not make him more mighty than that.

An increase in corporate power is probably the last thing that those who call for greater "corporate responsibility" would want. Yet that, paradoxically, is precisely where some of their prescriptions lead.

TOKEN ACTIVITIES

Predictably, there has been a considerable gap between business' glowing accounts of its own accomplishments and the actual magnitude of its achievements. Newspapers report many cases in which their public relations men have run far ahead of what companies have actually accomplished. *Newsweek* reported the case of a company with the

". . . only industrial mill in the U.S. to have been the subject of separate air and water pollution abatement hearings before Federal authorities whose advertising asserted 'it cost us a bundle but the Clearwater River still runs clear' . . . what [the firm] neglected to mention was that the picture [in the advertisement] had been snapped some 50 miles upstream from the . . . plant [where] it dumps up to 40 tons of suspended organic wastes into Clearwater and nearby Snake River every day."[2]

After citing several other such cases, the article goes on to report some more routine examples.

Even without bending the facts, companies may inflate their ecological contributions with half-truths. FMC Corp. recently took out double-page spreads in national publications to boast of its participation in the $3.8 million Santee, Calif., water-reclamation project, which converts sewage into water fit for swimming and boating. Conveniently omitted was the fact the FMC did no more than sell the project some $76,000 worth of pumps and equipment. Nor was there any mention of the company's inorganic-chemical plant in West Virginia which daily dumps more than

[2] *Newsweek*, December 28, 1970, pp. 49–51.

500,000 pounds of wastes, mostly toxic, into a nearby river, according to the Federal Power Commission.

Similarly, Union Carbide began an ad boosting its efforts to reduce auto pollution with the observation that 'Driving through this beautiful land of ours, you can get all choked up.' To the residents of the Kanawha Valley in West Virginia this is hardly news. So much smoke billows from the chimneys of Union Carbide's main ferroalloy plant there—28,000 tons of particulates a year—that a nearby Roman Catholic church had to encase an outdoor statue of St. Anthony in a fiber glass case to protect if from corrosion.

The conclusion to be drawn from this and the many other illustrations that can be cited is *not* that businessmen are particularly dishonest. Having associated with many businessmen over the years, I have come away with the impression that their personal integrity, their good will, and their distress at injustice does not differ notably from those of other groups. Of course, the honesty and the degree of concern with social issues will vary from one businessman to another, as it does elsewhere.[3] But even with the best intentions, given the rules of the game as they are today, there is little the individual businessman can do.

It is the prime virtue of the competitive process that it leaves little up to the good will of individual managements. The firm that is inefficient or that does not provide the public with the products it wants is given short shrift by the market mechanism. It is a merciless process which has no pity for the weak, ineffectual businessman. The chiseller who undercuts an inefficient concern is the consumers' best friend, though he is anathema to the firms that long for the quiet life and its permissive mediocrity.

But that same competitive process which prevents laziness or incompetence also precludes voluntarism on any significant scale. The businessman who chooses voluntarily to spend till it hurts on the environment, on the training of the handicapped, or in support of higher education is likely to find that he, too, is vulnerable to the chiseller without social conscience who, by avoiding such outlays, can supply his outputs more cheaply.

In the words of Edward L. Rogers, general counsel of the Environmental Defense Fund, "If I were a company president right now, I wouldn't do any more than I had to on the pollution front, because that would hurt my company more than its competitors."[4]

---

[3] Note that consumers' records of voluntary compliance in these areas are no better than those of business firms. It is easy to document cases in which there has been a response that is less than spectacular to voluntary programs for recycling of solid wastes, for the increased use of car pools, or for installation of inexpensive emission control kits in automobiles.

[4] *Newsweek,* December 28, 1970, p. 51.

The invisible hand does not work by inducing business firms to pursue the goals of society as a matter of conscience and good will. Rather, when the rules are designed properly it gives management no other option. Adam Smith was acutely aware of this. The famous invisible hand passage is often quoted, but, for some reason, the two critical sentences that conclude the paragraph are often omitted: "I have never known much good done by merchants who affected to trade for the public good. It is an affectation, indeed, not very common among merchants and very few words need be employed in dissuading them from it."

USE OF THE PRICE MECHANISM

Economists have long argued that when faced with mounting social problems one should not abandon the profit system or undermine its workings. Rather, if one is really serious about the social goals that are being urged upon business, one should use that powerful economic instrument, the price mechanism, to help attain them.

For example, it has been suggested that the reason industry (like others) has been so free in using the atmosphere as a dumping ground for its gaseous wastes is that clean air is a valuable resource available for use by anyone at a price far below its cost to society. Imagine what would happen if, say, coal or cloth or some other such resource were supplied free to anyone who wanted to use it, in any desired quantity and with no accounting for its manner of utilization. The resulting wastes and inefficiencies are all too easy to envision. But that is precisely what is encouraged when society, by virtue of long tradition, makes available on precisely those terms the use of its water, its air, and its other resources that are held in common.

Economists have, therefore, suggested that an appropriate remedial measure is to levy an adequate charge for the use of such resources. If made costly enough, their use will rapidly become more sparing and less inefficient.

There are many virtues to such a program which need not be gone into in any detail. Any such system of charges (e.g., a tax of x dollars per gallon on the discharge of certain types of effluents into waterways) is as automatic as any tax collection process. It does not involve the uncertainties of detection of violations and of the subsequent judicial process. It does not rely on the vigor of enforcement agencies, which seems so often to wane rapidly with the passage of time. It offers its largest rewards in the form of decreased taxes to the firms that are most efficient in reducing emissions. It thereby makes use of the full force of the market mechanism as an instrument of efficiency. It may be added that these are not all the virtues that can be claimed for such an arrangement. From the point of view of the businessman himself there is a great deal to be said for it.

First, it is a natural extension of the profit system, which he should welcome as a means to strengthen its workings and its social acceptability in the long run.

Second, it protects him from the notion that he is engaged in criminal activity when in the course of his productive operations wastes are unavoidably generated. By making him pay the full social costs of his activities, including all of the resources he utilizes in his operations, it becomes clear that he is engaged in a normal and commendable productive process, rather than the antisocial activity of which he is all too easily suspected under current arrangements.

Third, such a set of rules protects him against undercutting by competitors when he does behave in a manner consistent with social objectives —there is no room created for undercutting by the chiseller when everyone is subject to similar costs imposed for the protection of society.[5]

Finally, and this should in the long run be most important of all to the businessman, the proposal avoids completely the imposition of direct controls by the government. A management is not told how to run its business—whether to install taller smokestacks or to recycle or to adopt a higher-grade fuel. Rather, emissions are made highly unprofitable and the businessman is invited to decide for himself the most effective ways of reducing them or of eliminating them altogether. There need be no acceleration in the process of erosion of the freedom of enterprise. Changes in prices of inputs are a normal business phenomenon. Fuel can be expected to grow more expensive as its scarcity increases, and other inputs grow cheaper as innovation improves their productive technology, but neither of these changes undercuts the prerogatives of management. Similarly, the imposition of a charge corresponding to the social costs of the use of environmental resources does not interfere with the managerial decision process. It merely changes the structure of the economy's rewards to the company, increasing the profitability of the behavior desired by the community.

CHANGES IN RULES

This proposal is not, in itself, my central point. Rather, it illustrates what I mean by a change in the rules of the game. Many other types of changes in rules are possible.

[5] Of course, if such a rule applies only in a small geographic area, it does not protect the firm from the competition of suppliers located elsewhere. But this argues that such rules should cover as large a geographic area as possible, not that they should be avoided.

The type most frequently talked about is direct controls: for example, quotas assigned to firms or to municipal treatment plants, specifying maximum quantities of emissions and standards of purity which they must meet before they can be discharged into waterways. All sort of things can be specified by direct controls. They can require the installation of specified types of devices which limit the emissions of automobiles; they can make mandatory the use of various safety devices. The range and variety of such regulations should be obvious enough.

Besides such direct controls, whose enforcement is left to government agencies, other changes in rules are also possible. For example, legislation authorizing legal suits by interested private citizens has often been advocated. Something intermediate between direct controls and the fiscal methods described above is represented by the construction of treatment facilities by governmental agencies, whose costs polluters are then required to bear.

The essential point is that all of these procedures involve changes in the rules themselves. The firm is not expected to do anything as a pure act of benevolence. Rather, it is faced with a new set of conditions under which it and its competitors must operate, and they must adapt themselves as effectively as they can. The two most important characteristics of such changes in the rules, as far as we are concerned, are that there is nothing voluntary about following them, and that it applies equally to all competitors. In this way, it frees management from pressures to undertake a role in the policy-making process which it has no reason to want and which society has every reason to fear. Moreover, it protects the firm from attacks by those who stand ready to undercut it at the first opportunity, an opportunity which would be opened were the firm to bow to social pressures for the voluntary pursuit of its social responsibilities.

THE RESPONSE OF BUSINESS

With such potential advantages to the firm, to the free enterprise system, and to society, one might have expected that at least a substantial segment of the business community would have welcomed such changes in the rules with open arms. After all, does not that constitute a true acceptance by business of its social responsibility, through an arrangement that elicits desirable behavior from everyone and avoids the ineffectiveness and inequities of voluntarism?

But nothing of the sort has in fact occurred. Only recently have there appeared a few breaks in the solid opposition of the business community, when one automobile manufacturer (Ford) and one gasoline distributor (Mobil) joined those who question the desirability of the Highway Trust

Fund as currently constituted. However, such defections are still very much a rarity.

Let me illustrate the point. When I first undertook the preparation of this paper it seemed appropriate to see what might be suggested by the newspapers. For the next twelve days I searched the *New York Times* for relevant materials and encountered not a single example of industry support for anything that could be interpreted as a change in the rules designed to strengthen the protection of the public's interests. But I *did* find a profusion of pertinent cases in which industry took the opposite position. These are summarized in the following excerpts:[6]

Example 1. Consumer Protection

Legislation to create a consumer protection agency which would represent consumers before federal courts and regulatory agencies died on the Senate floor, a victim of a filibuster. The bill, regarded as the most important consumer measure of the present Congress, commanded majority support in the Senate; but it ran into intensive opposition from industry.[7]

Example 2. Regulation of Phosphate Utilization

Administration officials reported today that Governor Cahill will push next month for final legislative approval of a controversial measure that would give New Jersey the power to ban phosphates from detergents and other cleaning agents. . . . State officials reported that the Senate's Republican leadership now favors the measure, which died last year in committee at the hands of the detergent industry and organized labor interests in the Legislature.[8]

Example 3. Control of Strip Mining

Legislation to provide for regulation of the strip-mining of coal and the conservation and reclamation of strip-mining areas was passed by the House today and sent to the Senate. The vote was 265 to 75.

The House measure would give the Interior Department authority to issue cease-and-desist orders against any surface-mining of coal when the health and safety of the public or employees is involved; to designate cer-

---

[6] I do not mean to suggest that this is a random sample, i.e., that this represents the number of such stories one would encounter in a representative two weeks. The period that happened to be chosen encompassed the adjournment of Congress and so the number of pieces of legislation whose fate was settled was unusually high.

[7] J. W. Finney, *New York Times,* October 8, 1972, Sect. 4, p. 1.

[8] R. Sullivan, *New York Times,* October 11, 1972, p. 1.

tain areas as unsuitable for strip-mining if lasting injury would be caused to the environment; and to issue and revoke permits for strip-mining.

Six months after enactment, no coal strip-mining could be conducted without a permit. Except for reclamation plans, any permit application would have to have the written consent of the owner of the surface of the land.

Carl E. Bagge, president of the National Coal Association, representing coal operators, said the bill was a punitive, unrealistic measure which would reduce the nation's production of coal by 25 percent almost overnight.

Mr. Bagge assailed the bill as an "arbitrary, simplistic solution" to a complex problem. He urged the Senate to reject it, contending that it was too late in the session to amend the House bill to one that was satisfactory.[9]

Example 4. Safety of Drug Products

In an effort to persuade the House to narrow the legal remedies in a pending product safety bill, Thomas G. Corcoran, a Washington lawyer who represents major drug interests, pointed out that the bill could overburden the Federal courts with new cases. The drug industry was leading the fight against the bill, which is now nearing enactment.[10]

Example 5. Inspection for Disease-Carrying Pets

When the polyethylene bag was invented, the tropical fish industry ballooned. Its bubble may burst, pet supply wholesalers say, because of a proposed Federal law affecting fish imports, modeled after other regulations restricting the sale of turtles and banning the import of certain birds to prevent communicable disease.

"We recognize the need for inspection and regulation," says Richard Kyllo of Saddle River, vice president of the newly organized tropical Fish Institute of America. "But the new codes were enacted in a state of panic. They are so loosely worded that they leave an open road to any kind of interpretation."

New Jersey is among many states that recently passed restrictions on selling turtles unless they were found free of salmonella, a bacteria that causes intestinal disease. The regulations were a reaction to the death in 1969 of a 9-year-old turtle owner in Connecticut.[11]

Example 6. Information on Restaurant Sanitation

The New Jersey Public Health Council tonight ordered all restaurants in the state to post the results of their state sanitary inspection reports

[9] *New York Times,* October 12, 1972, p. 1.
[10] F. P. Graham, *New York Times,* October 14, 1972, p. 1.
[11] J. Marks, *New York Times,* October 15, 1972, p. 96.

conspicuously near their entrance, in an effort to open heretofore confidential inspection files to public scrutiny.

"We have kept intact our promise to provide consumer health protection unequaled anywhere in the country," Dr. Cowan said.

As a result, the restaurant industry, which bitterly opposed the open posting of inspection reports at a public hearing here last month, is expected to contest the council's order in the courts.[12]

Example 7. Water Pollution Control

The Senate and House of Representatives overrode today President Nixon's veto of the Federal Water Pollution Control Act of 1972, which thus becomes law and authorizes $24.6 billion over three years to clean up the nation's lakes and rivers. During nearly two years of Congressional deliberation on the bill, the White House had supported industry's opposition to many of its provisions, particularly the goal of no discharges of industrial pollutants by 1985 and the setting of limitations on effluents for classes of industry.[13]

Other illustrations are easy enough to provide. The billboard industry, the manufacturers of plastics, of tetraethyl lead, and many others have all played the same game. The outcries have become familiar: proposed regulations are "punitive," "unworkable," "staggeringly expensive," and even "ruinous." Said a representative of the pet fish industry (in the October 15 article just cited) "if [the bill as it now stands] passes, I'll be completely wiped out and so will the industry."

But we rarely hear of industry representatives who volunteer drafts of alternative regulations which really prove to be effective. Certainly I have never heard of an industry representative arguing that a proposed piece of legislation is not sufficiently strong!

RESPONSIBILITY AND VOLUNTARISM

We can only conclude that business still has a long way to go before it will have succeeded in a program of effective cooperation with the duly constituted authorities, the only bodies that do have any authorization to decide on social goals. Of course, the fault has not been entirely that of the businessman, but the illustrative cases of the preceding section suggest to me that so far he has done remarkably little to try to make such a process work, and that he has often effectively served as an accomplice to the undermining of any workable measures for the treatment of a number of the more pressing social ills.

[12] R. Sullivan, *New York Times,* October 17, 1972, p. 1.
[13] E. W. Kenworthy, *New York Times,* October 18, 1972, p. 26.

I am aware that there is an element of inconsistency in my position. On the one hand I have argued that business should have no truck with voluntarism which, at best, offers the illusion of effective activity and, at worst, poses a threat to the democratic process. Yet at the same time I am urging businessmen to cooperate voluntarily in the design and implementation of effective legislative measures as the appropriate medium of social responsibility. However, though both processes call for voluntary acts on the part of managements, the two differ completely in their potential consequences.

The adoption of new rules differs in two fundamental respects from a regime of pure voluntarism. First, it involves no takeover by business management of powers of decision that belong more properly to others—government retains the final authority on matters of social policy. Second, because what is involved is a change in rules that applies equally to everyone, there is no reason why a well-designed action of the variety under discussion need turn out to be ineffective. For the market mechanism, instead of undermining such a program, certainly need not interfere with it, and in some cases will actually serve to implement it. With competitors all subject to the same regulations, competitive pressures will not forestall the program, and if the structure of rewards and penalties is so modified in the process as to make failure to cooperate highly unprofitable, then the profit motive becomes the automatic force behind this program.

Thus, in my view, the true social responsibilities of business can be met only by a new spirit which may be called "meta-voluntarism"—systematic cooperation in the design and implementation of measures which are basically involuntary.

Let me not be misunderstood. I am not suggesting that all companies call in their lobbyists and turn their instructions about by a full 180 degrees. Such a goal is neither particularly attractive nor achievable. It would surely be unreasonable to expect the representatives of industry to spearhead a drive to impose the costs of public interest programs on themselves. And I am not particularly attracted by political activity on the part of corporations, no matter what it may happen to favor.

Rather, I am suggesting that, once the issue has been raised, and once it seems clear that some sort of government action is about to be undertaken, the time is ripe for constructive participation by the business sector. That is the time for voluntary participation by the business sector. That is the time for voluntary cooperation in the design of more effective changes in the rules drawn up so that they are not unnecessarily burdensome to anyone. By concerning itself with the last of these matters, business will still look after its own interests as well as those of the general public, but then it will do so in a manner that is fundamentally constructive and that can help to lighten the clouds of suspicion that now hang over the business community.

Editor's Commentary

Professor Baumol's proposal that socially responsible corporate leaders assent to changes in the rules that govern business performance and cooperate in the design of the rules to assure their effectiveness and efficiency in achieving desired performance goals suggests important and interesting questions of perception and motivation. As he observes, specific efforts to change the rules in such areas as environmental pollution and product safety typically meet strong opposition from the industries that will be directly affected by the changes. At the same time, some leaders of major corporations and publications of such leadership organizations as the Committee for Economic Development and the U.S. Chamber of Commerce are recommending to managers a heightened sensitivity to the ills of society and voluntary initiatives by business toward ameliorating many of those ills. Between these two responses there is a considerable gap, a critical lack of understanding, on the business side, of the inevitability of society's requirement for a new contract with private business, and, on the public side, of the complexities and costs associated with many of the proposed changes.

It is this misunderstanding that leads some business leaders to view the total problem as fundamentally a matter of improved public relations. This assessment does not lead most executives to the conclusion that all that is required is to persuade more people to swear allegiance to the private enterprise system, although this simplistic solution still appeals to a dwindling minority of managers. But it does appear to incline a significant proportion of businessmen to the conclusion that the appropriate strategy is to take a certain minimum of socially responsible actions and then publicize them vigorously. When programs to "tell the story of what we are doing" fail to ease the pressure—and even more when critics of business performance express skepticism about the validity of the claims or the adequacy of the effort—there are bruised feelings in the management camp and a sense of dealing with ignorant and hostile forces.

On the public side, particularly as embodied in activist leaders and their organizations, a comparable misunderstanding encourages the judgment that the business system should not be trusted and its leaders should be treated as adversaries. One result of this view is that voluntary initiatives by business are denigrated and business participation in the formulation of governmental actions to change the rules is resisted with references to the fox-in-the-chicken-coop cliché.

Both perceptions are dead wrong. On the public side an interesting, probably valuable, book could be written on the dangers inherent in actions by legislators and government administrators to regulate business performance without participation by and contributions from managers who understand the potentials and limitations of technology, the relation of costs to change, and the timing of change. But this is a book addressed to executives concerned with the problems of managing the socially responsible corporation. Furthermore, enlightened managers are in a better position than public officials to take the initiative, and it is in their interest to do so.

The issue facing corporate leaders today is not one of philanthropic voluntarism and not one of superficial public relations. As Professor Baumol and John Diebold observe, business organizations will not serve the national interest (much less their own) by undertaking to behave like philanthropic institutions. Such a transformation is neither feasible nor desirable. Recognition of this fact does not, however, support any of the following conclusions: (1) that the appropriate business strategy is to undertake to enlighten the general public on the virtues and values of the capitalistic enterprise system; (2) that the appropriate business strategy is to respond minimally to social demands for changed performance and call maximum attention to its "socially responsible" actions; (3) that the appropriate business strategy is to accept passively the creation by governmental bodies, largely guided by a mix of well-intentioned and ill-intentioned activists, of a set of new rules for business behavior; or (4) that the appropriate business strategy is to oppose all specific efforts by public authorities to change individual rules by taking up an adversary position that identifies business interests as committed to the defense of yesterday against today.

The first option above is totally unresponsive to current social problems and related needs. It is not the private enterprise system as such that is under critical attack, but its impact on the environment, on consumer interests, on open and equitable access to economic opportunities, and all the other issues that are involved in the emerging new social contract between American society and business institutions. Most reasonable people believe they can retain the enterprise system while changing some aspects of its behavior—and this is exactly what they want to do.

The second option invites, and has already begun to receive, identification of the essentially cosmetic character of the response. Further, it helps to destroy for all business that level of credibility in the general mind which business needs if it is to be allowed to participate in shaping the evolving American society, and which the society needs if it is to benefit from the technical contributions that experienced managers are uniquely capable of giving.

The third option is a prescription for economic decay, if not disaster. If what is at stake is truly a new social contract, as it appears to be, the issues are too important to be turned over to some combination of ignorant enthusiasts for social betterment who have no better than amateurs' grasp of the relevant technologies, costs, and motivations.

The fourth option prescribes an ultimately hopeless adventure in negativism which will surely end in defeat not only of the specific business interests involved in each adversary position, but also of all trust in the social goodwill of business leaders. We have been reminded by those who have known the experience that there is nothing so powerful as an idea whose time has come. American society in the 1970s has arrived at such a time with respect to an array of human values which are influenced by business performance.

Each of these four options has supporters in management ranks today. However, none of the options is advantageous for business in the face of the emerging social expectations of business behavior. Indeed, no single strategy is attractive in the context of the complex circumstances in which we find ourselves. There is room for individual and cooperative business voluntarism in certain situations. There is a requirement for government to act in other situations. The task for the imaginative corporate leader is to distinguish between these situations and design a strategy of multiple elements.

It is advantageous for the individual corporation acting independently to initiate socially responsible policies and programs that promise to be profitable in the long run—within a time span consistent with the organization's regular investment pay-out horizon. It is not advantageous for the individual corporation to take apparently socially responsible actions that will place it under substantial competitive cost and profit handicaps. It is advantageous for the individual corporation to seek cooperative and coordinated commitments for socially responsible behavior from other companies with common interests (in some circumstances, in the same industry; in others, in the same geographic locations), within the constraints of law and industry disposition. It is not advantageous for the individual corporation denied such cooperation to assume a passive posture. It is advantageous for the individual corporation to move affirmatively to participate fully and promptly in governmental programs to ameliorate social ills to which business has contributed and whose removal will improve the social environment for business.

Overall, a passive and static posture for business in a period of deep social change cannot fail to be disadvantageous for both business and the society of which it is an integral part.

CHAPTER 5

Cost-Benefit Analysis in the Socially Responsible Corporation

David Novick

One essential requirement for effective administration of corporate social responsibility is measurement of inputs and outputs in terms that will support rational judgments about priorities, efficiencies, and return on investment. Since the programs—as well as some of the resource inputs and many of the results—generally lie outside the range of traditional business activities, they are seldom measured in business financial and cost accounting systems or reported in quantitative terms in nonfinancial audit procedures.

New measurement techniques for analysis and control are required therefore. One that has been applied with considerable success in military and other government programs, and in some business planning areas, is cost-benefit analysis. This chapter explores the possibilities of its application in the corporate social responsibility setting.

David Novick, one of the originators of the application of cost-benefit analysis to military resource planning decisions, under the title of program budgeting, is the author of this chapter. He is now retired after many years' service as Head, Cost Analysis Department, The RAND Corporation, and is President of David Novick Associates.—EDITOR

I N THE simplest terms, cost-benefit analysis is an attempt to determine whether a good or service to be purchased or produced is worth the anticipated benefits it promises. We are all familiar with the cost-benefit and trade-off situations in our everyday life.

Consider the example of the woman who has decided to buy a new vacuum cleaner. A wide range of brands and models is available for her consideration, and there are also differences in performance and cost. If she is a rational buyer, she will accumulate information through demonstrations, talks with salesmen, discussions with relatives and friends who have used the various brands and types, and possibly reading testing service reports. Then she will make a choice based on two considerations: (1) the cleaning capacity, durability, and other relevant performance characteristics (in aggregate, the benefit) of each of the machines; and (2) the price (or cost) required to obtain each available mix of the various capabilities.

However, when she informs her husband what she has decided to pay for the cleaner she has decided to buy, he may raise the level of decision making from the simple question, "Which vacuum cleaner?" to the more complex question, "A new vacuum cleaner, or a new suit, or paying life insurance premiums on an annual rather than quarterly basis with its attendant dollar savings, or a week's vacation, or . . . ."

At this point, husband and wife will have to investigate their individual and joint needs and desires, and go on to establish criteria and determine measures of benefit for a wider range of alternatives. The cost-benefit calculation for the vacuum cleaner is now only one input into a wide range of choices that are part of a complex decision situation. The question now is: how to maximize the benefit to the family from a given expenditure or cost.

PROFIT AS A COST-BENEFIT MEASURE

The classical view of cost-benefit measurement as applied to the corporation was that business had only one function: to maximize profits. This concept sometimes has been restated in terms that postulate that the most efficient use of corporate resources, i.e., that which produces the greatest net profit for its shareholders, also creates the maximum benefit for all of society. In this view, profit becomes the measure of the extent to which the corporation is discharging its social responsibilities.

Maximizing on this single objective function is still accepted by most businessmen, workers, professionals, legislators, and academicians as the appropriate cost-benefit measure to apply to the corporation. The rationale for this view is that under competitive conditions profit is the measure of efficiency. When recorded, it indicates that the value of corporate output to society is greater than the resources taken from society in producing the mixture of goods and services delivered to the market. Therefore, the achievement of maximum profit means that business is meeting its social responsibility in the fullest sense.

In the light of today's widespread demands that corporations accept responsibilities previously not associated with their operations, it is interesting to note that for many years common law held that the corporation existed for the sole purpose of making profits for its stockholders and that officers and directors had no right to "give away" corporate funds in the form of contributions for charitable, educational, artistic, or other nonprofit purposes. The subsequent change that made the use of corporate resources for these purposes possible under the doctrine of a clear and distinct benefit to the corporation was developed in a paper by Gerhard D. Bleicken, Chairman and Chief Executive Officer of the John Hancock Life Insurance Company.[1] The issue of the right of the corporation to use its resources to meet social responsibilities is raised here as an indication of the change that has already taken place in legal restrictions applied to the corporation and the substantial further legislative and judicial relaxation that may be required if many of the social responsibility claims now addressed to business are to be met.

MULTIPLE COST-BENEFIT DIMENSIONS

To this point, the cost-benefit calculation has been viewed in terms of a single objective—profit maximization. This limited criterion still guides many business organizations, but a growing number of firms have expanded their list of objectives to include growth, share of market, and corporate image, as well as others especially suited to particular managerial contexts.

Even profit maximization is a multidimensional function. A clear distinction can be drawn between short-run and long-run profit goals. In addition, it may be recognized on occasion that negative profit in some areas may be required to service selected corporate objectives.

When questions involved in accomplishing profit or other economic objectives are examined, it soon becomes clear that measurement and analysis are required to assist the decision maker in choosing among available alternatives. At an even earlier stage, measurement and analysis are essential to a meaningful formulation of objectives, as they also are in

---

[1] Gerhard D. Bleicken, "Corporate Contributions to Charities: The Modern Rule," *American Bar Association Journal* (December, 1952).

developing the alternative programs through which a company can achieve its several objectives. As the number of objective functions to be maximized increases, demands are greatly expanded for quantification and analysis to be used in implementing cost-benefit determinations.

Assume the relevant techniques and information are available to supply material for the decision maker who wants to select a course of action that will maximize on the corporation's multivariate functions (a most questionable assumption, indeed). With this as a given, we now introduce a new set of considerations to be used by the decision maker in the socially responsible corporation.

In this setting, the maximization process briefly described above is subject to several kinds of external constraints. These "externalities," as the social scientists describe them, are a part of the internal problem of business planning and in only a limited sense are "foreign," i.e., outside, unknown, or not recognizable, forces.

APPLICATION TO SOCIAL RESPONSIBILITY PROBLEMS

Literally hundreds of statements have been made by business leaders on the need for business to go beyond traditional internal profit analyses and respond to demands that business assume a variety of social responsibilities. One of the simplest and bluntest of these is that of Admiral Ben Moreel, former Chairman of the Board of Jones & Laughlin Steel Corporation: "I am convinced that unless we do accept social responsibilities, the vacuum created by our unwillingness will be filled by those who would take us down the road to complete statism and inevitable moral and social collapse." Admiral Moreel's statement implies that business can define "social responsibilities" and can do it better than other groups. He also implies that corporations can deal with these problems through their own actions.

I believe that businessmen can answer the question addressed to Professor Milton Friedman in the 1972 interview published in *Business and Society Review* in more meaningful terms than he used. His reply was: "When corporate executives talk about exercising their social responsibility all they are doing is engaging in window dressing." I believe that businessmen should engage in socially responsible programs not only because of public pressures, but also because such activity can increase the benefit side of their own cost-benefit balances. This can be accomplished by direct extension of the techniques of measurement and analysis now incorporated in management systems.

These techniques are presently applied at all levels of managerial decision making, at all organization levels, and from short-range tactical operations to long-range strategic planning. In day-to-day operations the questions to be handled are related to the simple issue of assuring the efficient conversion of inputs to outputs in such areas as production schedules, mailroom procedures, individual workloads. Over a longer period, there is opportunity to deal with more complicated problems of efficiency in inventory control, changes in activities performed or in ways of doing them, shifting emphasis from one kind of equipment to another—all relatively minor changes in direction of a flow of activities already in motion.

Since World War II, operations research and related mathematical and logical methods of analysis have been applied successfully to improving efficiency at these first two levels, where everyone has a fairly good idea of what "more efficient" means. However, when policy issues at a more abstract third level are involved, such as the determination of optimal organization goals and strategies for attaining them, analysis becomes more difficult.

As a former counsellor to President Nixon put it:

> Tracing the complex and involute interconnections by which inputs produce outputs in a large social system is not the work of amateurs. It is not now done in any area of social policy save in economics, and there, most economists would insist, it is done imperfectly. It is not done elsewhere because no one really knows how to do it. It is just that most persons who have considered the matter feel it has to be done, and accordingly someone will have to learn how.[2]

Moynihan was discussing cost-benefit measurement for public policy issues. We are dealing with the application of cost-benefit analysis by private enterprise. However, there is every reason to believe that methodology developed for one will be applicable (partially or wholly) to the other. The important point to keep in mind now is that in both situations we are trying to cope with an extremely difficult problem and we are just beginning to work at it in either government or business.

IDENTIFYING COSTS

The initial requirement in applying cost-benefit analysis is to establish a meaningful relationship between the two terms in the calculation. This introduces twin conceptual questions: (1) whose costs and whose benefits; and (2) what costs and what benefits?

[2] Daniel P. Moynihan, *Toward Balanced Growth: Quantity with Quality*, National Goals Research Staff (Washington, D.C.: U.S. Government Printing Office, July, 1970), p. 7.

A wide variety of terms distinguish one kind of cost from another and a similar variety is found in classifications of benefit. Whether any particular term is appropriate in a specific problem situation depends, of course, on the type of decision under analysis.

It is, at least superficially, easier to identify cost terminology than benefit terminology. In the cost area, on the assumption that the only significant measure of benefit is profit, effective methodology has been developed to facilitate analysis aimed at profit maximization. The apparent precision and scope of cost methodology can be deceptive, however. The first great impetus to the development of formal cost methodology came from the Sixteenth Amendment covering income taxation; the second, from the "cost-plus" contracts of World War I. The former created a requirement for records to measure both business profits and personal income; in the latter, when Professor Taussig advocated and got a surplus profits tax instead of detailed fixed-price contracts for the government's wartime purchases, he assumed the existence of business bookkeeping methods which, in fact, were not in place. The same mistaken assumption about business's cost-measuring capabilities was repeated in the price-control machinery of the National Industrial Recovery Act of 1933. Even at the time of Pearl Harbor, many companies still lacked modern accounting systems, perpetual inventory records, and other now familiar management tools.

All of this history points to the fact that although a company may know the total of its expenditures, it often has only limited knowledge of costs associated with a specific product in a complex product line. When the problem becomes one of estimating future costs, the level of ignorance and innocence cannot be exaggerated. The record on this point is clear beyond debate. In the early 1950s, for example, when nuclear reactor technology was first made available for peaceful uses, a major public utility contracted with an established boilermaker for an atomic core for a power plant. The public utility had long experience with fossil fuel and hydro-electric plants, but this was its first entry into the nuclear field. For this reason, even though the boilermaker was experienced in the atomic field through its contribution to the World War II Manhattan Project, the utility engaged a consulting firm which also had a long history as a technical consultant in the nuclear field.

The contract awarded by the public utility called for delivery of the reactor within four years at a price of $35 million. On the original delivery date the boilermaker had run out of money and was not able to make delivery. Delivery was made several years later and the cost overrun was some 200 percent of the original price.

Comparable cost overruns were experienced by one of the nation's largest communications companies when it decided to introduce a new transmission technology after World War II. Here again, although there had been an accumulation of knowledge over the years, the new technique selected for introduction was not fully developed, and time was an important factor. In this case, the time schedule was met, but the cost overrun was in the 300–400 percent range.

In the early 1950's, one of the country's automobile manufacturers decided to reintroduce an old body-frame concept. Although used previously by the company and currently in use by other manufacturers in both the United States and Europe, it was new to the company at that time. All went well until the first units were delivered to the company's proving ground. There, the front end turned out to be completely unstable and unmanageable. When the car was accelerated, the front end left the ground, and the vehicle went out of control. A quick fix was achieved by adding several hundred pounds of metal to the front end. This additional weight held the car on the ground, but it meant cost overruns of about $200 a unit. In the automobile industry where budgets are very tight, a change of even $10 per unit is large.

In the public field, the story of the cost overruns on the Rayburn addition to the House Office Building in Washington has been widely reported. An office building is not a very complicated structure. Standard grades of steel are used for beams, reinforcement rods, and mesh. Many suppliers stand ready to sell ready-mixed concrete, sheathing materials for the exterior, sash, flooring, roofing materials, and every other part of the structure. Yet many office buildings constructed for commercial account have experienced substantial cost overruns.

This history of cost overruns and cost methodology demonstrates the intellectual trap which involves the assumption that while cost measurement is well within the state of the art, benefit measurement lacks comparable development. It is no more difficult to calculate benefits than costs. The only significant difference in the development of methodology is that the prevalence of profit maximization as a primary management objective and the requirements of the Sixteenth Amendment have stimulated close study of ways and means of analyzing costs.

As indicated earlier, it is not at all clear that adequate cost methodology is presently available to cope with a list of functions expanded to include share of market, growth, and corporate image. When the constraints imposed by the emerging social responsibilities of the corporation are added, it is clear that work on both costs and benefits is at an early stage of development.

Let me turn now to two applications of the technique of cost-benefit analysis of which I have personal knowledge. The first is a military case and the second is from business.

A Military Application

The military case involves two kinds of decisions: (1) cost-benefit measured in terms of competing vehicles available to perform the strategic bombardment mission: and (2) cost-benefit analysis applied to the allocation of resources for the strategic program as weighed against competing demands for the tactical, transportation, defense, and support activities. The case covers the five-year program and financial plan for the fiscal years 1962 through 1966 in the Department of Defense. Since classified information is involved, data used are illustrative rather than actual, but they approximate the magnitudes in the decisions.

In early 1961, Secretary McNamara had the following (among many other) budget requests from the armed services:

1. Navy: Strategic—10 Polaris systems for $3.6 billion;
   Tactical—2 aircraft carrier systems for $5.8 billion.
2. Air Force: Strategic—50 B–70 systems for $6.2 billion;
   Strategic—300 Minute Man Missiles for $0.8 billion;
   Tactical—nothing;
   Transportation—26 C–140 systems for $1.1 billion.

Secretary McNamara set out first to establish the strategic requirements. To do this he had cost-benefit analyses made of enemy targets to be destroyed, the number of warheads that had to be delivered on target, and the capabilities and vulnerabilities of the four systems available: existing B-52 aircraft, proposed B-70 aircraft, existing Minute Man Missiles, and proposed Polaris submarine missile systems. For each of these delivery vehicles analyses were developed in terms of the cost of each complete system: dollars for aircraft or submarines, missiles, bases, personnel, etc. This required determination of:

1. Vulnerability at base (failure to get off).
2. Vulnerability en route (aborts).
3. Penetration of enemy defense (attrition).
4. Effectiveness of deliveries.
   a. Aiming errors.
   b. Equipment malfunctions.
   c. Damage assessment.

Factors (1) through (4b) were quantified in dollar-cost terms and compared with benefits measured in (4c) as targets destroyed.

This information led the Secretary to decide that on the basis of cost and benefit numbers:

1. The existing B-52 fleet was adequate for the long-range target systems.

2. The 300 Minute Man Systems were required.
3. The B-70 was not needed.
4. More Polaris Systems should be acquired for use against the nearer-range targets because:
   a. The submarine was less vulnerable as a launch base for missiles than aircraft at base and airborne.
   b. Increased numbers could be used to compensate for their smaller warheads.

These decisions in the strategic area led not only to reallocation of resources in that program, but also to other changes. On the basis of cost-benefit analyses, the Secretary also decided to budget nothing for the Navy's carrier-based tactical aircraft and, instead, to assign the tactical aircraft to Air Force land bases despite the lack of a request from that service.

He also decided that the Army should be made truly mobile, and therefore gave the Air Force several times the number of C-140 systems it had requested. In short, he saw the benefits of a mobile Army as worth the additional cost of Air Force transportation systems. Also, he determined that benefit in the form of support for ground troops would be greater and the cost smaller when incurred by use of land-based Air Force planes than by use of carrier-based planes.

A Business Application

The business case covers cost and benefit decisions involved in an actual automobile in the Chevrolet-Ford-Plymouth class. The time was early 1964, and the model year under study was 1967. Since the automobile industry does its analyses on the basis of actual cost of the preceding year's vehicle, calculated cost of the current year's product, and estimated costs of the following years' products, the analysis of the 1967 car was executed in terms of actual costs incurred in 1964 and calculated costs for 1965 and 1966.

In the case under consideration a major design change had been introduced in the 1964 model. This had caught competition flat-footed and sales had soared. It was anticipated that competitors would meet this change, but on the basis of cost-benefit analyses it was decided that the momentum generated by the 1964 innovation would maintain the competitive position of 1965 and 1966 models with only minor changes in trim, available colors, and upholstery.

When the competition was confronted with the reality of 1964 market gains, they turned to cost-benefit analyses. One company decided its negative benefits (market share lost) were sufficient to warrant paying a very high emergency-induced cost of about $150 per car. It brought out a model change in mid-year—a 1964 and one-half model—with resultant reduction in profits. The other company stood pat. However, both competitors were expected to copy the successful style change in their 1965 and 1966 models, so 1967 was coming up as a critical year.

The year in which the study was done was 1964. There was some talk about air pollution and safety, generally at a low interest level, but a decision had previously been made to introduce a new power train for 1969 at a cost of $250 per car in that year's models. This cost was excluded from consideration. Cost-benefit analyses, therefore, were in terms of what could be done with a budget of $35 additional per car. The potentials available for this kind of money were:

1. Longer or shorter body.
2. More bright-work trim.
3. Better seats, upholstery, and related interior changes.
4. New carburetor with resultant gas savings.
5. Simple antipollution devices.
6. New and safer brakes.

The following benefits were analyzed:

1. Retain or slightly increase market share.
2. Since costs were being raised:
   a. Maintain price with attendant loss in profit.
   b. Raise price to cover added costs with attendant maintenance of the profit level.
3. Select the item or combination of items that would have sufficient appeal to promise some sales and profit gains.
4. Recognize the company's social responsibilities and buy as much antipollution and additional safety in brakes as $35 could cover; this might mean:
   a. Reduced sales and profits.
   b. Constant level of sales and profits.
   c. Increased sales and profits.

The cost-benefit analyses, therefore, had to measure the customer's appraisal of each of the six changes available for the $35 budget in terms of the four categories of benefits to the company.

The analyses presented the following additional information to the decision makers:

1. Past experience and current surveys showed very little customer preference for either reduced air pollution or safer automobiles.
   a. For $35 per car in cost and benefit calculations there would be no significant impact on sales results. The calculated outcome was (4a) or (4b) above and a sure cut in profit and possibly market share.

2. Longer body models had lost their appeal.
   a. At best, the benefit would be maintained or slightly increased sales.
   b. Without a price increase, there would be a possible loss in profit, and, at best, only a holding of the profit level.
3. More bright work also seemed to lack appeal and the results would be the same as in the longer-body analysis.
4. An improved carburetor would appeal to a significant part of the male buyers, but to very few females. Women were known to be more influential than men in the typical purchase decision. Again, the results were as in the longer-body and more bright work cases.
5. Fancier seats, upholstery, and related interior changes would appeal to a substantial number of men and most women.
   a. Spending the $35 here indicated the highest probability of realizing a sales gain.
   b. If the changes were artfully selected and executed they promised:
      (1) To maintain sales at a higher price.
      (2) Highest probability of increasing sales at higher prices and thereby increasing pretax net profit.

Cost-benefit analysis indicated better seats, upholstery, and related interior changes as the preferred decision.

A Social Responsibility Application

The following hypothetical example simulates a cost-benefit analysis of an array of socially related actions for an executive who accepts such demands as among the cost options deserving study.

Our hypothetical company is a manufacturer of fabricated metal products whose fabrication requires highly skilled machinists. The plant has a total employment of 400, of which 320 are in high-skill categories. Total annual payroll is about $4 million. Annual sales are in excess of $12 million.

The city in which the company operates has a population of 200,000. In the last twenty-five years there has been a significant immigration of lower-income, limited-education, socially disadvantaged, white, black, and Puerto Rican families and individuals. The population of this migration numbers over 15,000 and creates problems in housing, schooling, and welfare. The company in our example already employs about 25 from this group among its 80 low-skill employees.

Because of the size of its sales, payroll, and plant area—more acreage than actually required in its long-range corporate plan—the company has high local visibility. The chief executive officer is active in community affairs and has now decided that his corporate social responsibilities include more than Community Chest donations and company-paid time-off for employees who volunteer for selected Boy Scout, Red Cross, church, and similar activities. He also has decided that the town doesn't know the real importance of the role his company plays in its affairs. He has therefore decided to budget $100,000 for the next year to meet the corporation's social responsibilities. The company's Planning Department has been asked to do a cost-benefit analysis which in the fixed-budget case means maximizing benefits for the $100,000 investment.

After several weeks of study, the Planning group has identified the most attractive benefit alternatives that are available. The first alternative is to further increased employment opportunities in higher-grade jobs for the hard-core social problem group. Three means are available for accomplishing this:

1. Train low-skill employees to qualify for jobs within the company.
2. Invest in an outside enterprise now operating in the city, using low-grade skills in the manufacture of inexpensive clothing products.
3. Introduce a new product line requiring medium- rather than high-skill workers.

Two more alternatives are:

4. Upgrade the appearance of plant, grounds, and parking lots. Then use the remaining funds—estimated at $60,000—to build a recreational center for daytime use by children and evening use by adults and children. Obviously, the center could be used not only by people from the low-income area that surrounds most of the plant, but also by others from more distant residential areas.
5. Engage in a local advertising and public-relations program designed to upgrade the company in the eyes of the community and portray the company as socially responsible. In this case, none of the $100,000 would be spent on either employment or plant attractiveness and the recreation center.

On the basis of cost-benefit analysis of these five alternatives the Planning group present the following information to the chief executive officer:

1. On the basis of past experience, $100,000 spent on training hard-core employees for higher skills will involve more than just the money laid out for wages and instruction in the following year.
   a. Although a few will meet existing work standards, most of those who remain with the company can be anticipated to be lower in unit output and higher in product re-work than current standards.
   b. There are indications that some of the existing work staff will resent the special treatment offered this group, while other present employees will refuse to work with them under any circumstances.

This will mean costs over and above the $100,000 to be incurred not only in the coming year but also in later years.

2. Investing $100,000 in the local clothing company could yield as many as 200 additional jobs.

   a. However, the created employment opportunities would not be readily identified to the investing company.

   b. The jobs offered would be labelled "dead-end" and resented by the hard-core leadership.

3. Creating a new subsidiary to make metal products, such as inexpensive files and saws, could, with leveraging of the $100,000, create 40 to 50 semiskilled and 5 or 6 high-skilled jobs.

   a. This would identify the company with products it has always avoided and downgrade its image in existing activities.

   b. The improved job opportunities would be at most a "drop-in-the-bucket."

4. Improving the exterior of the plant would have an immediate and enduring impact on local citizens, employees, and customers visiting the plant.

   a. The recreational center would have the following results:

      (1) Enhance the local image of the corporation.

      (2) Identify the company as having taken a socially responsible action.

      (3) Serve as a continuing symbol of the company's acceptance of social responsibility through first-rate annual maintenance and periodic innovations and renewals.

5. $100,000 spent on local advertising and public relations to improve the corporation's image would impress mostly upper-middle and high-income groups. Some employees and other local blue-collar people might be impressed. It would probably be resented by some stockholders and the few hard-core people who heard about it.

For each of the alternatives listed, the Planning Department had developed information indicating the benefits to be anticipated from $100,000 paid out in the next budget year.

The analyses submitted to the decision maker are plotted in the accompanying chart. This indicates that:

1. There are no visible gains from recruiting from the socially disadvantaged for skilled jobs until 70 percent of the budget has been spent and the benefits obtained for the full amount are not promising.

2. Investing in the clothing plant produces substantial benefits quickly but shows no growth from additional outlays.

3. The new product line within the company produces reasonable benefit but does not appear to build beyond its early growth.

4. The community center and plant appearance program produces fairly

Cost and Benefit Measurement of Five Policy Options

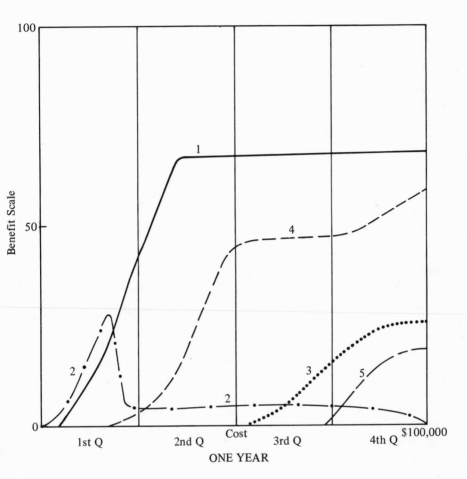

LEGEND:

1. Training low-skill employees for higher skills.
2. Investing in the local clothing company.
3. Creating a new product-line subsidiary.
4. Improving plant appearance and building a recreation center.
5. Engaging in an advertising and public relations program.

high benefits levels for relatively small outlays and promises increasing benefit when the program is completed.

5. The public relations program produces its major benefits with the early dollars after which additional outlays do not prevent declining benefits. More important, it is very low on the benefit scale.

Using the area under each curve in the chart as the basis of comparison, alternative 1 appears to be a dominant case. However, the promising upturn in the trend of alternative 4 indicates the desirability of further study of that option before making the final decision. This brings us to the elements of a cost-benefit analysis:

A. Objective: What is to be accomplished.
B. Options: Alternative means for achieving the objective.
C. Costs: Expenditures to carry out each alternative.
D. Effectiveness: Position on the effectiveness scale assigned each alternative in degree of achievement of the goal.
E. Criterion: Statement about cost and effectiveness which determines choice.[3]

Let us look at this list and apply it to our case. Is the objective purely humanitarian: to improve both the present status and the future opportunities for the socially disadvantaged? Alternatively, is it intelligent self-interest that aims at providing a desirable social service to the community while at the same time not penalizing profits, and also identifying the corporation as the provider of the service?

Alternatives 1 and 3 provide the means for improving the future economic opportunity for a limited number of the socially disadvantaged group. Alternative 2 offers the maximum benefit in terms of immediate impact on local employment.

Developing a community center and improving plant appearance (alternative 4) provides a desirable social service, identifies the corporation as the provider, and has potential business impact on customers who visit the plant. Alternative 5 appears to be purely a self-serving effort which makes no contribution to social needs.

Since we have normalized costs by use of the fixed budget and time period, this oversimplification does not permit exploring the full potentials of the community center program. At the same time, it suggests that further analysis is required before a commitment is made to what appears to be the obvious choice: investment in a local plant employing low-skill workers.

[3] Adapted from L. D. Attaway, "Criteria and the Measurement of Effectiveness," *Systems Analysis and Policy Planning* (New York: American Elsevier Publishing Company, Inc., 1968), Ch. 4.

Although businessmen are not specifically responsible for the larger society, they are responsible for the corporations they administer. For this reason, they may well be held accountable for the effect of corporate decisions on the larger society. It is no longer sufficient to tell either stockholders or society that the enterprise shows a profit. The socially responsible corporation now must be able to demonstrate to both its stockholders and the public that it has measured costs and benefits for its policies in terms significant to both the organization and the society in which it operates.

EDITOR'S COMMENTARY

Some of those who hold skeptical views about the possibility of implementing corporate social responsibility ground their doubts in the slippery and indeterminate nature of the costs and benefits associated with socially responsible activities. These are radically different, they argue, from the expense-revenue arithmetic of normal business operations. How do you measure, they ask, the costs to society, or to the individual company, of inequitable hiring and employment practices? Or the costs of environmental pollution? How do you measure the benefits of positive programs in these same areas? And how do you compare costs and benefits which have to be described in different vocabularies? Are we not up against the familiar apples-and-oranges problem so dear to grammar school arithmetic before the new math entered the scene?

David Novick's paper suggests that the measurement problems posed by these questions are not as novel and difficult as the skeptics seem to think. They have been confronted and handled in certain aspects of corporate strategic planning and, more recently, in military strategic planning. A large-scale effort is currently in process for applying the same cost-benefit approach to a variety of resource allocation problems in civil government and in not-for-profit institutions. In fact, the real difficulty may lie not in the nature of the new socially responsible programs but rather in our habitual intellectual fumbling when faced with the task of transferring a familiar concept to a new setting.

The first step in clarifying this indeterminacy is to recognize that the accountant's (and manager's) concept of cost as dollar expenditures, to be compared with dollar revenues, is a useful but incomplete measurement device.[4] Worse, it may even be misleading. Economists have developed a more comprehensive cost concept called opportunity costs. They use this term to identify benefits (or opportunities) forgone whenever one

[4] The following discussion is drawn from Gene H. Fisher, *Cost Considerations in Systems Analysis* (New York: American Elsevier Publishing Company, Inc., 1971), Ch. 3.

of several alternatives is chosen. The concept is taught in all basic courses in economics, with mixed results. The significant potential of cost-benefit analysis for making measurements of inputs and outputs of corporate social responsibility activities emerges directly in the opportunity cost concept. Specifically, since opportunity costs are benefits forgone, costs and benefits have a common conceptual base, a common dimension.

In spite of this shared dimension, it is frequently asserted that costs are easier to measure than benefits. A principal reason for this belief is that it is often easier to get useful dollar measures of costs than of benefits. But, it should be noted, there is a trap here; dollar estimates of costs may be incomplete. A second reason is the prevalent habit of dismissing costs not readily measured in dollars as not properly classified as costs for decision purposes, or of treating them as "qualitative factors," useful only at the fringe of decision situations. But one could apply the same simplifying approach on the benefit side, with comparable results.

If we think our way past the simplification trap, therefore, to the conclusion that costs and benefits are related as alternate sides of a common activity, we are part way toward grasping the potential contribution of cost-benefit analysis to measurement and decision making in the corporate social responsibility arena. The next step is to accept the notion that while the conventions of financial accounting require that all things included in accounting records be set down in a specific numeric vocabulary that gives a surface appearance of great accuracy (regardless of the gross estimates that lie beneath the surface), this precision is not always necessary for management decision making. Much of the traditional friction between controllers and line managers is generated by this distinction. A large proportion of all management decisions, including many of the most critical nature, can be and are made effectively with measures that yield valid comparisons of "more" and "less" without necessarily being accompanied by precise measures of "how much." This observation is not meant to denigrate the value of financial accounting which was, after all, developed in all its beauty to serve other ends than strategic decisions of resource allocation.

The third step is to grasp the idea that the purpose of cost-benefit analysis is to assist managers to make better decisions, not to make decisions for managers. (In actuality, of course, this should also be said about the analyses provided by financial accounting data.) The fact that some of the measures provided by the cost-benefit technique based on the concept of opportunity costs look imprecise should not be allowed to deter their use. Their function is to organize variables in a manner that heightens the rationality of choice among complex alternatives. In this setting, managerial judgment remains as a critical determinant, although functioning at a higher level of effectiveness because of the cost-benefit analysis.

The principal contribution of the cost-benefit technique, then, is its emphasis on isolating key elements on both input and output sides of alternative resource commitments, and ordering their relative weights in a common vocabulary of measurement. It should be invulnerable to the common criticism of subjective estimates, provided that the assumptions underlying the estimates are made explicit to those who use the information for decision making.

Viewed in this way, cost-benefit analyses can be a valuable adjunct of traditional accounting techniques (and their extension to the social audit process described in Chapter 6). They bring into the information inventory of the decision maker cost and benefit elements that are not readily captured by accounting techniques. As a result, they provide a broader and stronger foundation for resource allocation decisions, particularly in the relatively unfamiliar territory of social responsibility. Here, a major requirement is to strengthen managers' confidence that they can treat the new issues on a plane of rationality comparable to that applied to profit-oriented administrative tasks.

CHAPTER 6

The Social Audit Technique for Measuring Socially Responsible Performance

Clark C. Abt

A second measurement technique for analysis and control, conceptually related to financial accounting, is the social audit technique, which uses accounting concepts and procedures for measuring inputs and outputs. It is in the early stage of examination for possible application to management problems in the area of corporate social responsibility.

As with any new technique, there are complex problems of application that require creative innovation in adapting an old tool to new applications. The following chapter examines the case for and against the social audit technique and describes ways in which it can be used to build a foundation for rational managerial decision and reporting of results accomplished and return on investment.

*The author of this chapter is Clark C. Abt, President, Abt Associates Inc.–*EDITOR

THE GROWING concern for including social responsibility considerations in the decision process of corporate managers has its origins in at least two pervasive problems of contemporary American society. The first is the general awareness of grave social problems in our society and the inadequacy of attempts to deal with these problems on the part of governments at all levels and of individual citizens. Government officials, leaders of industry, private activist groups, and individual citizens have called on business organizations to help with social problem solving.

The second major source of concern over the social responsibility of corporations is anxiety over the survival of the present system of private capitalism. Particularly among the youth of the country, an observed decline in respect for the business culture and the attractiveness of careers in business threatens the society's confidence in the survival of its economy in more or less the present form. Public pressures from radical or youth groups, and also increasingly from the large centrist segments of society represented by consumer, labor, and church groups, are questioning the rights of corporations to act in any way other than with social responsibility.

The five publics most affected by the activities of corporations are the employees, the owners, the customers, the residents of the corporation's local environments, and the general public. All five of these publics are concerned, in different but related ways, with both the inadequacy of current governmental social problem solving and the survival of the corporation as a socioeconomic entity.

Employees are concerned about the major social problems of poverty, crime, drug abuse, race conflict, social inequity, and environmental pollution, because these problems directly affect the quality and security of their lives. The economic device of the corporation that offers cash income and related economic benefits in exchange for labor is increasingly regarded as an inadequate provider of the quality and security of life. Economic benefits are seen as insufficient if there is rampant crime, poverty, pollution, and mismanagement of general community services.

Employees are at the same time concerned with the survival of the corporation, not necessarily because they love it so well, but because they fear the insecurity of seeking their economic incomes, and perhaps their psychic incomes, elsewhere. Government and educational institutions together can offer only some 20 percent of the jobs needed, and individual proprietorships are difficult and risky. Even a shift to government employment in a socialist society would bring changes disrupting vocations and careers, as well as new constraints imposed on employees by a single all-powerful employer.

The owners of the corporations are concerned about the inadequacy of current efforts to solve social problems because, like employees (which most of them are), the quality and security of their lives are threatened. In addition, purely as owners or shareholders, they are concerned about the increasing inefficiencies and resulting reduced productivity of their enterprises as a direct consequence of unsolved social problems. These problems raise the costs of doing business, thus reducing earnings for shareholders. Crime increases insurance and other operating costs. Drug abuse raises labor costs by adding to recruitment costs and decreasing labor productivity. Racial and other intergroup conflicts increase personnel management and labor costs. Environmental pollution raises health, benefits, and production costs imposed by demands for pollution-free technology. In sum, unsolved social problems reduce profits.

Owners of corporations are also concerned about the survival of the corporation as an economic form. With increasing costs and declining profits as a result of social problems, and general public demands for intervention in the management of corporations to assure socially responsible performance, the corporation as an organizational form is seen by many as threatened by either unprofitability and bankruptcy, or absorption into the government by increasing regulation. With increasing regulation foreshadowing the possibility of ultimate socialization of industry, the game of picking the winners will be all over for shareholders. There will then be only one game in town and winning or losing will be determined in a narrow political system. The outcome could be a new elitism with a higher and narrower pyramid structure than liberal capitalism.

The customers of the corporations are concerned about unsolved social problems because they fear a decline in the quality, economy, and availability of goods and services. The higher costs of doing business created by social problems are passed on to consumers in the form of either higher prices or lower quality or both. Furthermore, as government regulation increases in response to these inroads on consumer interests, the availability of a variety of goods and services declines. Finally, with the complete decline of corporations into government operation, the variety and availability of products and services, as well as their quality, will be at the level of mediocrity available from most government monopolies.

The residents of the local environments of corporations are concerned about unsolved social problems because they are members of the other three publics—employees, owners, and consumers—but also in a special way as "neighbors" to activities whose side effects spill over onto their own lives and properties. The householder living near a chemical plant suffers directly from the neglect of such social issues as pollution control, unemployment, health, and housing. Furthermore, if local plants become unprofitable and go out of business, the entire local community tax base suffers, with attendant decline in the quantity and quality of municipal services.

Finally, the general public is concerned about the solution of social problems accomplished with the participation of industry because it sees little hope of the government doing it alone, and because of a general concern with the stability, survival, and growth of the country's traditional economic system.

DEFINING CORPORATE SOCIAL RESPONSIBILITY

Given the widely felt need for socially responsible performance by private corporations, how is such responsibility to be defined? Is it the responsibility of corporations to solve all of society's social problems left unsolved by government? Or merely to try to do so? Or merely to try to solve some of the problems? Which ones? How much?

Until government defines corporate social responsibility through legislation and enforcement, the definition must remain a matter for industry and individual company self-definition. In short, within the constraints of enforced legality and public opinion expressed through the labor and consumer markets, the type and amount of corporate social responsibility a company should implement will be determined by its owners and managers. This does not mean that corporate social responsibility cannot be defined, but only that it will be defined diversely with a relatively small core of commonly held criteria. Basically, within broad constraints, a company has as much and as many kinds of social responsibility as it wants to have.

Stating that definitions of corporate social responsibility are diverse does not eliminate the need for some kind of generally accepted definition, since criteria of standard social performance measurement and reporting must be based on some such definition. The following attempt to define corporate social responsibility is part of the general attempt to develop widely accepted, and hence widely applicable, standards of social auditing.

A comprehensive definition of corporate social responsibility should include dimensions of agreement, enforcement, comprehensiveness, precision of measurements and records, opportunity for and feasibility of corporate action, and support by extracorporate public opinion. To some extent these dimensions all express components of trade-offs among the goals of utility and feasibility.

The following suggested stratification of degrees of agreement have been developed from this writer's experience in working with corporate managers. They range from "widespread agreement" to "only a few advocates." Widespread agreement (among all or most industries in all or most areas) exists with respect to:

1. Responsibility for obeying major laws, particularly where the law also has widely accepted moral sanctions associated with it.

2. Responsibility for humane treatment of employees, usually but not always enforced by law.
3. Responsibility for honest, truthful, and fair dealings with other enterprises, consumers, and employees.
4. Responsibility for truthful financial reporting.
5. Responsibility for respecting the intent as well as the letter of contracts, in providing a reasonable quality and quantity of product or service for the price negotiated.
6. Responsibility for providing, or at least attempting to provide, a fair return on investment to shareholders by generating profits.
7. Responsibility for equal employment opportunity for entry-level jobs.

Majority agreement (among most industries in most locations) exists with respect to:

8. Responsibility for internal accounting and capital budgeting of all major expenditures, including those for social benefits.
9. Responsibility for obeying all laws, including those weakly enforced ones against pollution, unsafe practices and products, minimum wages, etc.
10. Responsibility for complete truthfulness in advertising.
11. Responsibility for the nonharmfulness of products and services.
12. Responsibility for the nonharmfulness of production processes to local communities in which they are situated.
13. Responsibility for employee benefits that assure family health, security, and welfare at least as long as employed, and afterward where employment ends with retirement.
14. Responsibility for making modest contributions to local charitable causes in kind or in cash, to the extent that these do not reduce after-tax earnings by more than about 2 percent.
15. Equal employment opportunity for all races and both sexes at all levels.
16. Responsibility for some recording of socially responsible actions and their disclosure to shareholders in at least qualitative form.

Minority agreement (among most industries in only some locations, or among only some industries in most locations) exists with respect to:

17. Responsibility for active efforts to achieve equal employment opportunities, both racial and sexual, at all levels including the officer level, regardless of difficulty and costs.
18. Responsibility for actively improving the local environment of the company by reducing pollution and other actions.
19. Responsibility for actively working to improve the quality of life of employees, consumers, and local residents by whatever means that can be made consistent with company financial requirements.
20. Responsibility for actively pursuing improved social justice and quality

of life for all by direct actions affecting customers, suppliers, lessees, and any other groups that are influenced by the company.

21. Responsibility for measuring, recording, and publicly disseminating detailed descriptions of social benefits and costs, and social assets and liabilities generated by the company on a regular, periodic, and quantitative objective basis, similar to annual financial reports.

The foregoing three levels of agreement on corporate social responsibility correspond approximately to those outlined by Eleanor Sheldon of the Russell Sage Foundation: first and widely agreed to, that "business has the responsibility to make a profit while dealing fairly and honestly"; second, and still probably obtaining majority agreement, that "business has a responsibility to society with respect to its employees and products, and a responsibility to mirror the ideals and values of the society within its own microcosm"; and third, that "it is a primary obligation of business to use its power to promote social ends perceived as moral." Breadth of acceptance within these levels moves up over time, and we may expect all twenty-one to be in the widely accepted category in a few years.

To some extent, degrees of responsibility for actions are independent of degrees of responsibility for measurement and recording. It is conceivable that the top management of a company would elect to be rather activist in its definition of its social responsibility, but eschew complex social audits for measuring the results of its efforts. One can easily imagine an old-fashioned benevolent despot of an entrepreneur dispensing with measures of social performance and insisting that his own judgment of what the social payoffs will be would suffice. On the other hand, a thorough and cautious modern manager trained in management sciences might elect to execute a most comprehensive and detailed social performance measurement program, not because of any liberal penchant, but purely for defensive purposes and perhaps for the sake of optimizing capital budgeting by getting more social responsibility payoff for less investment.

Any corporate manager—and the reader—may select his own appropriate degree of corporate social responsibility. My view is that the first eight aspects of corporate social responsibility listed as enjoying widespread agreement could be adopted forthwith as a bare minimum standard, or irreducible core. Beyond that core, companies should be encouraged to accept as much corporate social responsibility as they judge feasible and strategically desirable in view of the risks of inaction. Corporations still have the option of anticipating, and hence possibly rendering unnecessary, further government regulations in these areas.

Whatever a company's commitment to various degrees of corporate social responsibility, it would seem simply good management sense to develop a parsimonious statement of the company's social objectives (even if they are only to make money while staying legal), and then annually measure and record the estimated progress toward these objectives. For the most conservative companies, this will be little more than the annual financial audit and annual report to shareholders, plus a statement specifically disavowing any social objectives other than profit generated by legal means. Such conservatism should have the courage of its convictions, and it might even attract a few fellow conservatives as stockholders and employees.

In the case of my own company, Abt Associates Inc., I believe that I have the agreement of most of the employees and stockholders that our definition of our corporate social responsibility includes all twenty-one aspects described above. Furthermore, we do not believe that this larger and more comprehensive definition of corporate social responsibility threatens the financial responsibility or profitability of the company. On the contrary, we see powerful correlations between good social and financial performance, so that social performance is not seen as requiring any significant sacrifice of financial performance. Of course, this may be easier in the applied social research industry than in other industries.

It may be helpful to review a few operational examples of at least some of these degrees of corporate social responsibility, particularly because some are not as obvious as they seem. Consider first the core group of social responsibilities about which there is widespread avowed agreement (although not necessarily consistent corporate actions consonant with these responsibilities). Responsibility for "humane treatment" is a concept whose execution depends on the definition of "humane." Agricultural concerns may honestly believe that a $50-a-week wage for a field worker with a family of ten to support is "humane," particularly when the employer contributes "free" temporary housing in shacks with outhouses. Industrial corporations may consider it "humane" to terminate employees in their late fifties just short of achieving pension rights. Service firms may consider it "humane" to lay off women who become pregnant, and to refuse to pay medical benefits or provide continued employment to unmarried women who become pregnant. In each of these cases and similar ones, however, most of the general public would not consider the actions "humane." Thus, it is incumbent on a management at even this core level of corporate social responsibility to make public its own marginally "humane" actions, so that the public can appraise and respond to an inadequate or meager definition of humanity.

Responsibility for truthful financial reporting is a subject unto itself, but it would be unduly optimistic to say that, despite widespread agreement as to the desirability of this responsibility, and despite the best efforts of generally honest and skilled public accountants, most financial reporting is fully truthful. A company that overstates its earnings and thus stimulates stock price increases and/or investments which later turn sour as the less inflated truth is ultimately revealed, should be charged with a social cost of reduced credibility of current and future statements, as well as the cost to investors and others of the opportunity cost of the capital they would otherwise not have invested. This is a difficult cost to compute, but merely the effort to estimate it might deter some of the more flagrant "take the money and run" kinds of financial reporting.

Responsibility for attempting to provide a fair return to shareholders on their investment would seem too obvious to mention, and not ordinarily associated with corporate social responsibility. Yet there is responsibility toward small shareholders, who may have invested in a company—particularly a high technology, "growth" company—on the naive assumption that its management was dedicated to creating a competitive return on investment. Actually, the management may have been dedicated chiefly to achieving transient capital gains for its own holdings by promoting the future potential of a still untested concept or product. Again, if a company consistently fails to provide any reasonable return on investment year after year, and does not even give persuasive reasons for its wisdom in pursuing this path, then even a purely social audit should discount the net social worth of the enterprise by some amount estimated to represent the opportunity cost of capital to those investors who had mistakenly been led to anticipate a reasonable return.

The final example for the core group of corporate social responsibilities enjoying widespread agreement, in words if not in actions, is the responsibility for internal accounting and capital budgeting of major social benefit expenditures. Many large companies that expend considerable resources on socially directed activities, ranging from employee benefits to contributions to local charities, fail to account and budget for these expenditures on a level of accuracy and detail consistent with other expenses. A company might allocate 2 percent of its earnings to charitable purposes, but then give much less attention to accounting and budgeting for this amount than a similar amount expended on plant or equipment or labor—as if expenditures for social purposes were measured by their inputs (costs) rather than their outputs (benefits generated). This rather cynical practice would seem to impute no measurable output from some social investments, so that they are assumed to require no further accounting or budgeting attention. Unfortunately, this is something of a self-fulfilling prophecy, since where social investments are treated in this cursory manner the efficiency of the investment in producing socially desirable results is indeed likely to be low or insubstantial.

In the second group of corporate social responsibilities probably achieving majority agreement, the first one of responsibility for obeying all laws however inconvenient or poorly enforced is a surprisingly difficult one for many large corporations to accept in practice. Laws against water and air pollution are regularly broken by major chemical, oil, and power companies, who then pay modest fines for sustaining the privilege of breaking the law. Other corporate "scofflaws" include agribusinesses that violate labor and working-condition laws, consumer product manufacturers who repeatedly break laws concerned with truthful advertising and adequate testing of products, laws against collusion in pricing, and so on. Since penalties and fines for breaking most of these laws have not been set high enough to represent the real cost to the public of their infringement, many companies find it cheaper to continue breaking the laws and paying the fines. A social audit of these companies should include the social cost or liability imposed on the public by their operations in excess of the fines paid, making up the difference between the cost of the fine and the actual and usually much larger cost to the public interest of the violation of the law.

APPROACHES TO MEASURING CORPORATE SOCIAL RESPONSIBILITY

Given the needs for corporate social responsibility, and a range of widely and not-so-widely held definitions of the concept, there is an obvious need to measure it. Without measurement there can be no assurance of progress toward corporate social responsibility goals, no evaluation of the relative cost-effectiveness or efficiency of alternative social investments, no optimization of social investment mixes, no comparison among companies and industries to determine what is possible and what is standard, what can and should be corrected, and no criteria for corporate decision making in the interests of social responsibility.

It seems necessary first of all to clear the air of some misleading notions concerning the criteria of adequacy of audits in general and social audits in particular. Bauer and Fenn, in their recent *The Corporate Social Audit* state that

> there is no presently fixed notion of what a social audit is and, if the adequacy of an audit is to be judged by whether or not it served its purpose, then navel gazing cannot per se be ruled out . . . the question of whether a social audit is "possible" is now unanswerable because the term is still so undefined.[1]

[1] Bauer and Fenn, *The Corporate Social Audit* (New York: Russell Sage Foundation, 1972), p. 50.

We cannot accept these rather loose criteria for an audit, social or otherwise. Using the term "audit" in this way debases it beyond all intended and initial meaning in common usage. It would have been more correct to say that so long as there is no generally agreed-on definition of social audits, we must stick to the several that have been legitimated by effort and commitment and a reasonable resemblance to a financial and/or a management audit. Further, the question of possibility has already been answered affirmatively by the objective existence of several types of social audits. It is unreasonable to argue that, because a single definition for social audits has not been widely agreed to, no social audit can exist. That is like arguing that, because physicians cannot agree on the definition of the common cold, it does not exist.

The measurement of corporate social responsibility—by social audits and perhaps by other means as well—requires some *criteria* of measurement, for the sake of efficient design of measurement instruments and procedures. Below are listed some of the more obvious criteria:

1. Useful as a guide to decisions by managers (to do or not to do . . .), by employees (to accept or reject jobs), by consumers (to buy or not to buy products), by owners (to buy or to sell the stock), by reformers (to attack or to defend the company), by legislators (to attempt to pass legislation to control the company or the reverse).
2. Objective.
3. Reliable and repeatable.
4. Generally accepted.
5. Responsive to social concerns.
6. Feasible.
7. Quantitative.
8. Fully exploiting the available potential for action.
9. Offering maximum hard information and minimum cosmetic description.
10. Effective in institutionalizing social concerns in the corporation.
11. Transparency of assumptions and estimates (so user can make his own).
12. Full use of available expert and disinterested opinion.
13. Simple enough to be widely understood.

For measures of responsibility to be useful as a decision aid to managers, employees, consumers, owners, and others, they must deal directly with the issues of concern to these significant actor groups. Thus the issues to be dealt with, and hence the issues defining the variables to be included in any useful social audit, would include:

1. For *managers,* the total budget and its allocation among different social

responsibility programs, as well as the policies and procedures to be applied.

2. For *employees,* the quality of life, work, and advancement and fairness to be experienced on the job.

3. For *consumers,* the quality and efficiency of the products and services sold, compared to competing products, and the reliability and veracity of information about them.

4. For *owners* (stockholders), the overall prospects of the company in terms of expected future earnings and growth, as fully and honestly reported.

5. For *reformers,* the responsiveness of the company to changing standards and its willingness to respond to new social needs.

6. For *legislators,* the ability of the company to respond to public needs without enforcing legislation.

For measures of social performance to be objective, they must be verifiable by disinterested parties and not simply a way of showing the company in a favorable light. To be reliable and repeatable, the measures should be sufficiently universal to be applicable to widely different companies, yet provide meaningful information in all cases.

General acceptance of social performance measures is essential to their being commonly used, and effective. General acceptance requires that the measures relate to widely accepted concerns and are based on some already widely accepted principles.

Responsiveness to social concerns is essential if measures of social performance are to be taken seriously by all significant groups involved. Thus, social performance measures that deal only with environmental issues, for example, but not with equality of employment opportunity, will not win the acceptance of many of the minority and female individuals involved in company operations. The criterion here is that all major social concerns be addressed. Since social problems change in their relative saliency with time, this criterion implies that the agenda of salient social issues to be addressed in social performance measures must change with the times.

Feasibility has operational, financial, political, and technical components. Implementation of a given set of social performance measures must be possible without major disruption of the organization. It must cost some amount less than what can be readily afforded to take social measurements, and what the individuals affected would regard as a reasonable amount to pay for information. The social performance measurements must be possible to implement without so offending various affected groups as to render the exercise counter-productive. Finally, the measures must be implementable from the aspect of the latest social science state of the art for surveys, measurements, and the drawing of conclusions.

Social performance measures must be quantitative in order to provide a net result of benefits and costs, and of assets and liabilities, and a basis of comparison for the same organization through time and for different organizations concurrently. To see the disastrous effect of purely qualitative measures of social performance, it is only necessary to imagine the usefulness of an annual financial report stated in qualitative terms. For example, "This year we increased our income faster than our expenditures, so that net income was greater than last year. . . ."

The social performance measures should fully exploit the available potential for action on the part of the corporation, by addressing specifically those areas under its strongest control: hiring, personnel administration, production, advertising, procurement, marketing, investment, location, research and development. Any company makes an enormous number of decisions concerning where and from whom it buys what, what it does with what it buys (including labor and capital equipment), and whom it sells it to and how. All these decisions should be reviewed for the quality of their responsiveness to social issues, and hence the quality of the social performance involved in these decisions.

The criterion of offering maximum hard public information with minimum cosmetic description is essentially that of assuring a concern with honest action rather than boasting. If social actions are heavily exploited for their public relations value, not only will they tend to be heavily discounted by those most concerned, but consequent decisions may also be distorted. Sometimes the most socially productive decisions are not the most effective from an immediate public relations aspect, and sometimes the most immediately effective public relations decisions are not particularly productive socially. To maximize social net benefits, therefore, it would seem wise to provide public information with the minimum bias in favor of the source, lest the credibility and consequently the effectiveness of communications be compromised.

Effectiveness in institutionalizing social concerns in the corporation is required to assure continuity of the social performance effort. Without institutionalization, social performance efforts and the attempts made to measure them will tend to be one-shot efforts responding to a transient vogue, without consistent and long-term follow-up. Furthermore, the various levels of management in a company are unlikely to take completely seriously the directives of social performance and its measurement if these directives are not formalized in bureaucratic terms. The survival and growth of corporate social responsibility efforts require their formalization in some sort of institutionalized, repeated procedures.

Since the assumptions and estimates in any social performance audit are bound to be subject to change with advances in the state of the art of social auditing, and since different perspectives yield somewhat different estimates of social costs and social utilities, it is essential for the sake of objectivity and widespread acceptability that assumptions and estimates be transparent and clearly expressed. Only in this way can the user of the social performance measures either accept the assumptions of the measurer, or supply his own assumptions and estimates while still crediting the facts and logic offered.

The full use of available expert and disinterested opinion is a step towards the overall professionalization, legitimization, and widespread acceptance of social performance measures and audits. Without the full exploitation of the available state of the art and the available measurement experts, individuals from these sources will have reason to criticize the effort as not fully using the tools available. Furthermore, the measurement of many of the social variables involved is difficult even for experts, while at the same time being of sufficiently universal nature to encourage the confident naiveté of the layman (everyone, for example, is an expert on education, family health, working conditions, etc.). The use of expert opinion and professional methods offers some greater hope of applying the objective standards of scientific information gathering and inference while at the same time assuring comparability of information and logic (since statistical logic is everywhere the same).

Finally, the measures of corporate social performance must be simple enough to be widely understood, or they will not be used. One of the virtues of generally accepted accounting principles is that they can be understood after a few hours of diligent study (even if all the procedures involved in proper application take years to master). If social auditing becomes so complex that it requires multiple regressions, analyses of variance, major statistical, econometric, and psychometric skills, it will quickly become an academic curiosity.

Given these criteria, what sorts and degrees of measurement of corporate social responsibility can be developed? The first step would appear to be a simple qualitative statement of perceived significant social costs and benefits, and a qualitative estimate of the degree to which these desired social benefits have been achieved at indicated social costs. For the company assuming only the core group of social responsibilities, the simple qualitative statements of social performance are: (1) make a profit, and (2) stay legal. The simplest measurement of the achievement of these primitive social goals would be the binary determination of whether profit had indeed been generated, and whether the enterprise had indeed operated legally.

Beyond this simplest checking of social goals achievement, it is possible to make lists of specific social objectives, such as equal employment opportunity and nonreduction of local environmental standards, and to estimate whether negligible, little, substantial, or complete progress has been made toward their accomplishment. This is the checklist approach, and it is a useful quick and simple beginning. It also serves a kind of "consciousness-raising" function for executives who employ it, thus tending to mobilize commitment to more sophisticated measures.

The major limitation of the qualitative checklist, no matter how comprehensive, detailed, and elaborate, and no matter how many of its dimensions are expressed in some matrix, is that there is no logical way of determining whether any net social benefit results from the company's social performance. The net result of all the social benefits less all the social costs cannot be computed with only qualitative categories. It would be incorrect simply to subtract the number of discrete social cost items from the number of discrete social benefit items, because that would be making the improper assumption that each item is of equal weight. Therefore, the next step in the measurement of social performance is the quantification of social benefits and costs generated. This can be done with various degrees of sophistication, but within the current state of the art is likely to remain an approximation—although an approximation likely to be much more accurate than the simple qualitative checklists. The very simplest sort of quantification is to assign subjective weights to the various categories of social benefits and costs. This approach fails to meet the tests of objectivity and widespread acceptability, because weights are matters of judgment varying from individual to individual. What is needed is some external objective standard to rate the relative importance of various social benefits and costs, so that this will not be a matter of individual and inevitably variable judgment.

One such external quantitative standard, used by this writer in the Abt Associates Inc. social audit, is that of the equivalent dollar worth of the various social costs and benefits generated by corporate social responsibility actions. The dollar worth is determined on the basis of the traditional accounting principle of things being worth what is paid for them or what they can be sold for, whichever is less (lesser of cost or market value). This approach, while still only an estimation, has the virtue of relating social consequences to a common set of units that can be related to experience.

The current estimated ultimate measurement and reporting of corporate social responsibility is the integration of all these data with the financial measures and statements. This is still beyond the state of the art, but several companies are working on methods for doing just this.

There is obvious interest in integrating financial and social measures, since any mutual contributions or trade-offs of the two types of gains and losses *do* interact in intracompany and intercompany decision making.

Social Benefits and Corresponding Financial Benefits and Costs

	Social Benefits	Corresponding Financial	
		Benefits	Costs
To Employees	Employee fringe benefits	Increased morale and productivity, reduced turnover and training costs	Overhead costs
	Career advancement (more pay for more responsibility and productivity)	Increased productivity per payroll unit	Increased direct labor costs per capita
	Quality of working space and environment	Increased efficiency and morale improving productivity, reduced recruitment and turnover costs	Increased overhead cost of facilities
		Increased value of property beyond cost (in some cases)	
To Local Community	Taxes paid	Community services not required to be bought by company	Cost of taxes paid
	Environmental improvements	Decreased recruiting and selling costs	Costs of improvements
	Local tax worth of net jobs created	Increased labor capacity, reducing selling and sometimes production costs	Increased contingent liability of unemployment insurance and employee termination costs if overstaffed
To Consumers	Added value of services and products supplied to clients beyond their market price (consumer surplus)	Reduced sales costs and increased future revenues (customer good will), reputation and associated reduced cost of recruitment	Opportunity costs of providing consumer surplus
To General Public	Federal and state taxes paid	Federal and state services (e.g. law enforcement, public health, education) not required to be bought by company	Cost of taxes paid
	Knowledge created	Increased technical efficiency & competitiveness, thus reduced sales and production costs	Cost of producing knowledge not paid by clients
	Tax worth of net jobs created		

Social Costs and Corresponding Financial Benefits and Costs

| | Social Costs | Corresponding Financial | |
		Benefits	Costs
To Employees	Layoffs and involuntary terminations	Reduction of surplus or inefficient labor, reducing overhead costs of production	Decreased perceived employment security results in decreased morale, labor productivity Loss of training investment
	Overtime worked but not paid	Decreased short-term labor costs resulting in increased profits	Increased long-term labor costs from increased turnover and replacement cost
	Inequality of opportunity	Decreased short-term labor costs (from what they would be in an "equal pay market for equal work")	Increased labor costs from employee dissatisfaction and turnover, legal costs, possible loss of government contracts and associated increased selling costs
To Local Community	Local taxes consumed in services	Saving of costs of services that would otherwise have to be supplied by company	Costs of taxes paid
	Environmental pollution	Saving of costs of pollution-reducing devices and processes	Hostile community reaction, possibly resulting in legal costs, higher recruiting costs, and fines
To Consumer	Opportunity costs to consumers of unsatisfactory services and/or products	Revenues and associated profits	Loss of client good will, resulting in increased sales costs and reduced future revenues, increased recruiting costs from loss of reputation, increased cost of capital
To General Public	State and federal services consumed	Savings of costs of services that would otherwise have to be supplied by company	Costs of taxes paid
	Public (environmental) resources consumed		

There are also high costs associated with an integration of financial and social data. Because public accountants do not yet recognize social audits —they are not opposed, but rather uncertain and sensitive to the unresolved issues—they will not certify an integrated financial and social audit statement. This leaves a company desiring to integrate financial and social reporting the options of integrating them and losing certification of its statement by public accountants, or publishing both the conventional certified financial statement and the uncertified integrated financial and social performance statement. This latter course obviously incurs additional analytical and printing costs, as well as throwing some doubt on the credibility of the integrated statement.

But these latter costs are bearable; in money terms, the extra analysis and printing might cost at most a few tens of thousands of dollars. The greater difficulty, and for those who do not know how to approach it, the much greater analytical cost, lies in the theory and practice of actually integrating the financial and social performance statements.

The 1971 Abt Associates Inc. financial and social reports illustrate some of the theoretical and practical difficulties of integration that remain to be solved. Many of them involve gaps and overlaps of social and financial categories that would possibly result in double counts or noncounts of some items if the two statements were integrated. For example, the social benefits to the staff include career advancement in terms of added earning power, but the financial income statement carries only total costs of the staff as direct and indirect costs, excluding the incremental increase. A partial overlap also exists between "Overtime Worked but Not Paid" (a social cost to the staff) and the financial benefit of this work in terms of higher quality, reduced selling costs, and resulting reduced overhead and higher profit. The problem in sorting out this overtime effect is that it is only one of many contributions to profit—the familiar spillover or externalities problem. One possible approach would be to impute to overhead cost the equivalent salary cost of overtime work not paid, recompute profit, and then conclude that the difference between the actual profit and this lesser profit is the financial benefit balancing the staff social cost. Another approach, more complex and sophisticated, would be to relate individual productivity to overtime—which is not necessarily a monotonic function. Then a staff survey could determine individual productivity increases as a result of the efficiency-weighted unpaid overtime. This would probably produce more accurate results at somewhat higher costs than the linear extrapolation of labor productivity.

Other social costs and benefits that need to be translated into financial cost and benefit categories include at least those shown in the tables on the pages immediately preceding. As can be seen from the tables, every social benefit and cost has associated with it financial benefits and costs, and vice versa. Some of the quantitative relationships are shown. In a social audit they would have to be quantified to determine the net financial impact of a particular social benefit or cost and vice versa. For example, it would be necessary to compute the excess of short-term increase in financial profit resulting from decreased labor costs from overtime worked but not paid over the present value of the long-term cost of this activity in employee turnover, exhaustion, etc.

Another problem to be resolved in the integration of the financial and social performance audits is the possible difference between cost and market worth of various social benefits. They would vary among benefits, and would have to be determined by surveys.

INCENTIVES FOR INTEGRATING FINANCIAL AND SOCIAL AUDITS

If a company's net worth detected by a social audit exceeds financial net worth, and that excess consists of social benefits not captured by the company, why generate those social benefits, and why measure them? What is the purpose of generating and revealing this previously hidden asset of social consumer surplus unrecognized by the market valuation?

First, the corporation's incentive for generating social worth is the strengthened justification of the real worth of "good will," which is otherwise often only an accounting plug. Social worth helps to justify on a realistic basis the difference between book and market value, and conceivably could be legitimately used to justify an increased difference between the two.

A second major incentive for the financial expression and integration of the social audit is the justification of a corporation's capitalization of current costs expended for social benefits in the public interest that are expected to yield both social and financial returns in the future. The net effect of such a procedure could be to increase earnings per share because of the capitalization of social costs, or, alternatively, to permit increased social expenditures without damage to earnings.

One major effect of such a financially integrated social audit is therefore to decrease the apparent financial cost of corporate social responsibility activities, without reducing and, indeed, in most cases, with increasing long-term financial profitability.

To be absolutely clear, let me state that the capitalization of current social action costs is no shabby coverup of current losses or desperate delay of the recognition of current costs to avoid bottom-line decreases.

On the contrary, this financial innovation of the financially integrated social audit mobilizes the profit incentives of corporations for their own and the public interest!

If the social investments were not made, we would probably recommend a writing off of some of the good will of a company, because its social net worth would probably be below market net worth, reflecting an increase of contingent social liabilities. For example, if two chemical companies executed a financially integrated social audit, the one neglecting to invest in pollution abatement and equitable employment practices would actually be storing up future troubles for itself, to the detriment of its "real" good will. The socially responsible chemical company should and can, by means of the financially integrated social audit, invest in de-pollution and equal opportunity without reduction of current profits (because the expenses are capitalized) and with enhancement of future profits as well (because of the financial returns on the social investments, in terms of fines and legal actions avoided and reduced recruiting and sales costs to a favorable public).

Some typical social responsibility expenses that could be capitalized under a financially integrated social audit include:

1. Capital costs of de-pollution equipment, safety equipment, and environmental improvement.
2. Operating costs of minority recruitment and training, adjustments in salary for equal employment opportunity reasons (insurance companies, banks, employment of underpaid females), employee fringe benefits, contributions to knowledge, and any unusual losses on minority loan programs and suppliers.

SOCIAL AUDITS—THE STATE OF THE ART

The state of the art in the sciences is defined in terms of the state of the questions and the state of the answers. In this review of the state of the art of social audits, I will discuss the state of some of the questions, the state of some of the answers, and what can be done now.

The state of the questions concerns the awareness of possibilities for social audits and the most advanced theoretical thinking concerning the problems of their application. There are at least the nine questions below, a number of which demonstrate that the state of the questions is fairly well advanced, and indicates substantial awareness of theoretical possibilities and problems. Most of these questions pertain to some aspect of the integration of economic, sociological, and political theory with accounting and management science.

1. *How can social audits be executed and communicated in a form usable to decision makers?* This question seems decisive for implementation. If the managers of corporations and government organizations cannot use social audits to achieve their own management objectives, they are unlikely to do social audits. The uses of social audits are their reason for existence—without use, there is no point to them.

A cursory decision analysis of the issues of corporate and other organizational social responsibility and performance suggests that the major decisions to which social audits contribute are at least the following:

A. External to the organization:
   (1) How much resource (capital and human) should the organization allocate to primarily social responsibility activities? (How big should the pie be?)
   (2) How should the resources be allocated or distributed among various social action projects to maximize positive social impacts? (How should the pie be divided?)
B. Internal to the organization:
   (1) How should the regular business or government operations of the organization be modified or redirected to achieve positive social impacts, while still achieving the other organizational objectives such as growth, profitability, stability, and limited risk? (For example, how can a bank or insurance company reinvest its assets and reform its internal procedures, or how can a manufacturer redesign its products and production processes, to achieve positive social impact while maintaining growth of earnings?)

Management scientists have been concerned with such resource allocation questions for years. The general approach to the "How much total resource?" question is to choose that amount that seems to maximize return on investment while meeting organizational and other constraints, compared to alternative expenditures. This is also the approach used in distributing the total resource, and identifying the opportunities for modifying procedures, production processes, products, and services. Social audits theoretically can provide quantitative estimates of the costs and benefits of alternative investment levels and mixes under a variety of conditions. Without such quantitative estimates, social investment decisions, like any other investment decisions, are limited to qualitative, subjective, and unscientific judgments.

It remains to be determined what external and internal socially directed actions are of most interest to decision makers, and what is the preferred presentation format. At Abt Associates Inc., we have made the decision to include all known social costs and benefits and assets and liabilities significant for employees, clients, the local environment, and the general public. In order to facilitate quantitative trade-offs with financial performance requirements, and to determine the net social impact (excess of benefits over costs) of socially significant decisions, Abt Associates Inc. has elected to present its social audit in quantitative dollar units, in the form of a financial balance sheet and income statement. Whether these are the most managerially useful contents and forms for other, different types of organizations remains to be determined.

2. *How should the social audit reports be integrated with financial statements?* To be useful to managers as a decision-making tool, social audits must be capable of being related to financial statements. Where social actions by an organization compete for financial resources with its regular business or other activities, trade-offs between social and other objectives cannot be made without a common basis for measuring benefits and costs.

Socially directed actions may augment profits (or budget surpluses in nonprofit organizations), leave profits or surpluses unaffected, or reduce profits or surpluses. Since many larger social action programs often have a mixture of two or more of these effects, there is frequently the possibility of a positive or negative impact on the financial performance of the organization, and hence on its financial statement. Thus rational decisions about socially directed investments of financial or financially significant resources require some kind of integration of social and financial performance statements.

Integrative approaches suggest (1) inclusion of social costs and benefits and liabilities and assets in the financial statements; and (2) measurement of overall organizational performance in terms of the sum of net social and financial income (benefits less costs) divided by the sum of net social and financial investments—a kind of socioeconomic return on investment. These approaches raise several theoretical problems, some of which are outlined below.

The integration of social and financial reports, or even the effort to accomplish this, may result in the reform of financial statements themselves. Human and environmental assets and liabilities may soon be required to be reported in monetized terms in financial statements, substantially changing the quality of the balance sheets of many corporations. This reporting reform would have profound effects on the relative status of labor-intensive and capital-intensive industries, as well as service and manufacturing industries, with attendant impact on stock market values. It could—and should—also result in changes in tax policy. Users of public resources should pay user taxes, and contributors to public resources should be given tax incentives to do so.

3. *How can different social costs and benefits be made commensurate?* In other words, what common units can we apply to such benefits and costs as those of employee health, equality of employment opportunity, environmental improvements, product safety, consumer savings, improved knowledge, etc? One approach has been to monetize social benefits and costs in equivalent dollar terms, using the well-known accounting principle that things (or services) are worth their market or cost value. The shadow-pricing approach is not unknown to economic practice where exact prices for commodities have not been previously established, and it can be applied in social audits to services or things that have no established price or even cost.

One theoretical problem with monetizing social costs and benefits is that money is not worth the same to different persons at different times and circumstances. An economist would express it as a difference in the marginal utility of a dollar to a poor man and a rich man, or to a poor man living off the countryside and another one hungry in the city.

The same criticism may be made of the dollar units in the financial statement, however, so that this nonlinear utility problem seems no worse for social audits than for financial ones. The earnings per share may mean more for poor stockholders than rich ones, and the net worth of a company may mean more to presidents of small companies than to presidents of large companies.

What are the alternatives to money units as commensurate measures of social costs and benefits? If we used "social utiles" of some sort, we would have to translate the calculable dollar costs and benefits into such units at some widely agreed-upon equivalency of "utiles per dollar" or "dollars per utile." We would only create more work for ourselves, and still leave unresolved the nonlinear utility problem. To address the latter, we would have to create different social audits for different users and participants, a complication offering few decision-making benefits.

But even if we can approximate commensurability with monetized dollar units, and even with the use of shadow pricing and "cost or market" accounting for valuing known social costs and benefits, how do we estimate the costs and benefits? To put it another way, assuming we can by cost or market value estimates measure in commensurate units a project's or policy's social costs and benefits when we find them, how do we find them?

4. *How do we find social benefits and costs to measure, and then how do we measure them?* As stated above, when we identify a specific social benefit or cost that ensues from some organization's action or specific inaction, it can be measured by determining its equivalent market worth, or cost, by shadow pricing if necessary. But how do we identify the benefits

or costs for which we estimate a price? The problem here is that of the spillovers, or side effects, or externalities, as the economists say, of other actions contaminating the purity of effects of one's own social action.

For example, if a company puts a plant into a town with high unemployment, and unemployment drops by more than the added employment offered by the new plant, is this a secondary multiplier attributable to the greater expenditures of the newly employed, or is it the consequence of independent, parallel activities by other organizations or forces? It is not always easy or practicable to disaggregate the consequences of a given social action from other "external" causes.

This is a complex problem common to much social science policy research and evaluation. The usual procedure is to trace an action's (or a social investment's) inputs of objectives and resources through the processes of applying these inputs to the problem, to the project outputs, and finally to the impact of those outputs on the state of those socially significant variables the action was intended to change.

For example, a company might act to trace inputs of an objective of providing child care to all its female employees with preschool children, and the capital and human resources to operate a day-care center, through the processes of organizing and operating a day-care center on its premises, to the outputs of so many hours of child care, to the intended impacts of higher female employee productivity. Yet such a productivity increase might take place for an independent reason, or even not take place in the net because attributable improvements are more than cancelled out by concurrent negative factors.

The theoretical approaches to the problem of tracing causal chains in complex, interdependent systems (such as most socioeconomic systems) are either statistical or microanalytical. We can apply statistical methods to attempt to disaggregate the impacts of experimental from other variables, provided we have a statistically significant number of otherwise similar cases. But these are rarely available and always costly to analyze. Alternatively, we can analyze in minute detail the apparent causal chains, although this too is difficult and costly.

Given these difficulties, probably the most practical approach for industry and local government is to exploit the available results of large-scale federal government social and economic impact research—of which there has been several hundred million dollars' worth—and draw whatever useful analogies are possible between the contemplated social action and that already studied in government social research.

Even if social audits can be expressed in a form usable to decision makers and integrated with financial performance, and even if in doing so social costs and benefits are measured in commensurate terms, how can we do this for all organizations?

5. *How can individual corporate or other organizational social performance be related to national performance?* To express it another way, how can an individual organization's social accounts be related to the (yet undetermined) national social accounts? This problem is unsolved in economics as well, where the region between national income accounts (macroeconomics) and the economics of the firm (microeconomics) has been called "mezzoeconomics." Although there is a body of regional economic theory, there is no continuous theory from firm to nation, and the same problem exists in the social performance area.

Ideally, the net social benefits produced by all private and public organizations would add up to the net national social benefit, or at least some number directly related to it. As far as I know, however, no quantitative research has yet been done to relate the organizational to the national level of social performance, and of course we do not yet have a standardized set of national social income accounts. The question is significant for national and regional policy, since equity and efficiency would suggest that national public and private resources should be allocated roughly in proportion to net social benefits generated.

The more immediate issue for large-scale investors is that of estimating the social performance of different industries. The present state of the art permits estimating the relative social performance of different organizations within the *same* industry, because estimation of relative quantities of commensurable benefits and costs requires neither comprehensiveness nor precision. But to estimate the relative social performance of different organizations in *different* industries, or even different industries as a whole, common measures must be assigned to different constellations of social costs and benefits. This has not yet been done.

For example, it is now possible to estimate the relative net social contribution of different automobile manufacturers, if one makes certain assumptions about the social consequences of automobiles and automobile production that apply to all automobile manufacturers in common. Thus, whether we assume that cars are a social cost or a social benefit, or both to some degree, the relative social performance of automobile manufacturers will not depend on this assumption, but rather on the measurement of the relative values of such easily and objectively determinable variables as employee benefits, fair employment practices, and working conditions; automobile (product) safety, efficiency, and quality; community benefits such as employment and taxes, and community costs such as pollution; and general public benefits such as tax revenues and improved international trade balance and costs such as natural resources depletion and air pollution.

However, if we had to estimate the relative social performance of an automobile manufacturer and a pharmaceutical company, or even to estimate the relative social performance of the two industries, we would currently be limited to comparing their essentially non-product-related social performance actions toward employees, the plants' surrounding communities, and charitable contributions. The major component of the organizations' social impact—products and services—would have to be left out of the comparison or estimated by still highly controversial methods.

To measure comprehensive rather than partial social performance among different industries, we would have to determine the relative social impact of their principal product or service lines. In the example above, we would have to make some estimates of the relative social worth of automobile transport and pharmaceuticals. Ultimately we would be making judgments of the relative social utility of a certain kind of individual transportation and a certain kind of health. It is possible to make such judgments on the basis of aggregate market response to the two different product lines or by estimating their relative social impact on the populations in economic terms (employment mobility, secondary industries, reduced sick days lost from work, reduced insurance costs, etc.). However, such estimates would probably be quite reflective of individual values (health vs. mobility), age, income, and location. Whatever estimates are chosen would distort the values imputed to the products by groups other than those forming the basis of the estimates.

It is possible that sufficient value agreement exists at least among the members of particular age, income, sex, and locational groups to permit social utility estimates across product and service lines, but much further opinion research is required to determine this. In the meantime, estimates of the relative social utility or disutility of different products and services must be based on the incomplete indications of market prices or the hypothetical assumptions of social scientists striving nobly to limit the contamination of interpretive data by their own values.

It should be remembered that, although the example given above is for estimating the social performances of different businesses in different industries, the same reasoning applies to comparing the social performance of different government agencies supplying the same service (e.g. police forces in different cities) and different government agencies supplying different services (e.g., police services in one city compared to employment services in another). To date, government policy research has made it possible to compare the cost-effectiveness (or social performance) of different organizations offering the same services, but the comparison of the performances of different services is still at a very crude stage—again because assumptions about the relative social values of different services need to be made.

6. *How can we measure the contribution of an organization's regular business or service activity to national social goals?* In some cases, this is relatively easy to do, as in the measurement of an organization's progress toward the national goal of equality of opportunity or full employment. In other cases, such as environmental protection, health, and education, an organization's impact may be a complex of positives and negatives.

One approach to estimating an organization's contribution to social goals from its regular activities is to determine the degree to which it contributes a "consumer surplus" to the consumer of its regular activities. For example, if one drug company offers aspirin of the same quality as a competitor's, but at a lower price, other factors being equal in an imperfect market, a consumer surplus is generated. Particularly for companies offering services, the saving or new resources created for customers in excess of the costs of the services may be considered a social benefit.

The theoretical problem with even these crude approaches is that economic benefits provided consumers of products or services may not necessarily be social benefits. For example, if the economic savings are created for socially destructive purposes, then more savings result in reduced, rather than improved, social performance. One has only to consider the perhaps melodramatic examples of manufacturers of hand guns or heroin. They may be able to generate consumer surpluses through efficient production, but these economic benefits are likely to be translated into social costs, rather than social benefits.

These problems of the social uses of economic values are also related to the time when the economic or social values accrue. Just as a dollar five years from now does not seem worth as much as a dollar now (and in fact it costs about half as much now), so a social benefit several years hence may not be worth as much as it would be now.

7. *What is the social discount rate?* The social discount rate must be defined in order to make various future and present social benefits commensurate, much as the financial discount rate is used to give future earnings streams an equivalent present value. The problem is that the social discount rate may be quite different from the financial discount rate. Estimates for the social discount rate have varied from 30 percent to zero to negative rates in socialist countries.

If one values the quality of life of one's children and grandchildren equally with one's own, then the social discount rate should be zero, because social benefits in the future are worth just as much as social benefits today. If social benefits are believed to depreciate rapidly because rising social expectations tend to cancel much of the perceived increase in social benefits, then the social discount rate should be much higher than the financial discount rate. If, on the other hand, one is building a brave new world, and out of ideological idealism one attributes more worth to social benefits in the future society than in the present one, the social discount rate should be negative.

Whichever rate is selected will greatly affect the rate of social performance estimated. Social overhead investments with a relatively longer range payoff, such as higher education and basic research, would, with a high positive discount rate be relatively reduced in attractiveness compared to such early payoff investments as recreation and health care. If the social discount rate were considered to be zero—the assumption that future social benefits are just as valuable as present ones because we value the quality of our children's lives as much as that of our own—then the time when a social investment pays off will be much less significant than its benefit/cost ratio.

Thus the choice of social discount rates may significantly affect the choice of social investments. For fair comparisons to be made among different social audits without complex translating computations, it is most desirable that all social audits agree on the same social discount rate. Unfortunately, no such agreement exists today, even among the modest number of social scientists and socially concerned accountants who have thought about the social discount rate.

8. *How can uniform standards for social audits be developed and enforced?* Without some uniform standards of financial accounting, investors and tax authorities could not assess the financial performance of different organizations. Despite the wide variance in what are called "generally accepted auditing standards," financial analysts and lay investors still can get a general idea of the financial performance of a firm, even if in a minority of cases accounting has distorted reality. Furthermore, sophisticated investment analysts know how to discount some of the more blatant distortions included in "generally accepted accounting standards," such as capitalized sales expenses, excessive depreciation, and various ways of treating the income or losses of subsidiaries.

In social auditing, however, we do not have "generally accepted standards," even with a latitude as broad as the standards in financial accounting. Indeed, we do not yet have any "generally accepted" standard at all. We do not have the social auditing equivalent of the American Institute of Certified Public Accountants and its Accounting Practice Board to define "generally accepted standards" and to enforce them, however loosely.

Social audits are now in about the same category as patent medicine were a hundred years ago. The inexperienced corporate executive does not really know what they are, and if he asks two different experts he is likely to get two different answers with only some common elements. Truthfulness and accuracy of reporting are now a matter of individual conscience and competence. This is a situation that should not long be allowed to persist if the confidence of decision makers and the general public in social audits is to be developed.

One reason why such a slow start has been made in developing uniform standards is the lack of clear government mandates, standards, incentives to compliance, and legislated legal enforcements. The lethargy of the Congress's General Accounting Office in moving toward social audits of federal social action programs and policy research has not helped. The even slower response of the AICPA to the problem—despite numerous excellent articles on social audits and their components in the accounting journals—has also failed to give socially concerned CPA's much encouragement towards developing more uniform social auditing standards.

9. *What should the government do to encourage and standardize social audits?* The social performance of a private corporation has no direct current legal bearing on federal, state, or local taxes. Surely the socially productive acts accounted for in social audits and in support of national social policy—improved employee health, education, productivity, equality of opportunity, environmental protection, consumer protection, etc.—deserve some formal encouragement in tax policy. User charges for environmental pollution and tax credits for abatement need to be developed. Presently, there is no social investment credit, no social depletion allowance, as there well might be if the government were thorough in its pursuit of national social goals.

To this point the analysis has focused on the state of the questions in the state of the art of social auditing. What of the state of the "answers," or a least the responses to the questions? For all the above things that need to be done, what is being done now?

Responses to the problems of social audits are suggested below, representing in rough terms the state of the "answers." These include: a comprehensive social audit, human resource accounting, an example of security analysis from the social auditing aspect, the contributions of social science, government evaluation research, economics and management science, accounting and finance available data bases, measures of the quality of life, and current R & D sources.

An example of a comprehensive social audit is that undertaken by Abt Associates Inc. It presents in a financial statement format, in dollar equivalents, the social assets and liabilities on the balance sheet, and the social benefits and costs and net social income on the income statement, accruing to employees, clients, local community, and general public. Many of the numbers, although all carefully computed on the basis of actual records and data, represent management judgments about the relationship between one set of data and another. In the absence of "generally accepted" social auditing principles, there is no other alternative for an organization innovating its own system than to use its own best judgments concerning the meaning of its numerical data.

There are numerous theoretical weaknesses and incompletions in this social audit, which are being addressed in subsequent and hopefully improved efforts. For example, some of the social benefits, such as employee benefits, overlap with financial costs, while others, such as equality of opportunity, do not. Some of the benefits and costs accruing to employees also accrue to the community, such as new jobs and skills developed. An argument could be made for the employee net benefits to be included in the community net benefits, and for the community net benefits and client net benefits to be included in the overall net benefits to the public. The way in which this particular social audit has been structured represents a trade-off among the demands of theoretical neatness, clear communication of salient aspects of social performance, and maintenance of the analogy to financial statements. Other social audits could certainly express the same facts in a different format.

An example of what might be characterized as a partial social audit that, unlike the above, is integrated with financial statements is the human resource accounting of the R. G. Barrie Corp. of Ohio, developed with the aid of Dr. Rensis Likert, Director Emeritus of the University of Michigan's Institute of Social Research. This approach treats employee recruiting and training costs as an amortized investment rather than a current expense. Human assets are also "depreciated" and their replacement costs are included. Nevertheless, even in this example the human resources (financial and social) accounting is presented separately from the conventional balance sheet for lack of human resource accounting standards.

The investment community has recently brought forth several new investment funds whose ostensible purpose is to help investors make a reasonable return by investing in the more socially responsible corporations. To help identify the most "socially responsible" companies, these funds have applied a variety of very crude social performance measures which might evolve into social audits of potential investments. The Dreyfus Third Century Fund, for example, uses the simple and clear measure of corporate social responsibility of the legality of five types of a company's actions relating to employees (equal employment opportunity laws), work safety, environment, consumer safety, and honesty of advertising.

The simplicity and apparent nonambiguity of the Third Century

Fund approach to social auditing is a commendable first step. Most corporations violate one or more of these five types of legal requirements with the relative impunity of wealthy scofflaws paying trivial fines. If this approach results in some of the violators becoming more legal, that is all in the public interest. Unfortunately, this approach is capable of only crude discriminations, possibly even misleading ones.

The problem with five simple binary evaluations of corporate legality or illegality is that illegalities of minor social impact are equated with those of major impact. For example, under this approach a company guilty of minor infractions of work safety *and* consumer safety legislation resulting in a few thousand dollars' total worth of equivalent annual social costs would be considered less socially responsible than a company that was legal in all its actions except those affecting its environment, where its activities incurred tens of millions of dollars equivalent annual social cost.

These crude approaches fail to exploit the available and quite substantial results of contemporary social science and government evaluation research. The social and economic impact studies supported by the Environmental Protection Agency and the Army Corps of Engineers could be used to estimate the quantitative impact of corporate environmental actions. The social and economic impact studies supported by the Departments of Health, Education, and Welfare, Labor, Transportation, and Housing and Urban Development could be used to estimate the quantitative impacts of corporate health (employees and customers), education and training, and other actions.

Recent federally funded research on indicators of social change and measures of the quality of life could also be applied to more refined social audits than the binary legal checks of the Third Century Fund. The point here is that contemporary social research offers much more refined measures of social performance than the users of such measures in the investment community seem to be aware of.

Economics and the management sciences such as operations research have developed methods for imputing prices to any good or service, however intangible. Shadow-pricing and special scaling techniques are examples. Given measures of return on social investments using such shadow-pricing and the impact analyses mentioned above, the only major problem left for government and private investors in alternative social programs is that of optimal resource allocation, or optimal investment mix determination. Many techniques are currently available for doing this, from linear programming to statistical decision theory. Most of them make some use of the economics concept of optimizing a mix of competing investments by equalizing marginal utilities.

Accounting and financial practice also have much available and much to contribute to social auditing. The classical return-on-investment and discounted present value analyses are essential to rational social as well as financial investment. The classical accounting principles of establishing worth on the basis of the lower of market or cost is applicable to social benefits as well. The accounting concept of a comprehensive performance statement, both cumulatively (the balance sheet) and incrementally (the income statement), seems essential to retain for social audits, whichever format is used.

The data bases available for social auditing are numerous and impressive, despite many claims of data insufficiency. Consider some examples. Concerning equality of employment opportunity, there are all the data developed by federal regulation in the affirmative action plans required of all government contractors. Concerning environment, there are all the impact analyses of the Environmental Protection Agency and the Corps of Engineers, and the data collected by environmental groups such as the Sierra Club and the Friends of the Earth. Concerning employee benefits, there are all the actuarial and other data collected by insurance companies and unions. Concerning consumer and employee preferences and values, there are all the tools of survey research and the data collected by market researchers.

Given data on preferences and possibilities, the methodological research on the quality of life can be related to an empirical base. The work of Converse, Cantril, and the British Social Science Research Council, among others, suggests measures of desired qualities that can be used in social audits for estimating social benefits.

In addition to all the above, present resources of theory, practice, information, and data available for social auditing, substantial research is continuing. Some of the government agencies supporting this research are the National Science Foundation in its technology assessment work, the EPA in its environmental impact research, and the U.S. Office of Education in its long-term educational impact analyses. The General Accounting Office is also looking into social auditing.

Among private research institutions developing better methods of social auditing and its components are the Public Affairs Council, the University of Michigan Institute for Social Research, the Council on Economic Priorities, the Russell Sage Foundation, Harvard Business School, Yale Law School, Abt Associates Inc., and Arthur D. Little, Inc.

Given this state of the art of social audits, what can be done now? For all organizations, public and private, concerned in some way with social responsibilities, whether self-imposed or mandated by the public, at least the following five actions seem immediately feasible and desirable:

1. Organizations can and should do their own social audits, on a regular annual basis, at the most comprehensive and detailed level afforded by their intellectual and financial resources. Plenty of help is available if resources internal to the organization do not suffice. Technical assistance is available from university business schools and economics departments, and from firms specializing in social science research.
2. An organization's social audit should be directly related to management decision making, aiding in balancing the interests of stockholders (or voters), employees, customers, community, and general public. Not only the corporate charities and employee benefits programs should be included, but also personnel, R & D, production, marketing, and finance.
3. The social audit should be conducted as consistently as possible from year to year. As new, more comprehensive, sensitive, and precise measures of social impact are added—and they should be added as they become available—the previously used measures should be continued at least long enough for year-to-year comparisons.
4. Research and development directed toward refining the social audit should be carried out continuously, and cooperation should be offered to efforts to standardize the audits.
5. Management should use social audits in seeking a high positive social and economic impact for its organization, while keeping a low profile and modestly reporting results. It would generally seem wise to claim a little less social benefit for one's organization than one believes one deserves, to reduce the danger of the social audit being denigrated as merely a more sophisticated public relations device.

In summary, we have described the state of the art of social audits in terms of the state of the questions and the state of the responses or answers. We have also described briefly what we believe can be done now with social audits, and how they can continue to be improved. We remain confident that, despite the still primitive state of this art of social auditing, it is an art critical to the socially responsible management of public and private organizations, and that it will advance rapidly to resolve the issues raised above.

EDITOR'S COMMENTARY

The social audit has been described as an idea whose time has come but which isn't ready to be taken off the drawing board and put to work. Among those, in the ranks of business and academia, concerned about corporate social responsibility, there is rather wide agreement that it would be highly useful to have quantitative measures of external and internal costs and benefits associated with socially responsible policies and programs. Even a crude measuring instrument would contribute to more rational decision making in an area where judgments seek factual support and seldom find it. Yet skeptical reactions abound to proposals for converting adjectives to numbers. What will be generated, it is alleged, are bad numbers, and bad numbers are worse than no numbers when decisions involving large resource commitments are at stake.

Since Dr. Abt is a major proponent of the social audit concept and has gone farther than most in probing the technical problems in quantifying relevant costs and benefits and in applying the new technique to actual business operations, it may be illuminating to examine the opposition case. It stands on two foundations, one conceptual, the other technical. The two are not unrelated, because it would appear that if the conceptual issues could be resolved the technical difficulties would be substantially minimized, although not completely removed.

In the conceptual area, one important question focuses on the objective of the social audit. Is the primary purpose to enable a corporation to report its socially responsible activities in meaningful terms to an outside audience—its stockholders or the general public? Or is the purpose to provide data for improved internal management decision making and, possibly, to strengthen management's ability to respond in persuasive fashion to external criticism of its social performance? This is not an empty contrast. It can be argued that the two objectives lead to quite different quantitative measuring systems. The distinction parallels the distinction in traditional financial accounting between the information system requirements for reporting to tax authorities and investors (which themselves are not uniform), on one side, and the information requirements for internal management decision, on the other. As corporate controllers have long known, the composition and structure of the two sets of information requirements are far from identical and can be standardized within a single system only with some gross adjustments.

Another question arises in connection with socially responsible policies and programs that have no readily defined associated costs yet deliver significant benefits to customers and, often, the sponsoring company. Improvements in product safety and service-free performance, removal of dubious (although legal) advertising and promotional practices, and, for food products, increasing nutritional values are examples of such activities. Other examples can be found in equitable hiring and employment practices, improved pollution control that yields a profit over investment in control technology, and public service contributed without charge by executives and other employees.

Still a third question is suggested by corporate social inactivity—those policies and programs a company might sponsor but does not, possibly by specific management decision, often because of management inadvertence or lack of vision. Should these be brought within the scope of a company's social audit accounting, on the negative side? And what about inactivities that are not even recognized and identified? In a sense, this area can be related to the economic concept of opportunity costs, which are never reflected in traditional financial accounting and only occasionally in information systems for management decision making.

A broader, less determinate issue is raised by the question of public expectations of corporate behavior. There are no defined boundaries for the concept of social responsibility. A radical enlargement of the accepted definition is occurring in our time and we do not perceive a limit to the expanding scope. But if what is thought to be socially responsible in business performance is by no means defined nor fully specified, then how are the negatives to be quantified? The essential first step in all measurement schemes is to describe what is to be measured. Here we confront a shifting set of values which themselves can be described only in crude, possibly biased, terms. On this point the comment of John C. Burton is worth pondering:

> I have serious misgivings about the feasibility of attempting to identify and isolate elements of what management may not have done but which others consider it should have done. The disinclination of professional accountants to recognize or include "opportunity costs" in conventional financial statements is neither whimsical nor accidental. It represents recognition of the constraints of the objectively auditable and professionally certifiable acquisition (historical) cost-based data. The measurement of what ought to have been is limited only by the imagination of the proposer of alternatives.[2]

Finally, although still other issues could be identified, what conceptual disposition is to be made of the corporation which continues to operate a high-cost facility in a community in which it is the major employer because closing the plant down would inflict severe distress on individual employees and the entire locality? Here, cost measurements could be quite precise, but theory is slippery on the benefit side.

On the technical side, a comparable array of problems can be cited. Probably the most familiar—and, curiously, the easiest to dispose of—is the unassailable fact that many of the measurements inherent in any corporation's social audit must be gross estimates. Critics of proposals to institute the social audit point to the unavoidable soft data as a reason for not going ahead. The obvious response is that many of the data that appear in national economic and fiscal records are also soft (and so are

[2] *Business and Society Review/Innovation*, 4 (Winter 1972–73), p. 43. Professor Burton, on leave from his faculty position at the Graduate School of Business, Columbia University, was then serving as Chief Accountant, Securities and Exchange Commission.

many of the figures that appear in corporate financial accounts, as accountants and other financial professionals know). But their indeterminateness and even ambiguity do not prevent their effective use for a variety of appraisal and decision applications. It is, of course, essential that those using such data understand their limitations. But soft data present one kind of administrative problem when the objective is absolute measurement, quite another when the target is relative measurement. And much of the information needs of business executives are in the relative rather than absolute category. Estimating based on consistent measurement techniques can be as useful as precision counting in many decision situations.

A more challenging problem is the absence of proven techniques for dealing with cost and benefit measures along the full range of socially responsible performance. Interest in measurements of corporate social behavior is a recent development. There are no textbooks, no manuals of standard procedures, no record, even, of experiments and observed results. Any company attempting to account for its social performance to outsiders or for internal administrative use will find it necessary to invent its own measurement technique. Inevitably, the results will be open to criticism from both those who would favor a different technique and those who simply lack confidence in any specific applied procedures. It should be noted, however, that this technical deficiency does not apply to all aspects of the social audit. In a number of activity areas, standard financial and decision accounting procedures can be applied in existing or modified form. While costs of socially responsible programs are obviously more amenable than benefits to traditional measurement techniques, many of the external and internal social payoffs can be handled by imaginative use of the approved and familiar procedure of cost-or-market valuation.

A more subtle technical problem may well lie on the other side of the measurement barrier. Among those whose mental set tilts strongly to the quantitative approach to problem solving, there is a tendency to assume that what can be measured is important in decision making and what resists measurement is trivial. This can lead to gross error when unmeasured elements are central components in program results. Critics of the U.S. performance in Vietnam over many years made much of this disposition as applied to measures of claimed "success" based on bombing missions, areas under Saigon control, and similar fringe aspects of guerrilla warfare. But there should be no intellectual difficulty in combining quantitative and nonquantitative assessments in either reporting or decision making. The critical issue is to recognize both the potential and the limitations of any measurement technique, and to avoid the familiar fallacy of assuming that elements handled by verbal, rather than numeric, assessment are unimportant in ultimate judgments.

On balance, the skeptics have a case. In both the conceptual and technical areas there are serious unresolved problems that make it unlikely that valid, specific corporate audits can be carried out with currently available knowledge and skills. But the case is even stronger in favor of moving ahead to develop the requisite knowledge and skills. For both external reporting and internal decision-making purposes corporate managers need measurement systems that can be applied in deciding what socially responsible policies and programs to put into operation and what results follow their implementation.

Most of the problems, conceptual and technical, will be explored much more effectively through trial-and-error methods than through theoretical speculation and intellectual games. Without public announcement, without initial commitment to use the results, corporate managers would be well advised to start measurement projects. The beginning efforts should not be comprehensive. Rather, they should focus on selected activities that can be quantified on both cost and benefit sides with existing knowledge and techniques. Later, with useful numbers in view, more imaginative efforts can be undertaken to deal with other areas that will require new knowledge and skill.

Among the more obvious specific activities that should be amenable to measurement with existing techniques, the following stand out: equal-opportunity hiring programs, training programs for handicapped workers, day-care facilities for employees' children, programs to reduce or eliminate environmental pollution, job-enrichment programs, placement of business with and assistance to outside minority enterprise suppliers, and consumer protection and benefit programs.

The ultimate gains for the company that pushes a serious effort into measuring inputs and outputs in such areas will be substantial. First, management will have a growing stock of information for measuring efficiency of performance. Second, management will have the data essential for making resource commitment choices among competing socially responsible activities. And third, with the passage of time management will have a basis for specific reporting of its performance to its stockholders and the general public. As other corporations follow similar procedures, there will also be opportunities for comparing the range, effectiveness, and efficiency of competitive performance.

Reasonable observers should be willing to encourage this much progress, without criticizing the inability of corporate controllers to merge social responsibility accounting with financial accounting. That, too, may become feasible in time. But it is not essential today, and may never be an important information objective.

CHAPTER 7

Some Financial Implications of Corporate Social Responsibility

Dan W. Lufkin

Among the significant issues brought into view by social pressure for enlarged corporate responsibility is the effect of business responses on corporate financial performance and the criteria applied by investing institutions and individual investors in deciding where to commit funds. Return on invested capital as a sole valid measure of performance is coming under critical challenge as questions are increasingly raised about the policies and programs that create the return.

This chapter examines the implications of corporate social responsibility for both corporate financial performance and investing decisions.

Dan W. Lufkin, now retired from his founding partnership in Donaldson, Lufkin & Jenrette, and serving as Commissioner, Department of Environmental Protection, State of Connecticut, is the author of the following chapter.–EDITOR

W E ARE living at a time when the pace of change is accelerating throughout the world. It is one of those periods when the familiar landscape suddenly becomes strange. Old landmarks are obliterated. Comfortable relationships are tense and strained. Our maps no longer relate to the geography around us. In the past two years alone, we have seen the most dramatic shifts in world ideologies and alliances. Within our own country, the philosophical assumptions of more than a generation have been successfully challenged. Old power blocs have crumbled. And, what is perhaps most significant, new social contracts have been drawn up between the citizens and their government, between Washington and the states, and between society and private enterprise.

While it is still too early to comprehend the historical significance of the end of the Vietnam War, the changing relationships between the Communist and Western worlds, the tentative new ties between the United States and Russia and the United States and China, we can speak with greater authority about the meaning of events at home. The President has stated clearly his intent to fulfill his promises to that majority of Americans who elected him: fewer federal panaceas for social ills; more emphasis on individual effort; restoration of power to the states; and a breaking up of entrenched alliances between governmental bureaucracies and their traditional constituencies.

Not since the days of Franklin Delano Roosevelt has this nation experienced such a comprehensive "New Deal." The cards are on the table. But very few of us are sure of the rules of the game. One fact, however, seems certain. In the arena of social change—the rebuilding of the cities, housing, equal job opportunities, health services, education, the cleansing of the environment—there will be fewer grandiose attempts at federal remedies and more encouragement of local solutions by states and their subdivisions and, to a greater degree than ever before, the private sector.

The President's reading of his electoral mandate may be in error. The Congress may thwart his attempts at the reorganization of the federal establishment and the reorientation of our approach to national priorities. But it seems evident that the voters were saying something significant in November, 1972. And "attention must be paid" to the substance of their message.

What that message seems to be is this: somehow the social order in America has gotten out of balance. Greater affluence has not purchased or produced the paradise we were conditioned to expect. Instead, it has created a deteriorating environment, a disappearance of comfort and civility, a reduction in the perceived quality of products and services, and a growing distance between the ills of society and those who should be in a position to remedy them. Large-scale federal programs seem to have failed. Ten years and more than $200 billion later, there is still poverty, still inadequate housing, still unconscionable discrimination, still mediocre education, and still a cancerous spread of urban blight that is moving beyond the borders of our cities into what were once the healthy tissues of suburban and rural America.

THE NEW SOCIAL CONTRACT

In searching for solutions more immediately applicable to these problems, many Americans believe they have uncovered some of their causes. Out of these new perceptions of cause and effect, they are rewriting their social contract both with government and with that most powerful of all private institutions, American business.

Historically, as the Committee for Economic Development has pointed out, business has done what society required: fulfilling the needs and wants of people for goods and services at affordable prices and producing most of the wealth of the nation in doing so.[1] Since 1890, the total real national product has doubled every twenty years. Though population has grown three-fold and taxes have increased sharply, real disposable income per person has more than tripled, and hours on the job have declined by a third. Industry has not only produced the varied abundance America has desired; it has provided the jobs that paid the wages that purchased the goods that, in turn, provided the jobs that paid the wages—and on and on in an endless spiral of supply and demand. All of this was made possible by the generation of profits which provided not only the human motivation that powered the system but also the funds to underwrite accelerating growth.

Over the years, this basic contract has undergone many amendments: the rise of labor unions, antitrust legislation, the growth of regulatory agencies, tax laws, and similar phenomena have intervened to alter the fundamental laws of supply and demand, production and consumption, that characterized the relationship between business and society noted by Adam Smith.

NEW RESPONSIBILITIES FOR BUSINESS

The new contract is a radical departure from the original because it goes beyond placing restrictions on the actions of business within the context of the marketplace. For the first time—or at least so it appears—it establishes responsibilities for business *outside* the marketplace, endowing business with many of the powers and obligations once entrusted to government and holding business accountable for areas of concern which are unrelated to its primary commercial functions.

[1] Committee for Economic Development, *Social Responsibilities of the Business Corporation,* A Statement on National Policy by the Research and Policy Committee of the CED (June, 1971), p. 11.

Although all provisions of the new contract cannot yet be discerned, the nature of the public interest seems clear. Industry will be charged not only with the responsibility for providing goods and services, but also for assuring goods that are safe and well constructed and services whose latent effects are not harmful. If in the process of manufacture, industry pollutes the air and fouls the water, industry will be expected to bear the major costs of cleansing the air and water and restoring them to the public in usable if not mint condition.

Instead of providing jobs for those it chooses to employ, industry will be required to provide opportunity and training to social and economic groups traditionally excluded from the job market. And instead of merely paying taxes for the space it occupies within the geographical limits of a community, business will be expected to contribute to the community's social, cultural, physical, and spiritual, as well as economic, well-being.

William J. Casey has said that this new social contract is the result of a "revolution of rising expectations" on the part of the public.[2] These expectations are compounded of a disillusionment with the inefficiencies of government, a recognition that the problems are too vast for individual citizens to solve, and a feeling that business is a root cause of many of the problems and must be held responsible for solving them.

THE ACCOUNTABILITY OF BUSINESS

Daniel Yankelovich has conducted a variety of surveys among all segments of the American public. He finds deeply engrained in the national psyche an argument that goes something like this: "There is something fundamentally wrong in the country today. Business is the most powerful institution in the country today. Therefore, business must be responsible for what is wrong."[3] He concludes that as a result of this underlying sense of causality, "a changed and threatening social environment" now exists that challenges fundamental assumptions of the contract between business and society and calls "upon business to make decisions which do not have the profit maximization of the company as their objective."

The forces producing these pressures on business are not generated solely by radical minorities, as has been true during much of our history. The social climate in which business now operates has changed in kind,

[2] William J. Casey, "Corporate Responsibility As Seen from the SEC," *Business and Society Review* (Spring, 1972), p. 24.

[3] Daniel Yankelovich, "The Changing Business Environment," *NAM Reports* (January 31, 1972), p. 9.

not merely in degree. Quite simply, we *are* in the midst of a revolution brought about, Yankelovich asserts, by "the combination of vigorous leadership plus massive public support plus a new responsiveness on the part of the old regulatory agencies plus new laws, new regulatory agencies, new forms of penalties and new legal mechanisms."

I believe that all these forces added together form a "critical mass" which threatens the future of business—*if* it fails to be responsive to the widespread demands for a new social contract and a redefinition of corporate responsibility.

HOW MUCH RESPONSIBILITY

There are principles of law which state that a contract without consideration is not binding and a contract impossible of fulfillment is no contract at all. Some orthodox economists find no legitimate basis for any contractual agreement between business and the public except that which allows the maximization of profits on the part of business in return for its promise to provide society with an unending stream of goods and services.

"The only responsibility of corporate executives is to make as much money for their stockholders as possible," says Milton Friedman. And he denies the capacity of business to enter into a contract that imposes obligations other than profit maximization. "Only individuals can have responsibilities," he says. "A business cannot have responsibilities."[4] Thus, he denies that the new social contract is capable of fulfillment and holds that, as a consequence, it cannot be binding on the parties involved.

Professor Robert Dahl opposes this view.

> Today, it is absurd to regard the corporation simply as an enterprise established for the sole purpose of allowing profit making. We, the citizens, give them special rights, powers and privileges, protection and benefits on the understanding that their activities will fulfill our purposes. Corporations exist because we allow them to do so. And we allow them to exist only as they continue to benefit us. . . . Every corporation should be thought of as a social enterprise whose existence and decisions can be justified only insofar as they serve public or social purposes.[5]

While this may be an extreme position, I am not arguing its rightness or wrongness. I am saying that a majority of citizens seem to favor this view and, if necessary, seem to be prepared to support restrictive legisla-

[4] Milton Friedman, "Milton Friedman Responds," *Business and Society Review* (Spring, 1972), p. 6.

[5] Robert A. Dahl, "A Prelude to Corporate Reform," *Business and Society Review* (Spring, 1972), pp. 17–18.

tion commanding corporate responsibility, if business fails to uphold its end of the social contract. And there are politicians lined up ten deep ready to make political capital of the issue.

HOW BUSINESS VIEWS ITS
SOCIAL RESPONSIBILITIES

It also seems clear to me that business itself is increasingly recognizing its deep involvement in society. In a recent analysis of corporate annual reports for 1972, the Conference Board found that one out of three companies surveyed addressed themselves specifically to corporate social responsibility.[6] Some of the statements of corporate philosophy are startling in their departure from traditional profit orientation:

> *From an insurance company:* While our basic responsibility is to maintain and improve our primary business operations, we have both a clear intent and a corporate duty to apply our experience and skill in helping to alleviate social, economic and environmental problems.
> *From a banking firm:* Today more than ever, banking as an industry is aware that its growth and success are dependent upon the society it serves. The involvement of banks in community and national problems is not only a moral but an economic imperative.
> *From a food company:* We intend to continue to be a leader in public responsibility not only because it is good for the public but because it is good for business.

Such statements could be construed as lip service to mollify an angry public. But in every case they are supported by a record of social action not directly involved in the profit-making activities of the corporations. Clearly a very large number of American enterprises have been able to flesh out the new image of themselves as something more than "maximizers of profit." This new corporate dimension is neither separate from nor opposed to the profit-making function, but it is ultimately indispensable to its survival. This is a key point.

J. Irwin Miller has said, "I find highly offensive the argument that the business of business is to do business. You can call it a rule of thumb that where corporations do more than the law allows you have a good society."[7]

A number of economists and businessmen have pointed out that if corporations don't do what needs to be done using stockholders' or con-

---

[6] William R. Bradt, "Current Trends in Public Affairs," (New York: The Conference Board, 1972), p. 13.

[7] J. Irwin Miller, *New York Times,* February 10, 1971.

sumers' money, it will be done by government with taxpayers' money. I need not labor the point that at the prices government charges, it is far more efficient and economical to handle social responsibility through corporate channels.

Peter Drucker is the most prominent champion of the "reprivatization" of many of the social functions previously undertaken exclusively by government. He asserts that it is not so much a matter of morality as of practicality. The Friedman view may have been valid if we still lived in a simple time in a textbook world where there is "huge government surrounded by a society of small grocery stores owned by Papa, Mama and Rosie."[8]

But, of course, the real world today is not like that. Drucker holds that while the job of government is to propose directions for society and legislate the rewards and penalties into being, it is the role of enterprise to act, to manage, to innovate, and to bring about social change. This, after all, is what businessman have said all along they are good at doing. As a matter of historical fact, one of the reasons big government assumed many of the functions and obligations of business in the first place, and imposed much of the regulation that inhibits business today, was that private enterprise shirked its social responsibilities for so long.

Friedman says that any activity of business not designed to increase its profits constitutes the imposition of a tax either on its shareholders, its employees, or the public—a tax which it has no right to impose. But in this era when its social contract is being rewritten, business can impose far more of a tax on the public—and indeed risk its own survival—by failing to shoulder the burden of responsibility even while it is making a profit.

Robert Austin says that the corporation must take into consideration the interests of society in organizing its activities and calculating its value. And he responds to Milton Friedman with this formulation: "Business is responsible today for incredible technological change. This technological change will continue to cause social change. Social change brings demands for action to meet or mitigate the effects of social change. The top management today must be broadened to include an awareness of the social changes it causes."[9]

In other words, managers must be responsible for the second and third order of their decisions—a burden never before imposed on business to such a degree, if at all. Increasingly, they must be concerned with the social implications of their activities, not merely their impact on the bottom line. This establishes a whole new set of rewards and punishments

[8] Peter Drucker, letter to the author, October 29, 1970.

[9] Robert Austin, "Responsibility for Social Change," *Harvard Business Review* (July–August, 1963).

that can seriously affect the entire value system by which business operates and on which it has based its costs, prices, and resultant profits.

A polluter upstream who refuses to purify his wastes must recognize the impact of his actions and help ameliorate their effects on the people downstream who must drink the water he fouls. An employer who refuses to hire and train members of certain minority groups must recognize that he will inevitably have to bear the welfare or training costs for those whom he has forced to remain unemployed or underemployed. A buisness that neglects the welfare of its own employees must recognize that inevitably it will pay the price of loss of skills, productivity, and morale among the workers that remain with it.

Regardless of the private values and moral systems pursued by businessmen, both on and off the job, there is no line of the balance sheet or income statement for social ethics. After generations of the pursuit of profits to the exclusion of other seemingly tangential concerns, it is difficult for management to shift gears, reorient its people, and adjust its bookkeeping so that social responsibility is added to its already crowded roster of policies, procedures, goals, and costs.

PRIVATE GOALS AND PUBLIC RESPONSIBILITIES

In demanding that American business take on the added freight of social responsibility, while encouraging it also to pursue its own corporate goals, we have saddled it with a crushing paradox. Henry Ford II has expressed it very simply. If business concentrates on social goals at the sacrifice of short-term profit, it may find itself destroyed by its neglect of its long-term future. On the other hand, if it emphasizes profit to the exclusion of social goals, it may find itself abandoned and destroyed by the people it has ignored.[10]

The resolution of the paradox is a difficult one because the new social contract itself is so complex and, in many ways, so contradictory. We call upon the managers of businesses not only to maximize profit, but to increase social benefits as well. We ask them not only to enhance earnings, but to take on a wide variety of programs unrelated to their essential business activities. We demand that they not only increase productivity, but absorb constantly increasing costs of social welfare—without passing them on to the consumer. We expect them not only to grow, but to build

[10] Henry Ford II, "The Contract Between Industry and Society," *Harvard Business School Bulletin* (May–June, 1970), p. 15.

into their operations all the safety factors that reduce the harmful aspects of growth while at the same time inhibiting expansion.

Henry Ford II seeks to resolve these paradoxes by exploring the links between profitability and social action. He asks business to consider the ways in which it can make a profit from serving the public good. On the surface this may sound cynical if we define profit simply as financial gain. What is needed is a redefinition of profit: one that calculates gains and losses, net worth, and assets not only in terms of dollars but also in terms of people, of long-range return on social investments, and of economic benefits realized, or as yet unrealized, resulting from social actions.

As yet, most businessmen are unprepared to make such calculations, which are extremely complex and unquantifiable. And the organization and value system of most businesses are so oriented to short-term results as to not permit the luxury of a deep analysis of the social effects of business decisions. Therefore, what is happening in most corporations today is either an avoidance of social considerations, on the one hand, or the ignoring of economic constraints, on the other.

Each of these extremes can be destructive of an organization. Most positive decisions relating to social repsonsibility emanate from strong, externally motivated executives who can say, with authority and confidence, "If they don't like what I am doing, let them fire me." Unfortunately, it is only the rare executive who can influence an entire organization to think in new patterns and to act against immediate self-interest. As a result, responsible action as we have defined it never gets beyond the speechwriter's text.

THE UNCLEAR SIGNALS OF CORPORATE INTEREST

Most corporate expressions of social responsibility are tentative and superficial, seldom moving beyond patterns familiar to the business community. Recent studies have shown that most corporate social action takes place in a traditional arena through donations to universities, hospitals, museums, symphony orchestras, and similar institutions. The legality of these donations has been established by a series of court cases, so it is relatively secure from stockholders protesting the dilution of earnings. In addition, corporations on the average are giving only 1 percent of pretax profits to such socially beneficial programs even though they are permitted up to 5 percent under the law. With such limited financial backing, social responsibility can never be accepted by the organization as a significant corporate policy.

It is essential for the ethically motivated executive to remember that *budget is policy*. If insufficient dollars have been allotted to social programs, the signal to the organization is weak and indistinct no matter how lofty the corporate rhetoric. And such a signal can only evoke a response that says: "The boss thinks this is a good thing to do. Let's humor him just as long as it doesn't affect our normal business practices in any way. And this is fine because I know that it does not enter into the evaluation of my own performance." No organization will be energized by programs of social responsibility that simply float on the surface of budget tokenism. It takes a certain critical mass to produce corporate change, and the effectiveness of the response is in direct proportion to the funds appropriated.

The same is true of the commitment of people. Unless a critical mass is assembled, nothing happens. For, just as budget is policy, *organization is policy*, too. Most corporations are unable to achieve sufficient management response to social commitments because they are unwilling or unable to alter the structure and orientation of the organization, and the appraisal of performance within the organization, to achieve socially desirable objectives. Corporations seldom make major changes in their organization to handle social problems. Rather, they tackle these most difficult areas with ad hoc assignments to individuals totally out of organizational context.

It is not enough for top management to want to do good. The corporate system is designed to thwart activities which divert resources from short-term profitability *unless* they are given sufficient funding, *unless* they are assigned enough skilled people, and *unless* the socially responsible activity becomes a standard of evaluation against which staff and line executives can expect to be measured, compensated, and advanced. That is a second key point.

ORGANIZATIONAL ACCOUNTABILITY

Business organizations tend to measure their people by their short-run efficiency within the firm, and to shield them from the broader effects of their behavior by narrowly segmenting their functions and severely limiting responsibility. This is not to say that these effects will ever be harmful to society. It simply suggests that absence of accountability for the social results of private behavior tends to make both the individual and the organization essentially amoral and even antisocial. Obviously, society is finding this attitude increasingly intolerable. It is precisely why a new social contract is being drafted.

But the new contract will not work, and something only vaguely resembling the free enterprise system will be substituted, unless a new system of incentives and disincentives is created which will make it advantageous and rewarding for the members of organizations to become socially responsible at all levels. Some social critics, like Ralph Nader, have even urged that the concept of limited liability be revoked so that the businessman at every level can be held accountable for the second and third order consequences flowing from his business activities. If one thinks about that, he will realize the type of drastic solutions being suggested for the problem.

In place of radical surgery we need a new system of accounting which can translate social expenditures and their projected results into terms that the most pragmatic stockholder can understand when he questions the amount of his quarterly dividend, or that the institutional investor can rely on when he decides which corporate shares to add to or subtract from his portfolio. Without such a means of evaluating corporate social programs, they will continue to be extraneous to performance, and their value will be established only by sentiment or personal preference.

The assumption that you can measure business performance only by money standards—and its counterpart that you can't assess social responsibility in money terms—is like the assumption that the bumblebee can't fly. No matter what the aerodynamic engineers prove on the drawing board, it obviously does fly. The quantification of social gains, despite the abstract logic of some theoreticians, is proceeding apace. Robert Beyer (managing partner of the public accounting firm of Touche, Ross, Bailey & Smart in New York) has said:

> The degree to which basic human needs are reduced, and the time it takes for reduction to occur, is the acid test of a social program's success. Continuing measurement, reliably controlled in the best accounting tradition, provides a valuable instrument of continuing evaluation. The absence of this ingredient is responsible for the failure of more social improvement programs in the past than any other single factor.[11]

Mr. Beyer's remark is a direct rebuke to the doubters. Broadly, he is suggesting that if we apply the same skill and control to managing social improvement that we apply to managing businesses, we will be able to measure quantitatively the effect of our involvement.

Until then, however, the strength and health of a business organization will continue to be summarized on the bottom line of the financial statement. And this, for all its apparent precision, can be totally misleading, since it bears no relation to the social, environmental, or economic pressures which can threaten the very existence of the organization whose past record has looked so good.

[11] Robert Beyer, "The Modern Management Approach to A Program of Social Improvement," *Journal of Accountancy* (March, 1969).

Many old-line managers would like to publish this bottom line of the financial statement and nothing more, especially when it reflects a profitable year. All the verbiage surrounding these critical numbers in the annual report is considered "froth." To them, "How did we do?" is the central—in fact the *only*—question worth asking. "What did we do—or not do—and to whom?" is considered a frivolous irrelevancy.

Judging the business organization by the results of a single year is like giving credence to the statement of the man who fell from a thirty-story window. As he passed the seventh floor, he was heard to say cheerfully, "Everything's okay so far." The context in which every business operates is subject to such rapid and violent change that profit recorded on the seventh floor may become catastrophic loss on the first floor only a few moments away.

The bottom line reflects only *one* measurement of a corporation's responsibilities—the responsibility to make money. Without diminishing the primacy of this objective, there are many other obligations a business assumes when it undertakes to provide goods and services in the marketplace. Likewise, the stockholder who scrutinizes the bottom line so carefully is only one of the many publics the company must serve.

Because a business is always in motion in a constantly changing world, adaptability to change is probably a more important measure of corporate strength at any given moment than financial results, although it is much more difficult to measure. Corporate responsibility is a major factor in adaptation and must be tracked continuously by those within the company who set policy, and by those both inside and outside the company whose lives are influenced by it.

If management is alert to change and has supported its social policies with the budget and the organization to make them work, today's expression of social responsibility might well be the underpinning of tomorrow's profitability. This is not to say that every corporate act to improve social conditions must be profitable. It is simply to recognize that intelligent and relevant social policy will generally be rewarded by consequences favorable to the future operation of the business, while amoral or hostile acts will increasingly provoke public revenge, in the form of restrictive legislation and other expressions of outrage. As Paul Samuelson has said, "Once the public comes to believe that what is deemed good for General Motors is no longer good for the public, they will not wait for victory in the voting of shares and proxies. They will strike directly by legislation."[12]

Examples of both kinds of management decisions abound. On the side of corporate responsibility, a bank in New York began several years ago to train Spanish-speaking residents in its various employment skills. At

[12] Paul A. Samuelson, "The Businessman's Shrinking Prerogatives," *Business and Society Review* (Spring, 1972), p. 38.

the time, it seemed like an unnecessary and even fuzzy-headed expenditure of stockholders' money. In any given year, on any given bottom line, it could have been challenged as irrelevant to the essential purpose of the organization. But time and change are both in motion, and the composition of New York's population has altered radically. Spanish-speaking people at all levels of the bank's operation are now essential to its success. As a result, a socially motivated activity, apparently extraneous to current need, turned out to be a significant business decision that undoubtedly has had a favorable impact on corporate profitability. On the other side of the coin, we see how shortsighted employment and promotion policies on the part of AT&T have resulted in the awarding of back pay and other compensatory benefits in an amount that can only have a depressing impact on both earnings and credibility.

Not all socially oriented activities can be perceived so clearly as good or bad—even in hindsight. But, as a class of business decisions, they represent an awareness of the total environment and a capacity to adapt to change that are unmistakable characteristics of a successfully managed enterprise. Thus, even if the individual act of social responsibility cannot be quantified on the bottom line, it nevertheless creates a resonance that may energize and inspire the entire organization. It may create a more positive image in the marketplace and produce heightened morale and self-realization directly translatable into profitability in other areas of business performance.

RESPONSIBILITY AND THE INVESTOR

These less quantifiable vibrations can lead not only to better internal performance; they can even influence the price of a company's stock. Studies of the paper industry conducted by Alice Tepper Marlin show a direct correlation between early attention to pollution problems and the current price of stock. The reasons for this are complex, but in part they center around the investors' confidence that management which recognizes social and environmental problems early and acts swiftly to head them off is entitled to a higher multiple than management which ignores its changing environment and drags its feet on social problems.

Similarly, Tom Theobald, Executive Vice President of Citibank, has observed that companies that follow enlightened policies usually have about them an atmosphere that is conducive to future growth. And this makes them highly attractive to the investor. Commenting specifically on the Xerox Corporation's new policy of allowing employees as much as a year off at full pay to pursue social service activities, he said,

While this may seem to be an overly generous corporate effort, we—and apparently many others—believe it represents a worthwhile investment. Exactly how its intangible benefits relate to future sales and productivity is something we will never know—but we do think this program has added to the creative atmosphere at Xerox and that atmosphere is one of the factors that has made Xerox one of our favorites in recent years.

Most institutional investors like Citibank are requiring their own analysts to scrutinize and weigh carefully any issues of social responsibility that could have major economic implications. This includes the safety and effectiveness of products, advertising practices, employment policies, and how the company relates to the communities in which it operates.

Investors will naturally continue to place their primary emphasis on the observable trend of earnings and growth potential. But the resonances —and not only the single line—are getting their increasing attention. And because corporate responsibility is having a growing influence on investment decisions, this feedback is having a healthy impact on company policy.

SOME CAUTIONARY VIEWS

Amidst all the governmental and citizen pressure for a new social contract between business and society, it would be suicidal for business to forget that its primary purpose still is to serve the public good by *remaining* in business. It cannot assume all responsibility for solving social problems without danger of capsizing. Management must operate according to priorities; and the first order of business, at least, must be business. This means an avoidance of those actions which cannot improve results; at the very least, it requires a weighing of alternatives in the absence of an ability to do everything at once.

In determining how much of its resources will be directed to social programs and in deciding where they will be applied, some sense of practicality must prevail. As one executive has said to me: "I believe business can fulfill the role expected of it by the majority. But it can't satisfy the militant minority, particularly those whose expectations have been inflated beyond the point where they can collect." To achieve a balance of interests, business must be able to weigh the countervailing pressures stemming from all social issues and determine those policies whose pursuit is purifying without being self-destructive. But it must do so honestly and forthrightly, always asking the question, "How much can we do?" not "How little?" And, even then, it must not be satisfied with the answer.

Kingman Brewster, President of Yale University, said, "Yale as an institution cannot let itself be 'mobilized' for any cause, no matter how noble, or for the achievement of a social objective extraneous to its purpose, no matter how worthy." This may sound like a stalwart defense of academic freedom, but it seems very close to the "cop-out" that business has been using for years to evade social responsibility in the name of maximization of profits. Moral neutrality is inevitably immoral. When a Yale or a Princeton, a General Motors or a Dow Chemical, attempts to stand outside the mainstream of social change, in the disguise of neutrality, it does not become invisible. To the contrary, it offers itself as a tempting target for the idealogues on all sides. If these outside pressures become strong enough, the organization, no matter how powerful, will inevitably be affected.

Campaign GM did not move General Motors to respond to the proposals of the insurgents, but the corporation's victory was a pyrrhic one. Several substantial institutional investors voted with the Campaign GM group, including the Oppenheimer Fund, a publicly held and freely redeemable mutual fund. Moreover, many institutions which supported management on the proxy issue were sharply critical of the company's efforts in the anti-pollution field. The Rockefeller Foundation, for example, criticized General Motors for not embracing the goals of the proposals which "are clearly pointed in the direction General Motors and every American corporation must move if they are to function effectively and responsively in the difficult years ahead."

Fortunately, the General Motors management was sufficiently alert after the fact to form a Public Policy Committee to inquire into all phases of its operations that relate to matters of public policy and to recommend actions to the full Board. Many less perceptive organizations will find that such inquiries, if not conducted by themselves, will inevitably be undertaken by Congressional committees preparatory to proposing and enacting appropriate legislation.

A SOCIAL INTELLIGENCE SYSTEM

Instead of waiting for such pressures to build and then responding by establishing a committee, a company is in an infinitely stronger position if it is organized to consider socially responsible actions before, not after, it has fixed corporate policy. Every corporation, as part of its routine planning functions, should establish a social intelligence system to provide a constant monitoring of social change, an evaluation of public and employee attitudes, and to recommend priorities on which policy making can be based. Only by creating such a system that integrates social responsibility decisions with profit-directed actions can a business steer a relatively safe and responsible course. Otherwise, it will be forced into constant confrontation with an angry public, the press, the Congress, the courts, or various federal or state regulatory agencies.

Such a social intelligence system should not be relegated to the window dressing of public relations. It requires both authority and participation at the very top, so that major profit decisions are linked to social concerns and social decisions take into account the corporation's business plans and profit objectives.

Companies projecting their growth in earnings over the next five years should be on warning now that the issue of social responsibility has come down from the speaker's platform and the pulpit, and is a real and present factor in the marketplace. When the rhetoric was limited to students, or consumers, or environmental activists, or the peace lobby, it was relatively easy for industry to remain secure behind a facade of business and profits as usual.

Now, even previously neutral establishments like the states are beginning to evidence concern with corporate decisions that can affect the society or the environment within their borders. Connecticut, for example, recently sent a corporate responsibility questionnaire to presidents of all corporations in which the state owns common stock. The survey asks such questions as:

"What is management's formal position concerning the corporation's effect on the environment and on local ecology?"

"What are the actual steps taken pursuant to such a position?"

"Is there pending a recent civil or criminal legal action against the company concerning environmental or hiring policies?"

Perhaps the classical economic theorists would say that the state's only responsibility is to get the highest possible return on its investment with no questions asked. But the state has a vested interest in the health and safety of its citizens and the preservation of its environment. And it refuses to be a passive observer of or, what is worse, an active participant in any company that is pursuing socially damaging policies.

This survey is more than an exercise in governmental curiosity. It is telling all industries resident in the state, doing business in the state, or invested in by the state, that its sense of corporate responsibility is very much a public concern, and therefore can have severe economic repercussions. Any company that fails to respond to this implied warning does so at its own peril. The state is recognizing its role as representative of the collective interests of its people. It is telling business that the right to function within its borders and the ability to look to the state as an investor are going to be limited by the nature of its commitment to those interests.

Through increased economic and legislative influence, companies will not be permitted to pollute. They will not be able to discriminate. They will not be allowed to avoid their responsibility to train minority and disadvantaged groups. The Connecticut policy underlying this survey is very blunt and very direct. "The Treasurer shall not knowingly invest or maintain holdings in those corporations which are in flagrant violation of the law or in stubborn disregard of the social welfare of society or do not recognize environmental responsibilities in their corporate actions and are not taking reasonable steps to overcome the situation."

This is a pretty good definition of the new social contract, suggesting the financial problems and opportunities that America's socially responsible and irresponsible organizations will increasingly face. Connecticut is saying, in effect, that while we encourage business to profit from its association with us and our people, we will insist that certain fixed codes of social behavior be adopted and certain affirmative actions be taken in the interest of social justice and environmental quality. The rewards can be great, for Connecticut is a rich and prosperous state. The penalties can be equally great: the end of public trust, the termination of public support and all that follows.

As other states, universities, church groups, institutional investors, mutual funds, and consumer and environmental groups apply similar criteria, business will be forced to respond. Not by rhetoric. Not by lobbying. Not by simply passing on the additional costs of doing business to the consumer. But by becoming more responsible to the changing spectrum of human needs. By becoming committed to further the people's aspirations for a higher quality of life. And by undertaking the challenges of social accountability with the same zest and creativity with which business has pursued its own goals of growth and profit.

We are indeed living at a time when the pace of change is accelerating throughout the world, when new alliances are being formed and new social contracts written. Mysterious and powerful worlds in which private ownership and private property do not exist are competing with us for world markets as well as for the minds of men. Their allure in terms of supposed social benefits will be seductive to many. Now, especially, American business will have to demonstrate that within the system of free enterprise, the interests of society as a whole, not merely the prerogatives of wealth and power, are furthered.

It is a time when the strength and resilience of the free enterprise system will be tested as never before. And I believe it is a time when public purpose and private property will find new meanings within the free enterprise system, to the greater benefit of all.

EDITOR'S COMMENTARY

The issue of investor pressure on corporations to implement socially responsible policies and programs suggests a number of interesting questions and speculations. Public interest activist groups have used the proxy process in many of the country's largest companies to oppose such practices as doing business in South Africa and to support antipollution and antidiscrimination measures in this country. They have also staged confrontations with management over the same issues in annual meetings.

Efforts have been made to persuade universities, foundations, and other large nonprofit institutions to switch investments from corporations engaging in a variety of alleged antisocial activities (including, notably, but not limited to, accepting defense contracts related to the war in Southeast Asia) to companies whose activities are, in the eyes of social critics, relatively unblemished. The very large pension funds of governmental units at city, county, and state levels have been the target of similar thrusts. There have been news reports of the launching of several mutual funds specifically dedicated to investing in corporations with what is regarded as positive social behavior. Beyond this, Mr. Lufkin's paper suggests the intriguing notion that profit-oriented investors should begin to pay attention to the social behavior of corporations on the ground that managements which demonstrate their visible sensitivity to the requirements of a changing society are likely to apply superior vision and competence in their administration of normal business operations.

Skeptics and opponents abound on the other side. Their primary argument is simple and straightforward. The proper—indeed the only— objective of those responsible for institutional investment should be to maximize returns at a level consistent with appropriate risk acceptance. Any departure from this standard involves a failure of trust with respect to those whose funds are at issue. At bottom, of course, this is the view for which Professor Milton Friedman has been the most articulate proponent, although his attention has been principally directed to the social orientation of decisions made by corporate managers. Short of this position, however, the view is often expressed that the managers of institutional funds are not specially qualified to be judges of corporate social performance. Nor are they knowledgeable about the attitudes of all or even a majority of those whose future benefits are bound up with the investment performance of institutional funds. Fund managers are neither informed nor authorized surrogates. They have no business making social judgments with other people's money.

A carefully reasoned assessment of this complex issue was presented in an article in the *New York Times* (May 2, 1971) by William C. Greenough, Chairman of the Teachers Insurance and Annuity Association and the affiliated College Retirement Equities Fund, with assets aggregating some $4 billion representing the retirement annuities of college teachers throughout the country. Background for the article was the vote by a thin majority (8 to 7) of the trustees of CREF to support with its 715,000 shares a proposal by the Project on Corporate Responsibility (opposed by the General Motors management) to compel General Motors to disclose its progress in minority hiring, control of air pollution, and automobile safety. In explaining the action, Mr. Greenough said that the CREF trustees recognized that GM had taken some steps toward being more responsive to demands that it give greater consideration to the social impact of its operations. However, a majority of the trustees believed that provision of "the greatest amount of information possible would be good for GM and the country and the colleges we serve." By a vote of ten to four, with one abstention, the trustees determined to vote CREF's shares against another proxy proposal which would have required GM to terminate its manufacturing operations in South Africa.

In his *New York Times* article Mr. Greenough said:

> Is maximizing investment return a fiduciary responsibility that is absolute and unqualified? There is a vast amount of trust law relating to this subject, but a good many of the questions involved are primarily economic and social.
>
> A major, perhaps the major, unanswered question is the time span over which maximization should be judged. To be sure, the name of the game is profits, but the game is a long one.
>
> Fortunately, most institutional investors are interested in long-term investments and long-term trends. This is true of university endowments, pension funds, insurance companies and bank trust funds.
>
> They are interested in tying into the development of the American economy itself in its broad economic and social trends. If this is done, then the institutional investor can support and nudge corporate managements in their efforts to solve ecological and social problems, efforts that may cause additional expenditures in the short run, but gain effective new sources of wealth and income for many companies in the long run, and make government mandates and requirements with rigid specifications unnecessary.[13]

[13] William C. Greenough, *New York Times,* May 2, 1971.

There is considerable persuasiveness in the argument that investment managers who take the long view cannot avoid considering a broad array of social issues related to corporate behavior at a time when society in transition is revising its views about corporate behavior. This applies with equal force to those who manage investments of profit-oriented institutions and those who manage university and foundation money. This position does not avoid the issue of whose judgment should govern when the long-term economic significance of socially responsible behavior is being assessed. But in the final analysis this would seem to be an unavoidable issue. It parallels the question of whose judgment should govern in making strictly economic investment decisions, to which there is a practical answer: the judgment of the investment officer or committee to whom this responsibility is delegated. If his judgment results in unsatisfactory performance, he can be replaced. A similar sanction is relevant in the assessment of social appraisals.

This conclusion leaves open, however, the question of how to express that investment judgment. Greenough goes on in his *New York Times* article to suggest that seven options are open to the institutional investor in voting shares, in addition to the obvious choice of selling the shares of a corporation whose social behavior is judged unacceptable for reasons related to long-term economic performance.

1. Simply abstain from voting the shares. He notes, however, that this policy probably is not acceptable when a large proportion of a corporation's stock is owned by institutions, as is increasingly the case. This would leave an undesirable vacuum in the exercise of corporate power.

2. Vote for management-sponsored propositions. Many investment managers see this as the only appropriate alternative to selling shares. "Such a policy," observes Greenough, "implies that if an investor wants to vote for one opposition proposal and vote for six management proposals, he should sell the stock because of his one negative vote. This is an extreme and unhelpful approach which does nothing to benefit the corporation, its stockholders or the public."

3. Vote selectively on proxy propositions. This has much to recommend it, provided that corporate management does not regard such voting as for or against management, as in a parliamentary situation, but rather as an expression of views on individual policy issues.

4. Abstain "actively" from voting, by communicating to management and possibly to a larger public the reasons for abstention.

5. Pass voting rights through to institutions' clientele. This is a technique worth examining, particularly if ways can be found to accomplish this at reasonable cost.

6. Initiate proxy propositions. "Its potentials for good are great, but so also are its dangers of misuse. . . . Institutional investors should not be trying to manage American business, nor to give specific directives through frequent sponsorship of propositions. But there are occasions when such initiative would be both practical and helpful."

7. For any of the above options, add a letter to management that would "explain the votes of the institutional investor on either controversial or noncontroversial items, and bring out the thoughts of the investor and his clientele. . . . Careful use of such a letter can be an effective way for an investor to try to change prevailing management attitudes even where the total of all votes on a proposition may be overwhelmingly in favor of management's recommendations."

The general thrust of Greenough's analysis is in support of the idea that the investor has a responsibility for encouraging positive responses by corporations to changing social requirements for business behavior, as well as an opportunity to implement that responsibility in meaningful ways that serve the long-term interests of both business and investors. I share this view.

A more subtle problem is presented when the investing institution has a kind of social responsibility of its own, as in the case of a university or foundation. The university's situation is probably the more complex of the two because of the multiplicity and diversity of its constituencies—trustees, alumni, faculty, students, nonacademic personnel, even community groups —and the difficulty of creating channels through which their sometimes diverse attitudes can be determined. This situation explains both the pressures currently experienced by managers of university endowments to apply social performance criteria to their investment decisions, including an activist approach to share voting, and the diversity of recorded responses to these pressures. Nevertheless, it is impossible to ignore the special position of educational institutions in the scheme of things, their leadership position in the world of ideas, and the rather powerful influence they command over widely held values.

Along all these fronts there appears a growing probability that institutional investors will play a more active role in the future than they have done hitherto. This probability is strengthened by the trend toward institutional ownership of a larger proportion of outstanding corporate shares. Corporate managers will find themselves under the influence of both their own judgments about the desirability of positive responses to changing social expectations of business behavior and the expressed views of their owners.

CHAPTER 8

Business Cooperation and Competition in Socially Responsible Performance

Eli Goldston

Between the limits of feasibility for socially responsible programs of the individual corporation and the general imperatives of governmental legislation and administration lies an intermediate zone in which groups of companies may find it advantageous to explore opportunities for cooperative or coordinated actions. The groups might include firms in a single industry, or they might be composed of clusters of firms of different industries in a single location. Obviously, there are antitrust and other public policy constraints on certain types of group activities under stipulated conditions. In addition, both advantages and disadvantages may be attached to group programs in relation to participants' competitive positions, effective impact on a variety of environmental issues, and other considerations.

Chapter 8 examines some of these issues in the context of societal pressures for a new range of business performance.

The author of the following chapter is Eli Goldston, President, Eastern Gas and Fuel Associates.—EDITOR

T HE IDEA behind this rather mouth-filling title recalls a Jewish folk tale about an old, balding rabbi who one summer was seated under a tree pondering great thoughts. Suddenly he felt something wet and warm on his bald pate and, rubbing it off, he saw that it was bird droppings. Leaping to his feet, he shook his fist and shouted at the responsible bird, "For the rich you sing!"

It is just such a viewpoint—*this* you do to the *poor*, while for the *rich* you *sing*—that a great many people hold toward what we loosely call "The Free Enterprise System." They look at the GNP defined as Gross National Product as something that goes in unfairly large proportions to the rich and the GNP defined as Gross National Pollution as something that goes in unfairly large proportions to the poor. They then may ask the questions I've been asked to discuss today: how can both intra-industry and inter-industry cooperation and competition improve the socially responsible performance of individual corporations? Once again, that's quite a mouthful, and I suppose it might be more simply asked as, "How do you housebreak a nightingale, or at least persuade it to wear a diaper?" Is it really true that the birds of free enterprise sing only for the rich?

I should emphasize that my comments will be almost exclusively devoted to that portion of our economic activity that we sometimes call the private sector or the free enterprise segment. The other portions of our economic activity are moved by different forces, and they must, therefore, be motivated and controlled by different methods. Take, for example, the problem of pollution around Manhattan. The largest polluter of air and water in New York City is the city itself with its antique sewers, inadequate incinerators, and other municipal facilities; and among the larger polluters in the Manhattan area, the city is the one that seems to have done the least about its operations. At the same time that the city Environmental Protection Agency Administrator has been demanding instant ecology from the private sector, he has been doing practically nothing about the city itself. In many of these areas of social responsibility it is important for us to realize that, in contrast to the private sector, there are no taxes and no criminal penalties likely to produce action from such entities as municipal governments. They have to be moved by a political consensus and, unfortunately, the political process by which we arrive at a consensus is often impaired rather than aided by personal ambitions for political office.

My colleagues at Eastern Gas and Fuel Associates, O. F. Ingram and T. J. Gannon, along with Sharon Oster of Harvard University, made a major contribution to the form and substance of this text.—*Author*

Officials who understand very well how to attract the attention of the mass media do not seem to understand either the technology or the economics of the environmental problem. What we really need in public office are officials who understand how an advanced industrial democratic society works and how to motivate it; officials who know that businessmen can be moved along by carrots of incentives, whips of legislation, and exhortations to good citizenship. They must also understand that denunciation has limited and often counter-productive results. A witch doctor may try to exorcise the particular demon he believes is the cause of the illness. But more often he tries to seduce the demon out rather than to tear it out.

PRIME MOVERS OF PRIVATE ENTERPRISE

Within the private sector, it is important to sort out three different strands in the free enterprise system. As I see it, the essential elements are these. First, it is a system in which resources are allocated through a market economy with profit for individual firms as a major determinant of how national resources are allocated. Second, it is a system with private ownership of property, although property rights have been greatly diminished over time by restricting the absolute rights of property owners to use their property as they wish. Third, it is a system marked by political freedom, conditioned by the existence of two major parties which operate to blunt polarizing issues.

Under this view of the free enterprise system with profit serving as the allocator of resources, with the private ownership of property, and with an open political structure, it seems clear that free enterprise is not a revealed religion but rather a socioeconomic system we have become accustomed to after many centuries of evolution. This view was recently expressed by Prime Minister Heath of Great Britain. In reply to criticism of his policies as not being consistent with the Conservative tradition which he was supposed to represent, the Prime Minister told his critics, "Free enterprise is a tool to be used by man, not a God to be worshipped." He went on to point out that there has been a considerable convergence in the attitudes of the socialist and capitalist countries of the world in the direction of national economic management. The doctrines of Adam Smith and Karl Marx tend to overlap when, in the Soviet Union, advocates of Libermanism suggest an interest factor for capital, and, in the United States, political forces call for social responsibility in decision making by managers of the private corporation. In the Dubcek regime in Czechoslovakia and the

Kadar regime in Hungary, one can see how the market mechanism by it
self will accomplish a good deal of the economic growth we commonl
associate with free enterprise, even in the absence of much private propert
ownership or of much political freedom.

The difficulty, however, is that one doesn't easily shed old definition
or old ideas. Adam Smith saw a world of busy proprietor-manager-entre
preneur businessmen, with an "Invisible Hand" guiding personal avarici
to accomplish public benefit. It was this maximizing by the individual pro
prietor that most businessmen were taught in college and business schoc
as the way the world works, and it is the language that they like to use t
describe, however inaccurately, the things they are engaged in doing.

This suggests two propositions. First, we are somewhat like the fellov
in Australia who bought a new boomerang and went crazy trying to throv
the old one away. No matter how hard we work at intellectual innovation
our old ideas keep coming back. We are incapacitated in part from accom
plishing some of our social goals by projecting this Adam Smith image o
a maximizing entrepreneur on today's large, publicly owned corporation
Second, most businessmen are actually energized by motivations mucl
broader and more complicated than those they feel they must express
When decisions are made on many business activities, the businessma
feels that he doesn't sound right if he doesn't talk in the Adam Smith lan
guage of maximization. The fact is, however, that most managements o
large public corporations today do not really feel they have the exclusiv
duty to maximize even though they feel they should sound that way. Char
itable contributions, voluntary allowances to retired employees not fairl
covered by existing pension practice, and reluctance to cut losses by closin
down old operations are all evidence of generosity or compassion o
inertia, but certainly not of maximizing. The difficulty is that businessmen
while performing responsibly, and business critics, while disparaging tha
performance, both talk maximizing language.

MAXIMIZING VS. "SATISFICING"

For a younger generation of students of economics, the theory o
maximizing has been replaced to some extent by an alternate theor
espoused by Professor John Kenneth Galbraith. Professor Galbraith claim
that the overriding philosophy of professional executives in the large cor
porations where ownership has been separated from management is "take
care of yourself." Since a corporation's managers are for the most part no
its owners, the "take care of yourself" maxim no longer implies maximiz
ing profits. Instead, managers strive to improve their own salaries, pres

ige, and other personal goals. Moreover, these managerial benefits depend more on size of firm and growth rate than they do on profits. The bigger he company, the better the lot of management.[1] Thus, profit maximization according to Professor Galbraith is no longer a compelling rule for business.

Professor Galbraith is far from being entirely wrong, and he can find support in academic circles and in business experience.[2] The Penn Central collapse did not happen because management there was focused, with monomaniacal concern, on maximizing the return on the railroad company's equity.

Many perceptive economists are coming to see the principal thrust of modern business as what is sometimes termed "satisficing."[3] Satisficing is something between profit maximization as seen by Adam Smith and the maximization of managements' personal satisfaction as seen by Professor Galbraith. It describes the business manager as essentially an economic politician.

According to this theory, business management regards itself as having a primary duty of simply managing to get something done. If you are managing to get something done, you aren't maximizing by trying to make the last buck on each individual transaction. The information costs of choosing the "optimal" point are simply too high. On the other hand, a manager who does not want to spend the little left out of a poor earnings performance defending himself from takeover bids and other insurgency by either shareholders or creditors has to earn a reasonable return on equity. As a consequence, he satisfices. He pays labor what he must, and once in a while he takes a strike in order to keep payments to labor in line with competition. He pays his executives what he must in a similar context. Once in a while, for reasons of harmony or compassion, he must overpay a few of them. He pays suppliers what he must to keep them alive and healthy, but he does not overpay them if competitive suppliers will sell at significantly lower prices.

Under this concept of satisficing, a very complicated society evolves with, on both analytical and personal grounds, very complex crosscurrents and trade-offs. For the manager, the core of satisficing is to earn enough on the equity so the stock will sell at a price decent enough to keep him from being thrown out of his job. This concept also defines a pair of brackets within which the socially responsible manager must work.

[1] John Kenneth Galbraith, *The New Industrial State* (Boston: Houghton Mifflin Company, 1967).

[2] A similar view is expressed by J. D. Williamson in "Profit, Growth and Sales Maximization," *Economica* (February, 1966).

[3] H. A. Simon, *Models of Man* (New York: John Wiley & Sons, Inc., 1957).

There is a floor which defines what minimum a manager must do; it is pretty much a legal floor—not the law as it is written in the statute books, but the law as it is being enforced at any particular time. After all, practically every manager today who is having trouble with water pollution complaints against his firm is being chased with a law that was passed in the last century but was not enforced until recently, the Refuse Act of 1899. So the floor of minimum social responsibility is pretty much what society decides will be enforced at the moment out of the full grab bag of rules and regulations then at hand.

But there is also a ceiling, and the responsible manager works below that top of the bracket. The ceiling is set by competitive pressures. I may love my employees and I may want to give them $10 a shift more than the going wage rates. That is fine if I have an economic monopoly or a patent. But if I am in a bitterly competitive, small-scale manufacturing operation, I really cannot pay them much more than a penny or two above what the competition pays and still remain in business. Usually, I find the competition is probably paying either the legal minimum wage or the minimum wage that the market permits. So I end up somewhere below the ceiling by paying that sort of a minimum wage.

There is, however, considerable leeway in most businesses between the ceiling set by competition and the floor set by legal requirements. Within that range lie not only a very large amount of resources, but also resources that can be focused on particular critical problems.

Consider, for example, the current fact that the average large corporation donates about one percent of its pretax income as charitable gifts. The Federal Income Tax Law, however, permits it to donate up to 5 percent and deduct that from its pretax income. If all American corporations increased the amount of charitable giving from one percent to, say, 2.5 percent of income annually, it would create overnight the equivalent of a half-dozen Ford Foundations, with that multiple of the immense impact that just one Ford Foundation has had on America and on the world.

In determining what any individual businessman can do within those brackets and deciding how much can be done by the entire private business sector of a country, two things must be taken into account. The first is that the leeway between floor and ceiling is under constant compression because of the requirement to show a growth in earnings. This might be called "satisficing at a growth rate." The distinction between "maximizing" and "satisficing at a growth rate" may seem like a meaningless academicism, but there is a significant difference in the way people think and talk and act if they recognize that the real pressure is not to earn the maximum amount of dollars. Under the maximum dollars premise, one percent would not be given to charity unless a business leader could rationalize that every time money was donated to charity, the public would think better of his company and would buy more of its products. This would lead to the conclusion that money donated to charity was a profitable short-term investment.

On the other hand, if one thinks in terms of the pressures on management to ratchet up the earnings a reasonable amount year by year, he then sees a constant struggle to keep the bracket in existence, but with space for doing things other than making the last buck on every transaction. There is space, for example, for a manager to increase charitable giving and perform in other socially responsible ways and still feel that he is doing a professional job. Therefore, the first thing to recognize in this concept of satisficing is that it is not all easy and it is not all static; there is constant pressure to increase earnings per share.[4]

Second, we have to recognize that many social problems are of such massive dimensions that they have, thus far, defied some rather huge efforts by government at solution. Furthermore, at least some of these social problems are rather unlikely to yield to unorganized attacks by a multitude of private corporations. But there is a range of problems which can be attacked constructively by the imaginative business leader trying to think through how his company can function responsibly in the modern industrial community.

PUBLIC WHIPS AND CARROTS

The whip, the carrot, and the exhortation each can motivate business decisions: the whip of the enforcement of law or even enforcement of community standards (few are willing to be thought ill of, let alone be put in jail); the carrot of tax incentives or direct subsidies; and the exhortation of good citizenship—all can move a business manager from the bottom of the bracket to the top. But it cannot move him much beyond his competitive ceiling. It is essential to recognize that many of the problems of our society are of a size and complexity that defy solution within such a bracket.

Consider, for example, pollution, an area that has attracted conspicuous attention. As I suggested earlier, when addressing the subject of pollution it is important to distinguish between industrial-commercial pollution and the other forms. A good bit of pollution comes from the public sector and a good bit of the public sector pollution is that which has the greatest impact on the citizenry. Many more people use the streets than

[4] I have stated the theory of satisficing at a growth rate in my *Quantification of Concern: Some Aspects of Social Accounting* (Pittsburgh: Carnegie Press, 1971).

use the rivers. Thus, both as a matter of health and as a matter of aesthetics, it is probably more important to have clean streets than it is to have clean rivers. The difficulty, however, of accomplishing this with an unruly citizenry is very great. It is almost impossible to persuade people to do individually what they desire collectively.[5]

BALANCING SOCIAL COSTS AND BENEFITS

If I decide to pay for cleaner air, the benefits accrue not only to me but to everyone else who lives in my area. This is really what distinguishes a "public" good from a private good. If I want a private good, I have to go out and buy it myself; if I want a public good such as better air, there is always the possibility that someone else will "buy it" for me. Naturally, if everyone feels this way, no one will buy the cleaner air, even though all of us really want it.

The Pepsi Cola Company, as an experiment in New Jersey a couple of years ago, marketed its product in some fourteen million, sixteen-ounce returnable bottles. In a few months, despite the 5¢ deposit, almost half of the returnable bottles had disappeared. In this short period, people were willing to spend one-third of a million dollars not to take the bottles back. Here is an instance where, since the returnable bottle is a cheaper way for the bottler to distribute his product, a socially responsible business might seem to be able both to make a profit and to appear to be a good corporate citizen. But somehow or other the citizens themselves must be persuaded to cooperate if the problem is to be reduced, let alone eliminated.

Those who favor instant ecology and 100 percent clean air and water have seldom thought through the issues. A totally unpolluted system is almost certainly not the optimal one because in eliminating pollution you must expend extra energy on the elimination process itself. Ultimately, you end up eliminating most of the production and, therefore, most of the consumption in order to eliminate all of the pollution. We have a choice in balancing the damage that is incurred by lack of cleanliness against the private and public effort and expenditure needed to accomplish this cleanliness. What we are actually saying is that some pollution is necessarily a good thing. Some pollution may be *wel*fare, not *ill*-fare, because the cost of getting rid of that particular pollution (in terms of welfare) may be unacceptable.

It is also necessary, in thinking through the technology of pollution

[5] This is an example of the "free rider" problem discussed by Paul Samuelson in "The Pure Theory of Public Expenditure," *Review of Economics & Statistics* (1954).

control, to recognize that there is a very steeply rising cost curve as more and more of the undesirable externalities of pollution are internalized. The first steps usually are very cheap and do not involve much in the way of an investment. The first step in controlling smokestack pollution at many American electric generating plants only a few years ago was simply to polish up the precipitators that had been installed for many years and had never been operated. There was no capital cost; there was simply a maintenance and training cost. In this case, the first bite was a cheap and easy one. Until the final steps toward perfection are undertaken, a fair amount of pollution can be controlled for an attractive trade-off cost. It is when you approach 100 percent effectiveness that the investment becomes very expensive. At this point, the desirability of living with some of the pollution must be weighed against the social cost of eliminating it.

Setting a floor for pollution, deciding how much is too much or how little is indeed too little, requires a political decision. It is really up to the community to decide if it wants to pay more for its electricity in order to breathe cleaner air. But it is important in thinking about these problems to fractionalize them, to recognize that we are dealing with more than the problem of how much in gross dollars to spend to accomplish how much reduction in gross pollution. We are also dealing with questions of how resources are to be allocated, with the definition of private property, and, finally, with the extent of political freedom.

Students of the environment in the Soviet Union have learned that it is considerably more difficult to achieve political trade-offs of cost versus cleanliness in that society than it is in the United States. In the Soviet system, it is much more difficult for the public to express its feelings to the official who handles the allocation of resources and who decides whether society should pay more for its electricity and breathe cleaner air.

ECONOMIC CONSTRAINTS ON CORPORATE ACTION

When we consider some of the problems of intra- and interindustry cooperation and competition in relation to pollution, an interesting question arises: why don't businessmen all get together and do something about social problems like pollution? Or, if they can't afford to do it individually within that little bracket I have described, why don't we just get some laws passed and raise everybody's bracket simultaneously. Then everybody can play the same competitive poker game, but with different house rules and higher stakes.

The solution is not quite that simple. Changing the pollution rules often changes the position of individual firms. Relationships among industries may be altered after the rules are changed. Within a single industry, pollution controls usually do not affect all firms equally. A company that has just completed a new nonpolluting plant will not be hurt as much by new pollution controls as another firm within the same industry with an older, polluting facility. Firms with new plants will gain relative to others in the same industry. For this reason, it will be difficult to convince the owners of the older plants that they should join with owners of newer plants to establish a new minimum level of pollution that, in effect, will substantially alter the intraindustry competitive balance.

Similar problems arise on the inter-industry scene. Controls on pollution emissions will tend to raise the prices of the products of a presently polluting industry relative to those of a presently nonpolluting industry. The market available to the polluters will shrink.[6] The head of a firm within a highly polluting industry will not be easily convinced of the merits of the National Association of Manufacturers' multi-industry pollution control program, because his whole industry, quite apart from his individual firm's situation within that industry, will be adversely affected. This was brought out very dramatically in the hearings on the possibility of meeting the emission control standards for automobiles. All of the large, profitable automobile companies testified about the technological and economic problems rendering compliance impossible. On the other hand, every small inventor of new automobile emission control techniques went to Washington and testified that if a large automobile manufacturer would give him $2 million for research or pick up his mortgage, now in default, the problem could be solved in a relatively short period. The pressure of the emission standards for automobiles had quite a different impact on Ford and General Motors than on all of the little garret inventors around the country.

This problem of a differential effect on various firms is critical for businessmen. Like so many of the big problems for businessmen, this really is not much of a problem for the economic theorist. Many economists believe that our problem, at least in part, has been the overproduction of polluting goods, an overproduction which results from the fact that the externalization of pollution costs has made the price of polluting goods cheaper relative to the price of nonpolluting goods. As a result, we have overused polluting goods. From the economists' perspective, internalization of pollution costs and the resulting change in relative prices would cut back the production of the polluting goods and everything would be

---

[6] A RAND Corporation Study, *California's Electricity Quandary: Slowing the Growth Rate* (Sept., 1972), documents this interindustry differential.

perfectly fine. People would now be responding to prices which reflected the *total* costs of production both social and private. This becomes a general economic problem only in terms of how best to get the businessmen to work together to do something about it.

One of the best devices to get businesses with plants of different ages together to support new restrictions is through grandfather rights of temporary exemption. In a sense, this converts a long-continued action which has been newly classified as a wrong into an amortizing vested right. The old plant is given five to ten years of life and this helps to bridge the gap between it and the newer plant. The regulator of new restrictions says, "Here, by God, is what we want to accomplish, but we are going to do it in stages of several years so that fellows with the older plants can say, 'We can only survive for so many years, but that is about all the life that is left in the plant.'" In this way, we move toward a socially optimal point slowly enough so that capital and labor can have a relatively painless and equitable adjustment.

My company had an experience like that in New Haven, Connecticut. We had a coke plant there—the kind of coke used to reduce iron ore to steel. It was an old plant, built in the 1920's, and was due to close in about three years. Every one knew it was closing because its physical life was ending. We had contracts for the output for just that period, and we had developed a group of workers and managers all of whom expected to retire on that closing date. It was like the legendary Deacon's One-Hoss Shay. At one moment in time the plant would fall apart, the business would fall apart, the contracts would expire, and all of the management and workers would retire. Our coke operations in New Haven would crumble just as in the poem: "All at once, and nothing first—just as bubbles do when they burst."

We then received an order from the mayor of New Haven to cease polluting. It simply wasn't economically possible to take a plant that was certain to expire in three years and do anything major about pollution. If forced to comply, we would have had to close the plant down three years early.

As we thought about the situation and discussed it with employees, it seemed clear that this was not a technical issue, or a moral issue, but a political issue. Somehow we must get recognition of the need for a trade-off between the different interested groups. So first, in cooperation with the union, we hired an ecologist who calculated that the pollution created by our coke plant roughly equaled the pollution created by all the automobiles owned by the freshmen at Yale. Therefore, in terms of a political trade-off, if Yale freshmen were made to walk, as much would be accomplished for the New Haven atmosphere as would be accomplished by closing our plant. At that time, Yale freshmen did not vote in New Haven's local elections, but, of course, union members did vote.

Next, again in conjunction with the union, we hired an advertising agency to prepare a full-page advertisement that expressed in simple, dramatic terms the choice between jobs for citizens and cars for Yale freshmen. Then we took a trip to City Hall and showed them our proposed advertisement. It is the art of an astute political leader to reconcile diametrically opposite demands. The mayor met the demand for instant ecology by ordering us to close immediately, unless within three years we could bring our plant up to certain standards. At the end of the three years, we closed the plant because we couldn't bring it up to such standards. Here, I would suggest, is an illustration of the importance of recognizing the differential impact of different desires and working out what is essentially a trade-off solution.

It is also important to recognize in considering pollution matters that one's choice among alternatives depends upon interest positions. To an employee of our coke plant, it was clear that a little bit of dust sprayed around New Haven was preferable to losing his job. On the other hand, to a professor in the Yale herbarium who is not going to suffer economically if some fellow five or six miles away loses his job, having bits of dust settle on his rare specimens arouses quite a different reaction. All too often, the real social costs of the unemployment that results when a plant closes are ignored by environmentalists.

WHO PAYS? WHO BENEFITS?

Along this line, I have been severely chastised by my more ardent ecological friends for having suggested that, if it were up to me, I would worry a great deal more about the rats in Harlem than the chickadees in Westchester. We have only a certain amount of scarce resources to be applied to our problems and we have to set priorities. Too often we set our priorities from our own selfish standpoint. And those with more affluence often have more influence. Consequently, what seems to be a societal choice is really a choice made by a relatively narrow segment of society.

The U.S. per capita disposable income in 1971 was $3,600. Of that amount it is calculated that we spent $50 for environmental improvement. That does not sound like much; 1.5 percent of per capita income. However, according to the Council on Environmental Quality, the expectation is that by 1980 this $50 figure will increase to $150. That isn't so much either—from 1971 to 1980 only $100 more per capita to clean up the environment. All of this is out of the average $3,600 per capita. But, of course, to a mother on welfare with six children, the $50 or the $150 per capita to clean up the environment would be a very serious financial burden. Taken in this light, you may be inclined to agree that the problem of rats in the ghetto is more significant than the problem of birds in the suburbs. There are many societal problems, not quite so apparent to the prosperous middle class, that should be attacked far ahead of much-publicized ecological problems.

A related point in examining pollution trade-offs is the question of the distribution of the costs and the benefits of pollution control. We must consider who pays the cost and who gets the benefits.

Let's take the cost side first. If pollution control is financed by state or local taxes, the effect is likely to be regressive and antipoor. But if an equivalent amount is financed through a federally funded program, it is more likely to be progressive and soak-the-rich. There is no study of any consequence on tax incidence which does not recognize that federal taxes are more pro-poor than are state and local taxes, in large part because about half of the federal revenue is generated by a progressive income tax. If we are concerned about the distribution of income, federally financed pollution programs seem to be preferable to locally financed programs.

There are other, often unrecognized, implications of pollution control techniques. For instance, if effluent discharge is taxed in order to force firms to internalize the costs or close down the older plants and build newer and more expensive plants, economic theory suggests that most of this tax or most of this cost will ultimately be shifted forward to consumers by way of higher prices. Since poor people have to consume all of their income, while the rich can save part of theirs, an overall price increase on everything in order to clean up the environment will hurt the poor more than it will hurt the rich. Moreover, price increases from pollution control are not likely to be spread evenly over the prices of everything. Some industries pollute more than others, and, therefore, there will be larger price increases on some commodities than on others. The production of electric energy is one of the larger sources of pollution. Since the poor spend a larger percentage of their income on electricity than the rich, and a lesser percentage on works of art, a rise in the requirements of pollution control will be adverse to the poor who are buying a lot of electricity and considerably less to the rich who are buying works of art.

Now consider the benefits side. The benefits from cleaning up air pollution do accrue in some cases to the poor more than the rich, since more of the poor live in congested inner-city areas where air pollution is concentrated. The rich who do live in the congested urban areas commonly have air conditioning. There is clear statistical evidence that air pollution exposure decreases as personal income increases. As income goes up, the air breathed becomes cleaner, and less in need of antipollution programs.

Water pollution produces quite a different situation. The health hazard from the current quality of water available in the United States is minimal. Almost nowhere in the United States does the drinking water supply create any health hazard at all. Moreover, it is far cheaper to purify the amount of water we drink than to try to purify the lake or the river source. So in water cleanup programs we are dealing almost exclusively with aesthetic and recreational purposes, which means that most of the benefit goes to the rich. The rich, after all, have transportation to the lakes, the rivers, the water facilities. And they have the income to use the facilities, to buy fishing equipment, boats, and water skis.

When we ask why corporations do not clean up the air and the water, we are asking a very complicated question. Cleaning up is costly, and consideration should also be given not only to how much it will cost, but who pays for it and who benefits from it. An apt illustration is the way the underdeveloped nations today are anxiously soliciting investment in aluminum reduction plants, blast furnaces, and petroleum refineries. In the more advanced nations, we are trying to chase these facilities away or require them to install levels of pollution control that make them uneconomic in international competition.[7]

Friends recently back from a visit to the People's Republic of China tell me that the Norman Rockwell of the Chinese revolution, an artist named Fu Pao-Shih, is perhaps the single most popular artist today in China. His prints are found in hotels and other public places, since he is one of the most approved of their contemporary artists. His work features two motifs: national monuments and landscapes that include industrial scenes with dark emissions pouring from the smoke stacks. It would seem that the desire for clean air comes only after the basic economic needs have been satisfied. Or, as has often been necessary to suggest to those who try to raise money for the arts, first you dine and then you go to the theater.

Turn now to my opening question of how businessmen can be persuaded to cooperate in housebreaking the nightingale. We must first remember that the response of the public to businessmen acting in concert

---

[7] This, of course, emphasizes that there is an international competitive pressure as well as a national competitive pressure which limits the ability to internalize social costs. Since the first steps of pollution control cost so little and the last steps cost so much, initial efforts to clean the environment may leave us competitive, but beyond a certain point we may become noncompetitive. A "pollution tariff" has been suggested to protect domestic plants which have internalized social costs from plants abroad that continue polluting.

has almost always been negative. Adam Smith, the patron saint of free enterprise, had this to say on the subject:

> The proposal of any new law or regulation of commerce which comes from industrialists ought always to be listened to with great precaution, but ought never to be adopted till after having been long and carefully examined, not only with the most scrupulous, but with the most suspicious, attention. It comes from an order of men whose interest is never exactly the same with that of the public, who have generally an interest to deceive and even to oppress the public, and who accordingly have, upon many occasions, both deceived and oppressed.[8]

The cry for businessmen to get together and do something must be measured with an eye to both the public reaction and to the antitrust reaction.

The complexities of the pollution questions I have been discussing indicate that businessmen cannot really be expected to undertake major cleanup alone. How much is too much pollution? Who pays for the cleanup? How do we arrange the cleanup? Government decisions, controls, and incentives are necessary when dealing with these major problems that thrust above the bracket within which a single socially responsible business manager can act on his own. A critical question, of course, is whether the government can find the needed sophisticated administrators and the understanding political leaders. We can only hope they will.

All of this may sound rather bleak, as though the possibility of corporate social responsibility on anything more than a trivial scale is hopeless. This is not true. Let me take another illustration from my own experience. When I first came to the Boston Gas Company I was interested in trying to integrate some blacks into our work force. I first attempted to learn the number of minority employees in our company. There were some 1,200 employees and I was told only four were from minority groups. Now, four seemed to me a small number, but it seemed about three more than I had seen in several months that I had been around. Persisting, I then discovered that the four included myself, because I was Jewish, an Irishman who was dating a Chinese girl, and a black who had retired a few years back. The fourth was never found.

When I set about trying to integrate the work force I discovered two apparent rules. The first rule was that one could not get a job unless one was Irish. The second rule was that the first rule did not apply to the good jobs. In order to integrate the work force by hiring blacks, we first had to face the problem of promoting the Irish. Very quickly we had our first Irish vice president. That was when I learned the difference between Prot-

[8] Adam Smith, *The Wealth of Nations*, Book 1, Chapter 11.

estants from North Ireland and Catholics from South Ireland, because the man we had made vice president was a Protestant from North Ireland. Very rapidly we had some other Irish vice presidents.

As a consequence of our efforts, however, today we have well over a hundred blacks working for the Boston Gas Company. Their average income is about $10,000, representing a million dollars of payroll going into a minority community that previously received next to nothing from this particular company, even though there were miles of gas mains and many gas meters and customers within the minority community.

By way of contrast, consider the one percent of pretax earnings that represents the average corporate charitable gift. The Boston Gas Company, at that time, was earning about $5 million a year before taxes. One percent of pretax earnings would have been $50,000. Five percent, if we had given the maximum that the tax law permits, would have been $250,000. A comparison shows that if we had given five times as much as American industry in general gives to this one minority group community, it still would have been only one-fourth of the dollars derived from wages. And it would have been income of an entirely different sort, without the training, the incentives, the opportunities, and the pride that earned income provides.

I conclude, therefore, that even on a small scale significant things can be done by a socially concerned management. But the major problems of pollution and the general quality of life are more difficult, and neither business nor government will solve them easily or quickly.

EDITOR'S COMMENTARY

Alexis de Tocqueville, that shrewd observer of the characteristic behavior patterns of the American democracy, noted the reckless enthusiasm with which a large share of the public could be encouraged to rush to support superficially attractive ideas without pausing to assess complex problems in putting the ideas into practice. As Eli Goldston points out, we are currently engaged in just such a romantic approach to the ideas of environmental hygiene and product safety. Oriented as we are toward popular science, we tend to ignore the fact that while technology indicates what *can* be done, economics offers a more reliable guide to what *will* be done. The proposition bites particularly hard if we add to cost-price constraints the deprivations required by the either-or choices, forced by resource limitations. Among the valuable potential contributions of socially responsible corporations to a more rational ends-means analysis in the years ahead will surely be the education of opinion leaders, and beyond them the general public, in some of the harsh realities that confront us.

Examples of the general problem are all around these days. Application of high standards of environmental protection in the interests of clean air and water, preservation of natural beauty, and population safety have slowed (often, in fact, halted) expansion of electric power generating capacity, petroleum refining capacity, and coal mining. The nation is beginning to feel the bite in brownouts and blackouts, as well as in fuel limitations for transportation and heating. The pinch will intensify. Costs and prices are beginning to rise inevitably along a sharply ascending curve. Here, as elsewhere, we rediscover the principle that there is no free lunch this side of paradise.

Engineering curves that relate potential environmental hygiene gains to the costs of accomplishing them, in industry after industry, reveal a strikingly uniform shape. The repeated message says that a considerable measure of environmental purification can be attained at a modest cost and with few either-or choices. A loose generalization suggests that gains of up to perhaps 75 percent of goals targeted by activists can be achieved with relatively modest investments in proven technology. Beyond this general level, small incremental gains are accompanied by high incremental investments which often require both new technology and hard choices in resource allocation. The cost-benefit relationship changes radically. What is at stake is not just high prices to consumers, but transformations in national consumption and living patterns. Implicit in these developments are questions of social values and of balances among the elements of the American culture.

A reading of history suggests that these complex issues are likely to be resolved in costly and irrational ways if events are allowed to pursue their normal course. The image of the swinging pendulum is often cited. During the great GNP thrust of the industrial revolution, resources were exploited with little regard for future requirements; environmental and quality-of-life considerations got scant attention. This behavior, which we can observe being repeated in today's developing nations, may well be judged an inevitable condition of rapid economic growth. Improvement in the economic content of the human condition satisfies a primary need. On the North American continent moreover, resource limitations did not compel hard choices among desired goals.

Now the pendulum is swinging the other way in an affluent society in which serious resource limitations are visible. The enthusiasm for quality-of-life goals appears to be pushing us into a region where choices probably will be made, without either adequate information on the economic, social, and cultural trade-offs or adequate preparation in using the information to support rational choices that reflect considered values. The practical outcome may well be that a large share of the citizenry will find themselves paying the costs of an uncontrolled pendulum swing—costs which they might have chosen not to pay if they had been helped to analyze the options at hand. Some people will learn by living through blackouts or curtailed use of automobiles that they don't really want that much environmental hygiene at that price. This will be a hard way to get an education in the shape of the engineers' cost curves, particularly since reversing many of the decisions will not be simple or swift.

There is an easier way: study the realities of the available options and make considered choices. This does not inevitably mean, of course, that the majority will opt for some modification of environmental goals in order to reduce or remove industrial and personal constraints. Lacking experience in examining popular values in a post-industrial society, we cannot predict with confidence what choices will emerge. To complicate an already difficult situation, the political institutions through which a democracy selects among options of this type are clearly not well adapted to accommodate the rather special decision process involved. The inherent deficiencies have already been laid bare by the results of widespread use of judicial institutions and procedures to service the conflicting demands of environmental and safety controversies. Yet our other established decision procedure, consumer choice in a competitive marketplace, is also poorly adapted for handling options which involve social and public rather than individual and private goods. We are going to have to be inventive in designing institutional adaptations to service new popular decision requirements.

Corporate leaders have a significant opportunity to educate the general public in the realities of the choices that lie ahead. The facts about the costs of developing and applying high technology to pollution control, safety, and similar issues along the last 20 to 25 percent of the engineers' curves need to be widely reported. These are not simple concepts to communicate, nor will credibility be readily established for the corporate message. Surely the greatest handicap to business credibility is a prior record of an adversary position established at an earlier stage of the quality-of-life debate. Executives in other industries could learn a lot from examining the recent experience of the automobile industry. Possibly unintentionally, the automotive giants for several years preceding 1973 created for themselves a public image of denigrating both the need for and the feasibility of using technology to control emissions and increase passenger safety. Their public actions in 1973 indicated a desire to reform their posture into a more constructive stance, with emphasis on technical problems, costs, and timing. Not only among the general public but even among their traditional friends in the Congress and the executive departments there was widespread skepticism about their motivations, the accuracy of their facts, and the general legitimacy of their case.

The inevitability of this reception could have been predicted. But the sequence of events that culminated in the reception was not inevitable. The simple rule is: if you want to be believed by the public, take up an early and visible position on the public side and never allow yourself to be identified as an adversary. Executing this strategy effectively requires, of course, the elevation of social forecasting to a level equal in importance to economic forecasting. The fact that in both areas what is practiced is still more art than science should not be allowed to inhibit the development. Managers have long since learned to work in a world of probabilities.

Socially responsible managers also have an opportunity to cooperate with public authorities in devising new machinery for decision making in the arena where social goals and economic costs interact. The judicial process, so valuable in the protection of individual rights and liberties, appears in the recent record to be considerably less serviceable in handling conflicts involving public goods. With the growing probability that a larger share of future production and consumption will occur in the public sector, broadly viewed, we need imaginative innovations in institutional arrangements that will both protect individual and group interests and concurrently open a path for the majority to work its will.

CHAPTER 9

Problems and Opportunities of Public Interest Directors

Leon H. Sullivan

While it has long been regarded as good practice to have "outside" directors on corporate boards, until recently the individuals selected for these positions have been drawn almost entirely from the business and allied professional worlds, with, on occasion, a university president as a special adornment. One of the current corporate responses to social pressure has been the addition of a different type of outside director, deliberately selected to represent interests other than those of the owners of the business, at least as owners' interests are commonly viewed. Where such additions are not designed for cosmetic purposes, they open up channels for communication and influence within the corporate structure through which the concerns of minority groups, women, consumers, and others can be articulated.

This chapter examines the role and opportunities of this new class of public interest director, with special emphasis on the black director who regards himself as the representative of his race within the corporate structure.

Leon H. Sullivan, the author of the following chapter, is Pastor of the Zion Baptist Church of Philadelphia, a successful initiator of national programs for creating job opportunities for blacks, and the first black Director of the General Motors Corporation.–EDITOR

THE PUBLIC interest director represents a new idea in corporate management and, like all new ideas, it may succeed or it may fail. If the idea works and is applied in many companies, it will help American business to respond more effectively to social needs and demands. This, in turn, will help to preserve the enterprise system with all its potential for dynamic advance in general living standards and opportunities for the self-realization of talented individuals through successful careers. If the idea fails, the likelihood will diminish that the business system will be allowed to continue in the form in which we have known it. In my judgment, society will not much longer tolerate a wide range of business behavior—including discrimination in employment and advancement through management ranks, contamination of the environment, inadequate protection of consumers against product and information deficiencies—that is inconsistent with emerging social values. Business will change its ways voluntarily, or society will mandate a new code of business behavior. And with such a mandate will come other undesirable restrictions.

"OUTSIDE" AND "PUBLIC INTEREST" DIRECTORS

We must distinguish at the outset between the old position of "outside" director and the new position of "public interest" director. For several decades the practice has been growing of appointing to corporate boards individuals who are not officers. The objective has been to bring independent viewpoints to bear on the determination of fundamental corporate policy and to provide a foundation for the objective appraisal of the performance of senior executives responsible for the day-by-day administration of a business. With relatively few exceptions, however, outside directors have been themselves full-time officers of corporations, or individuals steeped in the corporate world by reason of their work as lawyers or managers of financial institutions. Here and there a college president or similar nonbusiness type has been elected to a board, but the action was usually regarded by managers as cosmetic in character, however seriously the individuals involved may have taken their responsibilities. The critical fact was that outside directors, like inside directors, viewed themselves as responsible to the stockholders by whom technically they were elected. So far as corporate social performance was concerned, they contributed no new loyalties, no new attitudes, no new ideas.

When I speak of the public interest director, I mean an individual who takes up a position on a corporate board with specific intent to represent, at least initially and directly, other interests than those of the share-holders who own the business. I mean, to give a specific example, a black who comes on a corporate board with the clearly understood mission of getting more equitable treatment for blacks and members of other minorities throughout the business: more entry-level jobs, equal opportunity in advancing through ranks right up to the top of the management pyramid, an active effort to place more business with black suppliers, an active effort to open up more opportunities for black agents and dealers. He is there to put the corporation under unremitting pressure in all these areas. I happen to believe that, indirectly and in the long run, the actions of such a black director will also be extremely beneficial to the interests of the owners of the business, but that is not his primary short-term interest. In just the same way, I think of a woman serving as a public interest director with a primary concern for advancing the rights and opportunities of women in that company, all the way from first hiring up through management ranks. Or an individual whose great concern is with consumers and the service of their needs and rights. In short, public interest in the title refers specifically to a public interest, in contrast, indeed at times in apparent opposition, to the interests of the stockholders. In the long run, as I observed, the interests of the owners of a business and the interests of specific non-owning groups who work for or sell to or buy from a business *must* be identical if the business is to survive and prosper. But in the short run this is not always the case.

In analyzing the problems and opportunities of public interest directors, I want to draw heavily on my own experience as the first black director of the General Motors Corporation. I am drawing on that experience not only because I am familiar with it, but also because it relates to the broader experience of public interest directors in general. Whatever the constituency a public interest director serves, he encounters common problems and common opportunities. There is always the risk that the appointment may be treated as the worst kind of empty public relations gesture. There is always the risk that the conditions in which he functions as director may be so constraining that he fails to serve the interest of his constituency. There is always the risk that he may even be seduced into sacrificing those interests, so that he becomes a traitor in fact, if not in deed. And paired with these risks, there are always, for the right individual in the right corporate environment with the right desire of management to cooperate in every possible way, opportunities to help to create social benefits. These potential gains are not limited to what may be done by the business such a director serves. By example, the performance of one business may spread to others, so that the positive influence of a truly effective public interest director extends far beyond his immediate company.

INCREASING JOB OPPORTUNITIES
FOR BLACKS

Up to the time of my election to the General Motors board in 1970, I had experienced many associations with people in corporate leadership positions. My first contacts were negative; later I enjoyed more positive relationships. Let me relate a little of this personal history.

In 1959, discouraged by the lack of progress in the employment of blacks and members of other minority groups on an equal opportunity basis in business, I launched and led boycotts called "Selective Patronage Programs," beginning in Philadelphia. Our targets were large enterprises that had very few black employees in attractive jobs. During this boycott period, which lasted from 1959 to 1963, I organized economic withdrawal programs against scores of companies, one at a time.

Four hundred black ministers joined with me in these selective patronage efforts in communicating our appeals to their congregations. At the height of selective patronage programs in Philadelphia, it was estimated that a half-million blacks were participating in the programs. By mid-1963, three hundred major companies in the Philadelphia area had agreed to employ all minorities on an equal opportunity basis. A powerful new thrust for equal employment opportunity developed, not only in Philadelphia, but subsequently across America. I was able, at the request of Dr. Martin Luther King, Jr., to provide counsel and assistance to his efforts called "Operation Breadbasket" on a national basis. The results of selective patronage continued to have their effects across the nation.

During this period in my association with corporations and big business, I was looked upon as an enemy of the business system. It took time for business leaders to realize that my goal was not to destroy the free enterprise system, but rather to see that system working effectively for black workers and white workers alike. It was my aim to save the American system from itself, not to destroy it. In time, many business leaders who were against my methods began to understand my purpose. This change of attitude towards my efforts was significantly recognized later when the business community of Philadelphia presented me with the Philadelphia Award for "significant contributions to the promotion of industry and business for the City of Philadelphia."

When in 1964 jobs began to open for minorities in Philadelphia on a large scale, I found it necessary to alter my tactics because I could not find enough blacks with the skills to do the variety of jobs now open to them. I concluded that integration without preparation could lead only to frustration. Beginning, therefore, in an old abandoned jailhouse in

January, 1964, we started a program of training and retraining for the American black masses which we called OIC, the Opportunities Industrialization Center. Later, OIC was to become a training program for whites and blacks alike.

As a result of OIC, which represented to many industrial leaders a positive direction, a new kind of personal relationship began with American business leaders. As Industrial Advisory Councils were organized around OIC programs in cities, as they developed across the country to provide support to the training efforts, it was recognized that OIC was not only good for the poor, unemployed, and underemployed, but was also good for business, creating a new, trained, employment resource available to all business in all communities.

Since its brief beginning, OIC has developed up to now in more than one hundred cities in America and has become the largest private, independent, nongovernmental manpower training program operating in the ghetto and depressed areas of America. As a result of these experiences I developed, also, a new view of American corporate leaders. I was amazed to find how socially concerned many of these men were, and to discover that although I disagreed with them on many points, it was possible for us to work cooperatively on a concrete basis to achieve mutually desired objectives.

EXPERIENCES AS A
GENERAL MOTORS DIRECTOR

In December, 1970, I was asked to go on the board of General Motors. It was not the first time I had been invited to serve on a major corporate board, but I had refused previous invitations because so many other matters required my time. When James Roche, one of America's truly great business leaders, came to Philadelphia to invite me to membership on the board of General Motors, I went home and discussed the offer with my family. We decided I should accept to see what I could do to open new opportunities to minorities, and to help sensitize big business, in the largest industrial corporation in the world, to the needs of the poor. As I have said many times, for a company to make profits is not enough; a company must also help people, or one day the corporations of America will lose out to other systems in the world that want to see free enterprise destroyed. I am a free spirit and a free man who has as his goal the advancement of his people, and the progress and survival of America.

With respect to the role of big business as it relates to the needs of people, Mr. Charles P. McCormick, in his book *The Power of People* expressed my convictions in the following six points.

1. Business is primarily a matter of people. Men, not machines alone, have brought the United States to its dominant position in world industry. The machines would never be here if men had not inspired and used their minds and energies toward making these great contributions to mankind. No machine was ever invented that performed any useful function until people operated it and managed it.

2. Employees are human beings first, citizens of our nation second, and factors in production third. Labor is not a commodity to be bought, sold, or exchanged in the market place. Labor can never be really understood if considered solely in the mass. The great working force of any business is a collection of individual human beings, all with individual rights and individual problems worthy of consideration by management and government.

3. The United States is the bulwark of individual freedom and economic stability in the world today. Its greatness, its abundance, and its wealth place upon us the greatest challenge and at the same time the greatest opportunity ever known. There are definite signs of our realizing our responsibility.

4. The welfare of the people cannot be legislated satisfactorily by any government. Laws may regulate and control, but only free management and free labor, working co-operatively within the framework of our society, can initiate and maintain the long-range striving for the public good that is the aim of democracy. The government must always be impartial and just to all factions if it is to maintain the best for all groups.

5. The ability of American business managers acting jointly with American workers to preserve the dignity of man and freedom of choice for the individual is the only positive approach toward obtaining and preserving democracy throughout the world. We need human relations leaders. Our oncoming generation has a real opportunity to capitalize on our good start.

6. Finally, the destiny of man lies in being of service to others. No government or philosophy has ever lastingly endured unless it was based on a religious or service motive for bettering mankind. No man, however rich or powerful, can make his proper contribution to society unless his life is built around serving others. We were placed here to improve the society in which we live and that should be the goal of business and professional leaders today, tomorrow, and forever.[1]

Since being on the board of General Motors I can confidently say that General Motors is on the move. When I went on the board I said I wanted to see more black dealerships. We started with 7, now we have more than 20, and there are 24 blacks today being trained for dealerships. By the end of 1975, there will be 100 black General Motors dealerships in America, and this will only be the beginning—if the black man is good enough to drive automobiles, he is good enough to sell automobiles.

When I went on the board of General Motors I wanted to see results

[1] Charles P. McCormick, *The Power of People* (New York: Harper, 1949).

in upgrading blacks into salaried positions. I said I wanted to see a major number of such advancements in 30 months. Already, there have been 5,000 such advancements into salaried positions and we are shooting now for 10,000. I said I wanted to see General Motors assist black businesses and begin helping black suppliers. Several years ago there were only a handful of black businesses supplying General Motors with products, but today there are more than 400 with $20 million in annual contracts. Two years ago black insurance companies had no General Motors participation. Today, more than $1.5 billion in General Motors insurance business has been given to black insurance companies, and that is not the end.

We have done other things, such as putting money in every known black bank in America, and providing assistance to scores of black businesses through the GM Mesbic. We will continue to do much, much more and to expand our efforts. We are fortunate to have in Mr. Richard Gerstenberg a chairman who genuinely believes in advancement for minorities and in our cause.

I have also learned in these past two years of the intense concern and involvement of General Motors in working with environmental problems. Prior to my coming on the board, I was of the opinion that these men had a limited concern about matters such as pollution. I was wrong. Indeed, more than half of the board meetings were spent in dealing with questions of public concern and I found that hundreds of millions of dollars were being expended in the utilization of the best scientific and technical knowledge available to deal with problems of ecology, pollution, and emission. Of course, this is necessary for an automobile company, because the solution to pollution problems is, in today's climate, related to the survival of the automobile industry. It was interesting to note the degree to which I found this and a mounting interest in human needs and community problems among directors of General Motors.

General Motors is not doing all that it should do, and is not yet doing all that it could do, but it certainly is doing a lot better than it used to do; and you can be sure I will strive to see that they keep on doing more, because I will certainly keep on talking and doing my best to push the company along in these directions.

OPPORTUNITIES AND PROBLEMS

Now let me move out from my own experience to the role of public interest directors in general. I think they have an enormous opportunity to influence corporate behavior wherever they take directorships, provided they (1) recognize that they represent specific constituencies, (2) insist on being active representatives of the interests of those constituencies, and (3) are never satisfied with partial gains but forever keep insisting on further and faster progress toward their ultimate goals. To be sure, they must be realistic about the time it takes to get a big organization turned around. But this kind of realism in recognizing some of the facts of life in big corporations should never be allowed to lead to a relaxation of pressure.

Public interest directors must not be afraid of being regarded as difficult people by their associates. Any individual who presses for changes in practices of long standing will be regarded as difficult. But if what he is pressing for is inherently right, and if his fellow directors and line management know it is right, his attitude will come to be understood and he will be listened to and respected. In most cases, I might add, the public interest director who comes to his assignment with, possibly, rather limited knowledge of the policies and attitudes of established corporate management—as I certainly did with General Motors—will learn that most business leaders are willing to lift their sights and participate in formulating new policies and practices which are related to important social needs. And when business leaders accept these changes, they bring something of great value to the solution of the problem: they are action oriented, they know how to make things happen, and they know how to get results.

Public interest directors should also expect to encounter some problems. The first big problem will be right within the board of directors. Some of them may be hostile or indifferent to the introduction of socially responsible policies and programs. And some may be uncertain or skeptical about the competence and sincerity of their new board colleague. The new director will have to demonstrate that he is interested in the performance of the corporation as an economic enterprise with a profit-making orientation at the same time that he is beginning to apply his weight to steer the company toward changing policies that are adverse to the interests of his particular constituency. To a significant degree, he will establish personal credibility and command attention for his special concern by demonstrating that he understands that a business is not a philanthropy. It is critically essential that he establish this credibility and attention because he is a very small minority in the total group of directors. Even if a corporation has several public interest directors (representing, say, minority groups, women, and consumers), they will still be a small share of the full board membership. They must make their views known and accepted by patient persuasion. They can be unremitting in their advocacy of the interests they represent. But their ultimate power is the power to persuade through education, rational analysis, and accumulation of a factual record.

The next problem the public interest director must face and find a way of resolving is the supply of information. This has three aspects. The first is concerned with ascertaining the real facts of corporate posture and performance in the area of his principal interest. A black director must find out what policies and practices, formal and informal, exist that affect in any way employment and promotion opportunities for blacks in all parts of the business, as well as opportunities for black businesses to work as suppliers, dealers, etc. He has to find out the numbers and proportion of blacks in all jobs, ranks, and locations. A woman board member has the same need for her constituency. In the ordinary course of events, the required information is not part of the normal information system of the company. Special studies have to be made, and in a giant corporation this is no simple undertaking.

The second aspect of the information supply problem is concerned with getting reports on policy and program changes that result from the activities of the public interest director. The special target here must be, not top-level decisions, but rather the way in which the innovations are transmitted down through the organization and how operating managers are informed, motivated, and appraised. Middle management is the engine of corporate performance. Major changes in corporate behavior will not occur unless top-level policy decisions are taken seriously and executed wholeheartedly. The execution of policy in business, as in other organizations, does not follow automatically upon the leaders' decisions. Particularly if what is involved is a fundamental change in behavior that disrupts personal attitudes and practices and is viewed as possibly inimical to short-term management performance, there may be a disposition down through line management ranks to give only lip service to the new policies, or even to ignore them.

The third aspect of the information problem focuses on getting timely and accurate reporting up through channels on what actually happens as a result of top-level decisions and middle-management implementation. Again, what the public interest director needs to know is likely to be available only through new reporting procedures.

Throughout all three aspects of the problem it is important to establish the validity of the information reported. In my own experience I have found it desirable to create a special staff independent of the company, responsible to me, with top-level clearance to go anywhere in the huge General Motors organization and check on the facts. In other large organizations, a public interest director may want similar machinery for assuring that he knows all he should know about performance, and that what he is told is accurate in all details. The need for such verification machinery will undoubtedly diminish as time passes and the new policies and programs become ingrained in the mores of the business. In the early stages of change, however, they are probably essential, particularly in large, complex corporations in which operational details are not easily visible from the board level.

BUSINESS AND URBAN DECAY

Public interest directors must persevere, too, in urging our corporations to give major attention to ameliorating the basic problems of the inner city. All American businesses have a stake in what is happening in the inner city. Like a core in an apple that becomes rotted and diseased, and in time destroys the rest of the apple, so the rot and the socioeconomic disease of the inner city, if not dealt with swiftly and effectively, utilizing every resource available, will in time destroy American cities, including suburbia as well.

Unfortunately, in recent years, a great blackout has obscured the actual conditions existing in the ghettos of every major city in the nation. White America does not even know what is going on, because the blackout is hiding the truth and minimizing the severity of the situation. This very day 500,000 black, returned Vietnam veterans are standing on street corners, alone, unemployed, filled with anger because they believe the nation has turned its back on them. In every major city there are entire neighborhoods that look like bombed areas, with huge vacant spaces, surrounded by little fences, as evidence of the destruction that grows from poverty, deprivation, unemployment, and crime. There exists a situation of volcanic proportions in the ghettos of this nation, which, if not tended to, will erupt in disturbances that will make what happened at Watts look like a picnic on a Sunday afternoon.

Corporations will have to make a far deeper commitment to the solution of these problems, human and economic, even to the extent of arranging "paid" release of workers to participate in community programs to improve bad situations, along with a commitment of a share of profits to the removal of urban and rural deprivation, poverty, and ignorance.

HOPE ON THE HORIZON

I see a new hope on the corporate horizon. If the developing attitudes in General Motors are any indication of what is happening or can happen in other corporations, there is reason for optimism. I am continuing to look for benchmarks of progress, not only in General Motors but in all large American corporations. They must move beyond adding a black or a woman to the board, meaningful as this representation is. Our presence alone is important; but even more important, we must push and speak, and be determined that our presence on boards becomes a force for change. In an objective mood, and from where I sit, I do see progress. Not as much as I would like, but some.

Lyndon Johnson said to me when I talked with him on his ranch just a few months before his death, in speaking about OIC and our work among the poor and the unemployed in America, and about the possibilities in my association with General Motors: "Leon, I think we are going to make it." Confronting the many problems that stretch before us like a great Red Sea, I think Lyndon Johnson was right. It will take effort and time, and some praying too, but "I think we are going to make it"—because we must.

Editor's Commentary

The concept of the public interest director suggests an interesting speculation about possible future changes in the function of the corporate board. The traditional, and legal, role of the board of directors, of course, has been that of representative of the stockholder-owners, responsible for the general performance of the business. This has been translated in action into responsibility for designating and removing the chief executive officer, approving the selection of the chief executive's principal associates, approving fundamental corporate policies and commitments, and maintaining a general surveillance over operating performance. In practice, as has been widely reported by observers and critics of the corporate world, the work of corporate boards has generally been determined by internal power groups consisting of the principal line officers and key directors (both internal and external), and board membership has been self-perpetuating. Ordinarily, departures from this practice occur only when operating results are unsatisfactory, gross policy or personality conflicts surface, or clear evidence of illegal actions is revealed to the board or the general public.

The heightened attention commanded by issues related to corporate social responsibility and the decision by a small but growing number of corporate boards to add public interest directors of the kind described by Dr. Sullivan bring into view the possibility of a radical transformation in board function. This would reflect the emerging idea that the corporation as a business organization operating under public charter carries a dual performance responsibility. In addition to the traditional responsibility for producing an economic return to owners there is a new responsibility for social performance. The mounting dialogue between business leaders and independent observers of business institutions poses interesting questions about the object of the latter responsibility. Those who argue that improved corporate social performance is in the long-run economic interest of stockholders would hold that public interest directors have the same ultimate responsibility to shareholders as have other board members. Those who believe that improved corporate social performance is a long-delayed but proper return to society of valuable benefits as compensation for valuable benefits conferred by society through its grant of corporate charters would hold that public interest directors have a unique responsibility to elements of society other than shareholders.

Dr. Sullivan bridges these contrasting views. He suggests that the public interest director should focus primarily on creating benefits for the special group with which he is affiliated. If he is effective in his work as a director, he will over time shift corporate performance toward a more equitable balance between owner interests and social interests. In his view, this will have tangible short-run benefits for shareholders (for example, by improving the market for General Motors cars), as well as long-run benefits (by helping to preserve the private enterprise system). But he makes it plain that these stockholder benefits are no more than attractive and useful by-products of progress toward the primary objective, which, in his case, is jobs and opportunities for the advancement of blacks. He would expect a woman director to be equally concerned with opening opportunities for women, and a representative of consumer interests to focus on goals appropriate to that constituency.

The corporate board then becomes a forum in which multiple interests interact. There can be no assurance, of course, that this interaction will always find easy accommodation among diverse interests. The several public interest directors may well develop conflicts over clashing benefits for their respective constituencies. And as a group they will be likely, at least occasionally, to come into conflict with other directors whose primary concern is short-run stockholder benefits. This scenario suggests a politicization of corporate boards, with all the results that dynamic political conflict in other arenas so often brings into view. Drastic changes would certainly appear in the boardroom environment and in the agenda of board meetings. Difficult new problems would be created for corporate managers and for the fundamental decision processes involved in planning, resource allocation, and budgeting.

An objective observer of corporate behavior and performance could bring serious substance to the argument that developments of this nature might turn out, on balance, to be advantageous. Even one who shares Professor Friedman's philosophy might agree that if social pressures are going to force private business organizations beyond strictly for-profit operations, it would be better to have competition for resources debated at the board level among proponents of diverse interests than to compel individual managers to make choices between economic and noneconomic ends. The result would be an emerging model within the individual corporation of the politics of competing interests on the national scene. It would be an example of "corporate democracy" of a kind probably not envisaged by those who invented the term with reference to labor participation in managerial decision making.

The special public interests identified by Dr. Sullivan do not reflect the full potential of future developments in board composition and function. Not mentioned in his paper, but standing offstage and preparing to come into view, are representatives of the general public and of employees, two constituencies with a recognizable interest in corporate behavior. The first of these constituencies is beginning to make its claims heard at two levels. There are the interests of local communities in which corporations do business, notably plant communities, which are concerned with the environmental effects of manufacturing (or power generating, or transportation, etc.) operations, and the economic effects of changes in the scale of operations. There are also the interests of the national community which are allied to the movement to strengthen control over all aspects of the activities of large businesses which transcend the administrative grasp of local or state authorities. We even see the first vague stirring of discontent with the inability of national governments to establish effective control over the operations of giant multinational corporations. As for employee representation on boards, while not yet practiced in the United States—and not even advanced as a serious claim by union leaders—this is both a growing practice in a number of other countries and a legal requirement in some.

Those concerned about the future of the private corporation in the United States must, therefore, contemplate the evolution of board membership toward representation for local and national government and for employees (unionized or other), as well as for the kinds of special interest groups that are already beginning to supply directors. Support for government representation might well be strengthened by the argument that, at least in some industries, this would be a useful adjunct to public regulation though administrative agencies, as in the transportation, energy, and communications industries. A related development, identified by some observers, is the appearance of corporations financed by mixed private and public investment, with parallel mixed private and public management.

All of the foregoing possibilities are obviously speculative and one could get a hot debate going over the appropriate odds to assign to the probability of their occurrence as more than occasional curiosities of aberrant behavior. It is impossible, however, to avoid remarking the fact that the number of boards which in recent years have added representatives of minority and sex constituencies is growing and that the list includes some of the largest, allegedly best managed, and most successful American corporations. Many of the individuals named as public interest directors are, like Dr. Sullivan, people not disposed to serve cosmetic purposes. They will press hard, as he has done, on fellow directors and line managers to produce benefits for their constituents by changing corporate policies and practices. To the extent that they get visible results—an outcome which is already beginning to be reported—pressure will increase on other corporations to take similar steps. This pressure will be reinforced by related pressure generated at other points along the business-society interface. When minority and sex representation on boards is rather general practice, with widely reported benefits for represented constituencies (a time which may not be more than a few years ahead), it would not appear unreasonable to expect customer, community, and labor interests to advance comparable claims. In these areas, too, other influences along the business-society interface, identified above, will lend support to the asserted claims.

As one speculator, I would regard it as more likely than not that by the early 1980s special interest and general public constituencies will be rather broadly represented on the boards of the larger corporations. By that time, corporations will, voluntarily or by compulsion, be much more sensitive to claims for socially responsible performance. The composition of boards of directors will then be viewed as appropriate for the guidance of corporate affairs, as traditional boards have been viewed in the context of a different set of assumptions about the function of business in our society. And while the new arrangements will create novel and complex problems for line managements, they will probably also make important contributions to solving some problems of balancing economic and social interests that would otherwise be extraordinarily difficult to handle.

CHAPTER 10

The Socially Responsible Corporation and the Political Process

Patricia Roberts Harris

The practice of corporate social responsibility will require business executives to interact with the representatives of government along a broad interface of issues and interests and from national to local levels. To the extent that corporate responses to society's expectations and demands cannot be initiated by an individual company or by company groups for competitive cost or other reasons, elements of the new social contract for business are likely to be implemented through governmental action, as has been the case recently in such areas as environmental contamination, equal employment opportunity, product safety, and consumer protection. It will be advantageous for both business and society if managers who have the requisite motivation and skill participate constructively in the design of legislation and administrative actions; their contributions can help to accomplish desired ends with an economy of means. Presently, few managers have the training, knowledge, or experience to function effectively in this business-government arena.

The following chapter examines the need for greater business understanding of and participation in the political process, and proposes ways to make this participation more productive.

The author of this chapter is Patricia Roberts Harris, a practicing attorney in Washington, D.C., long active in and knowledgeable about the political process, and a director of several major corporations.–EDITOR

C LEAR THINKING about the relation of business to the political process requires a distinction between two aspects of business and two aspects of the political process. On the business side, we can distinguish between the traditional business activities of manufacturing and marketing products and services in a relatively unrestricted competitive environment and the activities and performance expected and increasingly required of business by today's changing American society. On the political side, we can distinguish between the activities of political parties, during and between elections, and the governmental process of legislating and administering in a post-industrial society in which new ideas are emerging about the quality of life and the general human condition.

With respect to relations between traditional business and the political parties the record of history urges a simple code of conduct. Business should pursue a policy of political neutrality. This would best serve both its own economic interests and the economic interests of the society in which it functions. Subject only and inevitably to the general rules of the game—unrestricted competition, protection of employee and customer safety, absence of fraudulent practices, etc.—the responsibility of business leaders is to seek maximum return on invested capital within whatever time horizon and incidence of risks are judged appropriate. In this context, businessmen's relations should be with governmental institutions and public servants only when the specific economic interests of individual firms or their industries are at stake. Corporate involvement with political parties in their partisan activities is likely to be counter-productive in individual instances. Viewed more generally, it invites contamination of the partisan political process, with serious attendant dangers for both the economic performance of business and the maintenance of general public confidence in the integrity of business and government institutions.

Altogether different issues appear, however, when we consider the emerging problems of corporate social responsibility, on one side, and the work of governmental bodies and processes, on the other. If constructive responses are to be made to the growing concern for the quality of the human condition, other than those aspects measured by Gross National Product statistics, in a society that continues to value the dynamism and freedom of private enterprise, business leaders cannot remain neutral or passive. Most business initiatives aimed at improving the quality of life require interaction with government agencies and personnel. The development of policies, programs, procedures, standards, and incentives car rarely occur totally within the sphere of unregulated individual companies or industries. Sooner or later, partially or totally, public institutions, which are the creatures of the political process become involved. An objective observer is led toward the conclusion that it is the socially irresponsible corporation which builds a network of relationships with political parties and politicians, and the socially responsible corporation which builds a network of relationships with public institutions and their personnel.

Business leaders who have developed, if not expertise, at least a certain familiarity in dealing with parties and politicians through campaign contributions may find themselves poorly equipped to manage their relationships with legislative and administrative institutions. They lack a clear understanding of governmental processes. They are ill informed about the critical channels through which ideas and information inputs influence legislative and administrative actions. This state of relative ignorance has been vividly demonstrated in recent years in such areas as environmental contamination, product safety, delivery of medical services, and employment equity. If social needs are to be served in the years ahead—and the democratic process will compel these needs to be served in some fashion—business leaders must develop a sophisticated understanding of this aspect of the political process.

It is no simple recommendation to propose that corporations withdraw from partisan politics and concurrently increase the intensity and skill of their relationships with public institutions. Yet it is only by this dual adjustment that the concept of corporate social responsibility can be implemented in a way that is also likely to preserve the benefits of the enterprise system. Subtly, but inescapably, the two parts of the recommended adjustment are related. The price of public acceptance of and belief in a legitimate role for corporations in helping to design new approaches to improving the quality of the human condition in this country is likely to be the abandonment of business subvention of political parties.

BUSINESS AND GOVERNMENT: ADVERSARIES AND PARTNERS

The relation of business to the political process has been the subject of controversy in this country since the beginning of the republic. As Mr. Dooley, that loquacious creation of Finley Peter Dunne, once observed in a later period:

> It seems to me that the on'y thing to do is to keep pollyticians an' business men apart. They seem to have a bad infloonce on each other. Whiniver

I see an Aldherman an' a banker walkin' down the street together I know the Recordin' Angel will have to ordher another bottle of ink.

Opposition to business has been as much a part of the history of the United States as support of business. In fact, the historic conflict between Thomas Jefferson and Alexander Hamilton included diametrically opposed opinions about business and manufacture. In his "Notes on Virginia," Jefferson made it clear that he opposed industrialism and its consequences. Although, as President, he was later to aid industry in the fledgling nation, his attitude toward manufacture was expressed in the statement "While we have land to labor . . . let us never wish to see our citizens occupied at a workbench, or twirling a distaff." But it was Alexander Hamilton who anticipated the American future and established the political philosophy of the new industrialism that he saw as essential to the development of the country for whose independence he had fought. Out of his experience in the Revolution, Hamilton brought a conviction that social stability rested on the firm alliance of government and business. His *Report on the Subject of Manufactures* (1791) enunciated principles for the encouragement and protection of business that have never been revoked.

Despite Jeffersonian skepticism, the alliance between business and government began with the nation, and acceptance of the Hamiltonian brief for a strong central government provided business with an ally that was to become even stronger. Federalism gave business not only the central government as an ally, but also the several state governments in varying numbers and strength. Wherever there was government, there were politicians to people and maneuver it, and despite the fact that the prophet of laissez-faire, Adam Smith, referred disparagingly to "that insidious and crafty animal, vulgarly called statesman or politician," capitalist and politician have formed alliances throughout our national history.

As the first Secretary of the Treasury, Hamilton applied his conviction that government and property must form a close working alliance. The battle over the application of this principle began in this country decades prior to the publication of the *Communist Manifesto* when Jacksonian politics attacked the most visible aspect of Hamiltonian policy, the Second Bank of the United States. Shortly thereafter, Daniel Webster emerged as an eloquent proponent of government support of big business. Arthur Schlesinger, Jr., has noted: "The nation never gave its heart to Webster. The merchants of Boston did, along with a share of their purses, and also the speculators of Wall Street and rich men everywhere." Calvin Coolidge's statement, "The business of America is business," would have been accepted by Daniel Webster, and is accepted by many present-day state and national legislators and administrators.

History indicates that American business has done very well indeed in its quest for political influence. Although the businessman's preference for the Republican Party is manifest in every report of contributions to political parties, the prevailing attitude about how businesses fare under the other party is found in the joke: "Business under the Democrats is like sex: when it is good, it is very, very good, and when it is bad, it is still good."

BUSINESS AND POLITICS

The reason for the essential well-being of business under both political parties is that the welfare of the nation depends upon the existence of a healthy economy, and American business is the American economy. As important as the all-encompassing nature of business today in American life is the role of business as the primary patron of the politician. Despite laws limiting business participation in the political process, business has been a major source of support for political candidacies, even including that of Senator McGovern in 1972. Despite the appearance of Senator McGovern's "skinny-cat" contributors, essential seed money for the McGovern campaign came from firms in the automobile and other industries. Senator McGovern's Democratic Committee Treasurer was a former partner in a well-known Wall Street investment banking enterprise, and his famous chairlady for the Democratic National Committee was a sometime absentee from the nonproletarian business activities of mink-breeding and construction.

Although Senator McGovern had some millionaires among his supporters, they did not, of course, match those of his opponent, or, in fact, those of his predecessor as a Democratic nominee, Senator Humphrey. While the defections of normally Democratic voters was felt in November, 1972, the flight of normally Democratic capital to the Republicans was already painfully visible in July. We have all heard of the huge campaign chest available to the Republican Party. It has been revealed that one hundred people gave $14 million to that campaign. (One man alone gave $2.1 million and another contributor $1 million.) Among the top twenty-five Republican donors were several individuals who had been major givers to the campaigns of Hubert Humphrey.

The third largest contribution to the Republican campaign chest came from the dairy industry, and another sizable contribution came from the National Association of Real Estate Boards. James R. Polk, of the *Washington Star and Daily News,* described the Nixon donors as "ranging from billionaire oil producer to a factory owner in Erie, Pa." and including

"Wall Street and the oil, electronics, medical and drug industries" with "others who made their fortunes in everything from hamburgers to retread rubber."

The availability of such large sums from a single group in American society is fraught with grave dangers. Recent revelations about business gifts to political parties provide grounds to believe that business is using its access to enormous amounts of money to influence and even obstruct the enforcement of the law. The charge that a major corporation offered a political contribution in order to insure a result favorable to the corporation in antitrust enforcement has highlighted the extraordinary danger of present-day influence of business upon the political process.

Outright bribery of individual government officials in order to achieve business goals still occurs on the national level, but is more likely to be found in local government. Chicanery such as Collis P. Huntington's buying of the California legislature and bribery of congressmen to promote his business interests, as well as similar activities in the nineteenth and earlier parts of the twentieth century, are widely known, and the jail sentences from scandals such as the Teapot Dome have made businessmen wary, and have made intelligent businessmen honest. Nonetheless, the financial resources available to businessmen, especially heads of expanding corporate giants who have need for either help or benign neglect from government, give businessmen a potential and a real influence in politics beyond their numbers.

The availability of political contributions from business is an inducement to try to secure the contribution. Otherwise honest politicians understandably do not wish to antagonize a class that can buy television time, billboards, and handbills for their opponents. The validity of this concern about not driving the "fat cats" into the arms of the opposition was confirmed nationally in the 1972 Presidential election.

Political figures concerned with the welfare of all of their constituents must be particularly concerned with the welfare of those who can play so decisive a role in the life and death of their political careers. Whether it is business or labor (union political funds being the only significant alternative to business money), those who contribute to a political campaign do not expect to be insulted if they have a concern; if they contribute enough, they will not be. Where there is no countervailing pressure, those who make political contributions are not likely to find themselves offended by the hostile vote of those whom they support.

Presidential candidates are not the only candidates seeking and receiving funds from businessmen. Candidates for mayor, congressman, senator, and points below and in between must have money for printing, postage, newspaper advertisements, and radio and television commercials.

The wealthy businessman is a prime fund-raising target of both Democrats and Republicans, as, of course, is the well-to-do lawyer, writer, or physician, although the professions are generally underrepresented in the Himalayas of political contributions. Thus from City Hall to the White House, the need for money for the next campaign and the greater need to see that one's opponent does not secure too much money insure friendliness to businessmen at all levels of government.

More important, the rush of business money to those who have already proven their amity to business puts the opposition in a difficult position. Sometimes, however, a spectacular rush of business money to one candidate can lead to an overabundance of riches, with attendant errors of judgment based largely upon that overabundance; this is probably as good an explanation of the Watergate affair as any; it may have destroyed at least one senatorial candidate through overexposure on television made possible by these excess contributions.

BUSINESS INFLUENCE

The fact that so much money flows from business sources leads to understandable expectations on the part of the contributors that their economic interests will not be hurt by adverse legislation. Curiously, in the face of this record, there is a general sense of ineffectiveness among businessmen at all levels. They doubt their ability to influence national economic decisions. This surprising view of the impact of businessmen upon events and attitudes was apparently shared by Lewis F. Powell, a former Richmond, Virginia, lawyer, and presently Associate Justice of the Supreme Court. In a memorandum to the Chairman of the Education Committee of the U.S. Chamber of Commerce, dated just two months before his nomination for the Supreme Court position, Mr. Justice Powell, ignoring the traditions of Thomas Jefferson, the trust-busters, and the populists, claimed to find something "quite new in the history of America," an "assault on the enterprise system." Powell singled out Ralph Nader as "perhaps the single most effective antagonist of American business. . . ." This citation of Mr. Nader as a threat to American business is the best indication of the political problems of U.S. business that we can have. Mr. Justice Powell quoted a *Fortune* magazine article stating that Mr. Nader's "passion . . . is aimed at smashing utterly the target of his hatred, which is corporate power."

A reader of the *Fortune* excerpt or the Powell memorandum would never be led to remember that Mr. Nader's "passion" was initially directed at corporations that failed to make certain that their products would not kill consumers. In the preface to *Unsafe at Any Speed,* the first cannonade of the modern war against business irresponsibility, Mr. Nader said:

> A great problem of contemporary life is how to control the power of economic interests which ignore the harmful effects of their applied sciences and technology. The automobile tragedy is one of the most serious of these man-made assaults on the human body. The history of that tragedy reveals many obstacles which must be overcome in the taming of any mechanical or biological hazard which is a by-product of industry or commerce. Our society's obligation to protect the "body rights" of its citizens with vigorous resolve and ample resources requires the precise authoritative articulation and front-rank support which is being devoted to civil rights.

Opposition to a man whose concern is so articulated may explain why businessmen have little credibility in politics, and why so many businessmen believe they have little credibility. The efforts to discredit Nader's motives, and the attacks on his personality in place of a response to the basic issue he raises—the right of the public to safety in using products which produce a profit for their manufacturer—shows a human as well as a political insensitivity on the part of his opponents.

A Louis Harris survey, reported in the *Washington Post* of Monday, February 5, 1973, found that the area of greatest slippage of confidence in business reputation was a perceived deterioration of the quality of products and services offered to the public. Although the Powell memorandum suggests that Nader and his colleagues created this condition of suspicion, the reality is that his ideas fell on the fertile soil of recognition by every consumer who has had to take his automobile back for service of defective parts only a few days after driving it from the showroom, or by the consumer with the dripping wash in the new, but defective, washing machine. Understandably, the public wants business to perform better. But the fear, expressed in the Powell memorandum, that there is growing public support for government ownership of business is refuted by another Harris survey, reported February 12, 1973, which shows that people oppose a government takeover of business because they think "government running things" would be even worse "than having business run them as it is now."

Nonetheless, the sense of ineffectiveness persists among many business leaders. The result has been business opposition to change in the interest of maintenance of the status quo. This political opposition reflex was commented on by Thomas J. Watson, Jr., former Chairman of the Board of IBM, at a dinner of the Advertising Council in which he catalogued business opposition to the social reforms of the last forty years. The other substantive thrust of business that is most apparent to the general public is the attempt to secure direct benefits from the government, as in the case of the Lockheed Corporation.

BUSINESS INTEREST AND
PUBLIC INTEREST

A growing section of the public sees the impact of business on politics as essentially hostile to the public interest, and this public judgment has led to defensive responses by business. One of the least pernicious of these defensive responses is seen in the Powell memorandum which urges extensive public relations and educational activity to regain the regard the public once had for business. Similar to this is the institutional advertising campaign asserting that we all need the railroads, or that private utility companies are important taxpayers. Infinitely more dangerous is the response of behind-the-scenes maneuvering to secure special privilege. As major contributors as well as important community figures, businessmen have an ease of direct access to government officials that is denied to most members of the general public. Although many responsible corporation executives eschew such contacts as counter-productive in the long run, others take full advantage of the status resulting from their occupation and income to try to influence political decisions. The aspect of this influence-peddling belonging to what President Eisenhower called the "military-industrial complex" is especially visible as the result of recent examples in the aero-space industry, but other special business interests for purposes of self-preservation have formed alliances with sections of the government, national and local. The danger of these alliances comes to full fruition when political figures support the validity of these essentially furtive relationships by attempting to regularize and institutionalize them.

The belief of many responsible businessmen that they are not politically effective suggests that the present political role of business is not satisfactory to responsible businessmen, and it clearly is not satisfactory to a large share of the general public. The only way to end the chronic dissatisfaction with the special position of business in political influence is to remove the incentive for both business and politicians to provide that special position. So long as business remains the primary political patron, through the device of contributions from business leaders, the temptation to demand, and the temptation to grant, special consideration to business will exist. Instead of business contributions, tax dollars should be used to finance political campaigns, and the major modern campaign cost, television time, should be eliminated so far as political candidates are concerned. One of the costs of securing the benefit of the use of television and radio channels for private profit should be the requirement of the dedication of specified time on these channels, during political campaigns (including the pre-primary period), to political candidates. Other campaign costs should be financed from a public pool, appropriated by legislatures, and administered by bi-partisan commissions. Voluntary tax return check-offs are a beginning, but are not adequate.

Business will not suffer from the requirement of alternative means of financing political campaigns. What has prejudiced the general community against business has been the continuing appearance of the purchase of political preference through the ability to finance the political process. By removing the temptation to politicians to demand such financing, and the temptation of businessmen to buy political insurance through these contributions, it may be possible to restore the faith of the electorate in the political process, and to remove the suspicion of corruption that still haunts honest businessmen and makes them the undeserved target of those who would render businessmen mute on the political issues about which they should be vocal. If the suspicion of the purchase of governmental favors is removed, the basic tendency of the American people to protect the business goose that lays the golden egg of the U.S. standard of living will reassert itself. Shareholders of U.S. corporations, small businessmen, and the majority of us who are dependent on American business in so many ways, represent the best protection business can have.

BUSINESS PARTICIPATION IN THE POLITICAL PROCESS

Business leaders will always have a superior opportunity to participate in the political process as individuals with special skills and perspective. Thomas J. Watson, Jr., in his speech to the Advertising Council cited above, exhorted the next generation of businessmen to use these special skills for affirmative, rather than negative, action:

> I think businessmen in the future have got to take the lead in enlightening social legislation in this country. For too long we as a group have been against almost any change or law which restricted our freedom of movement in any fashion. As you look backwards, we've been against an awful lot of things that most of us accept today as being necessary and desirable.
>
> We've been against the minimum wage, the 40-hour week, the five-day week, equal pay for women, social security, and all of you in the room can name a good many more.
>
> And so I would say to the young businessmen coming up in the system and taking responsibility for bigger and bigger decisions today that if I had to capsulize what I've learned in 35 years in the system in a single sentence, I would say try to be *for* things rather than *against* things when they relate to the national welfare.

This advice from one of the giants of American business indicates that there is a role for business in politics. Such general social concern does not preclude the use of the political process to protect business interests, but it suggests that business interests on which politics should be brought to bear extend beyond wage and tax policy, beyond dividend and profit concerns, to the total context within which businessmen operate. A broader perspective will serve to legitimize the political activity of businessmen and will serve as the best protection business can have in a society that trusts business more than government, but is prepared to let government intervene when it can no longer trust business.

Most business leaders have little experience in this new relationship, little understanding of the influence channels through which constructive participation in the amelioration of social problems can be developed, little knowledge of the political processes through which legislative and administrative organizations get their work done. These are critical handicaps not only for executives who want to apply business resources, knowledge, and skills in support of programs that will reverse the erosion of the quality of life in our high-technology society. On a broader front, they threaten the continuance of the private enterprise system in anything like its present form. Our democratic institutions of government will inevitably respond to social needs as energized by pressure groups that are often more enthusiastic about action than knowledgeable about solutions that will work. At best, the outcome will be inefficiency in the use of resources, which translates into unnecessarily high prices for realized social gains and constrained advances in living standards. At worst, ill-designed and unduly restrictive controls may drain the dynamism from the business system.

Examples of what can occur when uninformed social improvers compel government action can be found in many of the areas of current discontent with the performance of business: delivery of health services, product safety, environmental contamination, protection of consumers in the marketplace. The characteristic chain of events that culminates in clumsily drafted and off-target legislation—often prescribing standards of technical performance compliance which generate unacceptable future social costs—begins with a widely recognized social problem growing out of the creation of an economic good in response to a market need—such as the environmental contamination associated with production of electric power. Underlying the spreading public discontent is an economic reality: the production of electric power has traditionally been accompanied by the transfer of certain costs from the utility to the society—in as simple terms as increased laundry and cleaning bills for those who live downwind from a fouling smokestack. Individuals and groups complain, protest, and propose remedial and protective actions.

The businesses whose activities have created or substantially contributed to the societal problem typically ignore the complaints (if they can), deny the seriousness of the problem (if its existence cannot be challenged), call attention to the allegedly unacceptable economic cost of removing the source of the problem (if its seriousness is beyond doubt), and argue that the state of the art in the relevant remedial technology is incapable of curing the problem (if all other arguments fail). When substantial economic interests are at stake, large sums are spent on advertising and public relations campaigns to communicate these views to the general public and to governmental officials. This line of defense may achieve success for a while—sometimes for many years. The American Medical Association held off Medicare for decades in precisely this way. The AMA called it "socialized medicine" and communicated at a multimillion dollar annual cost the several messages that it was unnecessary, impossibly expensive, and subversive of traditional doctor-patient relationships and, more generally, of the American way of life.

Ultimately, if the social problem is real and affects large numbers of people, the citizen interest groups, which are the activating yeast in the otherwise inert social dough, command growing attention, enlist support, and arouse the sympathetic interest of legislators and public administrators. Legislation is proposed to cure the problem, often embodying standards of technical performance by the offending producers of economic goods that reflect ignorance of either the limits of available technology or the unfavorable cost-benefit trade-off. At about this stage it is common experience for representatives of the offending industry to come forward with offers to help draft the legislation, define the appropriate technical standards, and formulate the administrative rules and procedures. (Just before the passage of Medicare legislation, this is exactly what the AMA did.) When this happens, the typical response of activists and most public officials ranges from skepticism about the honesty of business intent to outright rejection. (This was precisely the response to the representatives of the AMA.)

In short, the adversary position taken up by the offending firms or industries, their challenge to the existence or the seriousness or the feasibility of solving the problem, destroys their credibility in the public mind and in the minds of government officials. They are viewed, not as valuable and technically competent partners motivated by a sincere interest in working for an improved society, but rather as an enemy who, having lost the first battle of propaganda against protective legislation, now intends to win the war by sabotage. The electric power and the automobile industries have maneuvered themselves into precisely this position in recent years.

There is an obvious lesson for corporate management in this characteristic sequence of events. In the long run, the response of governmental institutions to widespread social discontent in a democracy is inevitable. When this response is influenced, even specifically designed in its technical aspects, by activist groups who lack technological expertise, firsthand knowledge of resource management systems, and cost-benefit data, remedial legislation and administration is likely to be inefficient and even ineffective. The corporate leaders who command the relevant technological expertise and understand how to use resource management systems to achieve desired goals can establish the credibility base necessary for open participation in social reform only by demonstrating social concern early. If their adversary behavior identifies them as opponents of social action who convert to proponents only after defeat is in sight, they will not be allowed to participate in the design of solutions.

Not only business leaders but all of us pay the price for this failure to establish credibility. The inefficient and ineffective solutions spread their costs throughout the society. Emotional and uninformed adversary behavior on both sides of the fight over the expansion of electric power generating facilities will create widespread discomfort and loss of jobs through brownouts and blackouts throughout the country in the years ahead. And this is only one of several areas in which knowledge has been sacrificed to emotional enthusiasm because those who possess the knowledge have not understood either the American political process or the cost-benefit advantage in a reasoned approach to participation in that process.

This kind of participation in the American political process is a long way from the traditional business role of funding political parties and their campaigns. It requires knowledge and skill radically different from those hitherto required to build a successful career in corporate management. But it is precisely this knowledge and skill that in the years ahead will be essential ingredients for successful performance of corporate leadership responsibilities.

EDITOR'S COMMENTARY

Advising business leaders to become active participants in the political process because it is the machinery through which many aspects of corporate social responsibility will inevitably develop brings into view the familiar gap between policy and implementation. Experience and observation have taught many executives to regard the public bureaucracy with distaste, if not some stronger emotion. They are accustomed to dealing with it through intervening buffers: lawyers for the Department of Justice and the regulatory agencies (and their equivalents below the federal level), lobbyists for the legislative branch, and checkbooks (or less visible cash) for the political parties. With few exceptions, they understand neither its organizational structure nor operational process. To the extent that some managers think they comprehend how the machinery works and where the levers of power are located, they are likely to be mistaken. Neither education nor experience has prepared most businessmen to interact confidently and effectively with public bodies. Understandably, those who are aware of their deficiencies are inclined to avoid such relationships.

The kind of knowledge a business leader needs about how the political process works in drafting legislation and formulating administrative rules and procedures at any level of government is not to be found in political science texts, legislation defining agency responsibilities, organization charts, or job descriptions. Only to a limited extent, and only for the broadest policy issues, does the political process of public policy determination operate as if the government or one of its major units were a functioning entity. Nor is it commonly the case, particularly at the federal level, that specific intervention by an individual or a small group interacting with one or a few high officials generates a major influence on complex legislative or administrative action.

The importance of acquiring and using this knowledge is emphasized by the fact that the business interest in and potential contribution to improvements in the quality and equity of societal conditions are very much more likely to be found at the operating than at the policy level. Very few people, managers or others, are disposed to argue today, for example, that it is undesirable to take action to reduce environmental contamination. The policy decision is obvious and, at least superficially considered, simple. The complexities arise when the question is put: what is the most effective and efficient way to reduce how much contamination when? This quickly brings specific problems into view. Is it better to upgrade industrial performance by incentives or by penalties? What cost-benefit trade-offs should be identified along the path to total decontamination? How far will the existing state of the art take us, and what investment should be made in research aimed at developing superior technology? Since many solutions to social ills, like many therapeutic drugs, have undesirable side effects, what accommodation should be made in the mainstream effort to prevent unacceptable ancillary developments? There is probably no arena in which the quality and equity of the human condition can be improved in which questions of this kind are unimportant. They are operational and technical questions, rather than policy questions, and they are best handled by people who have operating and technical competence.

The complexity of the operational and technical aspects of quality-of-life programs explains the dominant role played by supporting staff personnel in both legislative and administrative organizations. Particularly when new legislation or administrative rulings are on the drawing board, staff experts who understand the operational and technical issues and who also enjoy the confidence of members of legislative committees or senior administrative agency officials exert critical influence on what will be done and how it will be done. They formulate standards, select the motivational devices, design the administrative machinery, determine objectives and schedules for their accomplishment. That all of their work is tentative, subject to approval or amendment by superiors, is not a significant qualification. By and large, their proposals emerge relatively unscathed in final legislative or administrative decisions. None of this should be surprising to corporate leaders. It parallels how things work in their own organizations when the problems under attack are novel and the important considerations are understood in depth only by staff experts. The history of the introduction and use of computers in business organizations illustrates this universal experience.

Two points stand out when we consider the business interest in the operational and technical aspects of government intervention in corporate social performance. The first is the large potential contribution the affected businesses can make to the design of legislative and administrative machinery that will accomplish desired results effectively and efficiently. The second is the necessity for business to establish credibility in its good faith so that, when offered, its knowledge and skill will be accepted and used.

The record of production controls in World War II yields persuasive examples of the extent to which the effectiveness of control systems imposed on private industry is directly related to similarities between the control systems and the normal operating and information systems of the affected industries.[1] Controls designed to incorporate maximum feasible conformity with industrial procurement, inventory management, production scheduling, and information recording practices were generally installed rapidly and operated to secure desired results with minimum friction. A control system that compelled an industry to change its accustomed administrative practices radically usually encountered serious delays in attaining operating effectiveness, imposed unnecessary costs on controlled companies, and experienced a high rate of error in record keeping. The history also indicates that industry compliance was considerably better with consonant than with dissonant control systems.

In World War II experienced managers were the best source of information on administrative practices in particular industries. In precisely the same way, experienced managers, in the years ahead, can be the

[1] David Novick, Melvin L. Anshen, and William C. Truppner, *Wartime Production Controls* (New York: Columbia University Press, 1949).

best source of information on the operating and technical issues involved in designing legislative and administrative actions which are aimed at removing or discouraging business behavior that erodes the quality of life and, on the positive side, compelling or encouraging behavior that contributes to societal gains. Operating and technical managers in such historically contaminating industries as steel, chemicals, paper, and electric power know what can be done to reduce or eliminate contamination in terms of both technology and economics. Their experience can also yield constructive ideas about control methodology, standards, and scheduling.

It is in the common interest of business, government, and the whole society that this knowledge be offered and used. Business has nothing to gain—indeed, it has everything to lose—from taking up an adversary position in any situation where the ultimate thrust of social change is clear to an objective observer. With equal logic, it can be stated that government has nothing to lose—and much to gain—from inviting business to contribute its knowledge.

Beyond a recognition of the key role of legislative and administrative staffs in the design of public controls, which leads to the recognition of the importance of establishing working relations at that level, the challenge to corporate leadership is to make its willingness to participate constructively a credible posture. The adversary or minimum-cooperation attitudes that have characterized much of recent business behavior will have to be abandoned. All they have generated is distrust. They fuel the criticism of business performance by antibusiness activists, in addition to encouraging a general lack of confidence in business intentions among millions of citizens who, innocent of knowledge of the cost-benefit balances at stake, simply find it impossible to believe the public statements of many business leaders. In this setting, pronouncements by leaders of the automobile industry about technological and economic constraints on eliminating exhaust pollution, by executives of electric power companies about trade-offs between additions to generating capacity and environmental contamination, by leaders of industries selling commodities for household use about product purity and performance are simply not trusted. Too many in the citizen audience remember earlier business hostility to or silence about these issues.

The worst possible long-range strategy for business is to present itself as opposed to the interests of the society which holds the ultimate power over the terms of business operations. A healthy, growing, prosperous business cannot survive within a hostile social envelope which sees the private interests of business as fundamentally opposed to the public interest as that interest is perceived by a large share of the population.

Since the public interest finds expression through the political process in our democracy, business must meet and serve that interest in social performance in that arena, in addition to serving its customers' wants in the marketplace. To do this well, it will have to achieve an understanding of the political process and an ability to work within it equal to its demonstrated understanding and ability to respond to customers' wants in the marketplace.

Labor Relations in the Socially Responsible Corporation

A. H. Raskin

The acceptance and implementation of corporate social responsibility create substantial challenges and problems for union leadership in its own house, as well as for corporate executives responsible for labor relations. In both areas, traditional ideas and practices will be modified either by independent initiatives taken by imaginative leaders or by social forces acting through the institutions of government.

This chapter examines the areas where change must occur, by option or compulsion, in the context of historic commitments and existing practices.

The author of this chapter, A. H. Raskin, for many years the distinguished labor reporter for The New York Times, *is presently Assistant Editor of the Editorial Page.–*EDITOR

B Y WAY of preface let me acknowledge that my remarks are sure to impress the reader as being somewhat one-sided. If I do not seem to be belaboring corporations with the same vigor I apply to hitting unions over the head, it is not because I feel business has a vast edge over labor in social responsibility. Let me just say that many unions still nurture an atavistic hate-the-boss spirit that militates against leaping at the idea that management walks with God, no matter how unctuous its outer garb. Not all of it is atavism either. The gulf between cant and performance in management remains great, and each new evidence of profit-grubbing or ethical backsliding anywhere in industry confirms all the old prejudices and makes genuine, sustained cooperation for the public good that much harder to achieve.

LABOR VIEWS OF SOCIAL RESPONSIBILITY

George Meany never tires of describing organized labor as "the people's lobby" or "the conscience of America"—the only group in the community that fights indefatigably not only for the wearers of union buttons but for all the nation's millions of helpless and disinherited outside union ranks.

That description is put forward with total sincerity. Regrettably, as with so many similar self-congratulatory expressions by corporate executives, it bears about as much resemblance to reality as the Nixon Administration's current assurances that it is standing 1,000 percent behind the 5.5 percent guidepost for curbing inflationary wage increases. Labor leaders have an infinite capacity for becoming captives of their own hallowed shibboleths long after these have ceased to have much validity. For that reason any discussion of the union role in helping to make corporations more socially responsible must start with some assessment of how socially responsible unions themselves are in their own approach to both the economy and the community.

The sad fact is that much of the idealism and much of the creativity that went into the formation of the mass production unions nearly four decades ago has drained out. It is true that the AFL-CIO remains the most steadfast force lobbying on Capitol Hill for expanded social programs in education, housing, health, mass transit and most of the other things Mr. Meany's new-found soulmate, President Nixon, wants to scale down. But there is a ritualistic quality to its call for things it has been backing since the early New Deal, things for which a rank and file gone middle-class and intensely tax-conscious seems to retain no discernible enthusiasm.

Born as a voice of dissent in industrial society, organized labor has become a mainstay of the status quo in a period when even the staidest organizations—educational, corporate and governmental—have felt obliged to take a critical look at all their most cherished precepts and scrap those made obsolete by changing technology and mores. Its leadership is frozen, its ideas stale, and, to make it all much worse, the smugness which is its worst affliction is currently being aggravated by the vast deference it is receiving from the President and Congress.

That is bad because labor's instincts remain sound, however benighted the occasional abuse of its power or disheartening the rigidity of its approaches to an era of meteoric technological and commercial readjustment. Collective bargaining has become a sterile exercise, a meaningless tug-of-war over illusory wage increases which evaporate before the worker can get to the supermarket to spend them. Yet unions shrink from turning the bargaining table into an instrument for tackling the much more fundamental challenges of worker discontent, which urgently require attention.

This reticence is certainly no expression of humility. The whole history of unionism has been one of pushing out the boundaries of bargaining whenever the union detected a pressing new problem. For a labor movement geared to the sanctity of the "work ethic," no problem ought to have higher priority than the mounting evidence that younger workers—blue-collar and white-collar alike—are becoming increasingly dissatisfied with dull, repetitive, and unchallenging jobs.

LABOR VIEWS OF THE ENTERPRISE SYSTEM

When a special study group of the Department of Health, Education and Welfare issued its recent massive report on how trapped and dehumanized many workers felt and how high was the attendant cost in low productivity, sloppy workmanship, absenteeism, sabotage, and quickie strikes, the reaction of most union leaders was just as negative as the Administration's own. It could be summed up in two words: "Drop dead."

Now there are two easy answers for that reaction. One, quite frankly, is that no union leader has any particularly good idea of what the answer is to boredom and alienation on the job. And not having the answer is a respectable enough reason for not calling everybody out on strike as a way of making them feel that they really are masters of their own destiny and that no boss can push them around. The other explanation, for which I have no sympathy at all, is that many top unionists consider all the talk about the need for relieving the workers' sense of emptiness and frustration as part of an elaborate management speed-up plot, a scheme to get more work out of fewer workers. Without doubting that more efficiency is an obsessive concern of every employer, I nevertheless feel unions have at least as big a stake as management in finding cures for the "blue-collar blues."

I suspect that one major factor in their reluctance even to acknowledge the problem's existence is that the average union chief is at least as conservative as any pillar of the NAM when it comes to crossing the line into worker control over operations of the business, even on such matters of immediate concern to the worker as the design of his job. The conviction is growing that a fundamental rethinking of jobs to make them more human will involve new forms of industrial democracy that may eventually carry American industry almost as far toward co-determination as many enterprises in Western Europe have gone. In West Germany unions are legally guaranteed one-third of the seats on the supervisory boards of all publicly held companies and in coal and steel they have half the seats. The Common Market Commission has recommended extension of that model to all nine countries in the expanded market.

Any such idea is, of course, anathema to American unions. In the words of Jerry Wurf, the somewhat irreverent president of the State, County, and Municipal Workers Union, the thing that distinguishes American unions from any others in the free world is the totality of their acceptance of the capitalist system. When Meany says "ideology is baloney," that is the one ideology he does not reject.

This devotion to the system can sometimes be carried to excess, as it was by the Teamsters and many other groups on the seamier side of unionism in the shenanigans so exhaustively probed by the McClellan Committee fifteen years ago. At that time a learned labor historian, the protean John Dunlop, went before the labor law section of the American Bar Association to put all the rackets into scholarly perspective. He chided not the crooks but the public for expecting the labor movement to measure up to exaggerated standards of moral probity.

> We are proud that our labor unions are strong supporters of *free* private enterprise and admirers of our business system, but in recent days it appears that the community expects labor leaders to be economic celibates, to be a group called out and apart from the rest of the community akin to government employees and the clergy.

So spoke John Dunlop, and he went on:

> It is no accident that "business unionism" became the dominant kind of union organization in the A.F.L. The labor movement found by hard experience that it could not organize and retain members nor could it long survive in the community with a program radical to the basic features of the economic and political system.

In truth, the labor movement to its credit did not embrace so forbearing a doctrine of what should be swallowed under the rubric of adapting to the economic environment, and Jimmy Hoffa, Johnny Dio, Tony

"Ducks" Corrallo, and assorted other free enterprisers were exiled from the House of Labor. That was the AFL-CIO's shining hour, even though Meany and his fellow paladins of the Ethical Practices Committee found that ouster did not strip the pirates of their power—a discovery that has impelled the Federation to keep its shiny suit of moral armor in moth balls, unused for more than a decade.

MAKING JOBS MORE INTERESTING

It will be tragic now if fears of fracturing the no-trespass line into management's preserve seriously inhibit efforts by labor to address itself to the problems of job dissatisfaction. Thus far the most imaginative assaults on the problem—and also the most fruitful—have been made in companies without unions.

One of the most successful cases is Texas Instruments, with headquarters in Dallas and 57,000 employees in forty-four countries. It has been altering the power structure in its plants for fifteen years, with increasing reliance on drawing teams from its production lines and letting them figure out ways to do jobs more efficiently and with greater satisfaction to themselves. In 1967 when the company found that it could not hope to fulfill its delivery of airport surveillance radar on schedule because the research phases of the project had taken too long, it put the problem up to seven hundred employees working in natural teams with their supervisors. The results were so astonishing that the production rate tripled and the customers got a price cut—in addition to getting their radar on time.

This kind of job enlargement through problem solving has given Texas Instruments a productivity improvement rate of 13 percent a year for each of the last three years, far beyond the United States average. And it has been done without any jelly beans in the form of piece rates or suggestion bonuses. However, the company does have a profit-sharing plan, which gave the workers 3.6 percent over their normal earnings last year and which is about to be made more generous. Just to prove that money isn't everything in such plans, officials cite a transistor manufacturing machine that used to require a four-man crew. When the company asked the workers how to make it more productive, they volunteered the idea of eliminating one worker by hanging a magnifying mirror at one position. The others look in the mirror to see if any monitoring is needed at the vacant position, and everything works fine. The displaced worker has been switched to another post.

Another pioneer establishment in this fight against ennui on the job is a General Foods plant making Gravy Train dog food at Topeka, Kansas. When the plant opened two years ago its workers were split into ten-man teams, each with a team leader. Through meetings each team decides how to meet its goals, a scheme so successful that productivity is about 30 percent above expectations and absenteeism is down to one percent. "The guts of the thing," says the plant manager, "is that each man has autonomy to decide how we're going to do things. He shares his problems with his peers."

Perhaps the most radical departure of all has been made by Procter & Gamble, never known for social adventurism, at its highly automated plant in Lima, Ohio, employing 125 people. Charles Krone, the head of organizational development for the huge soap company, told David Jenkins, author of the forthcoming book, *Job Power,* that the plant had been designed from the ground up to be democratic. The basic principle is that every worker has "growthful potential" and that nothing in the physical or organizational structure of the plant should constitute a barrier to such growth.

There are no job classifications and each individual defines the direction in which he wants to grow. They all develop specialties but they also must perform community tasks in day-to-day operating duties. There are no time clocks. The members of the community work out their own salaries and all the salaries are known to everyone. They also work out the plant budget and keep its financial records. The experience is so good that the same system has been installed in most new plants built in recent years. About 10 percent of the 28,000 Procter & Gamble employees are now on this "open system" method.

And when will the unions get around to making some small independent contribution to this effort to humanize the workplace? From the tone of recent comment, their forward movement will not be breathtaking, but it cannot be delayed forever. After all, forty years have passed since Charlie Chaplin immortalized the horrors of the assembly line in "Modern Times." The United Auto Workers came into being largely on the slogan of fighting the brutalizing aspects of the speed-up. As far back as 1964 the union was describing General Motors as a "gold-plated sweatshop." And the 1970 contract negotiations started with 38,800 local grievances littering the bargaining table—these on top of the 250,000 grievances a year processed through the normal grievance machinery.

Two years ago, a 36-year-old black employee at Chrysler's axle plant in Detroit pulled an M-1 carbine out of his trouser leg and went on a shooting spree. "He's firing at everyone in white shirts!" a man alongside him yelled. In a couple of minutes three men were dead: a foreman who had suspended the assassin for insubordination an hour earlier, another foreman, and a job setter. When a union committeeman subdued the killer, he muttered: "They took me off the job I had held for two years and put a man with less seniority in my place." Ten months later a jury found the man innocent by reason of temporary insanity. That judgment was based on two factors: the man's early life as a sharecropper in the South, and the destructive conditions of factory life, including violence, unsafe surroundings, and harassment from the foremen. "Did you see that cement room in the plant?" one juror asked. "Working there would drive anyone crazy."

Malcolm Denise, Ford's vice president for labor relations, made a private talk to management officials three years ago which the union got and circulated widely. It warned that employees in the 1970s would be less and less willing to put up with dirty and uncomfortable working conditions or with the unvarying pace and functions on moving lines. Already, he noted, large numbers of new workers were finding factory life so distasteful that they quit after brief exposure. Yet, with all that long history of awareness that irritation was getting stronger and the reinforcement provided by the recent upheavals in GM's dream plant at Lordstown, Ohio, Leonard Woodcock still says: "If any of the companies suddenly said to the UAW, 'O.K., we agree; we want to humanize the workplace, you do it,' we wouldn't know where to begin."

Fortunately, the union is not being as totally negative on the subject as one might gather from seeing Woodcock take off after "elitist" academics whom he finds guilty of "writing a lot of nonsense" about job enrichment. The union is cooperating with the automobile companies in some small-scale experiments. One involved taking a twenty-three-man team from assembly operations at the General Motors Truck and Coach Division and assigning its members to assemble a truck from scratch. The first truck took twenty-three hours to put together. By pooling their ideas and energies, the group eventually cut the time required to less than two hours. Absenteeism, which had been quite high for some members of the group, dropped almost to zero. Characteristically, nobody on either the union or management side seems to have thought very hard about what would happen to these men when they went back to the same old grind. In Woodcock's words, "they squawked like the devil" when the experiment ended and they returned to conventional assembly techniques.

In general, new approaches adequate to meeting the need for modifying authoritarianism in industry and giving the worker what Professor Chris Argyris of Harvard calls a chance, through his job, to "experience some meaning and fullness, some growth in his life, a chance to grow" will come only when the present generation of septuagenarians and octogenarians in command of labor give way to a new generation.

The trouble even there, however, is that labor believes wholeheartedly in the one-party system so that the leaders coming up are mostly organizational yes-men steeped in the same barren traditions of doing everything the way the founder did it. Labor is not much for duplicating the huge sums industry spends on leadership training. On the contrary, the few unions that did anything ambitious to develop new talent soured on what they got. The saddest case was that of the International Ladies Garment Workers Union, a union with a glorious tradition. Its former president, David Dubinsky, decided twenty years ago that the union needed to go outside its own ranks for future business agents and staff members and draw in idealistic youngsters of the kind who flocked into public service in the early Roosevelt New Deal period. He was very happy with the record of the new training institute until he discovered that some of its graduates were organizing a union of their own to demand better salaries and working conditions from their employer, the ILGWU. In Dubinsky's book, that was turning the union into a business. So he declared war on the new union and finally beat it in the NLRB and the courts. At the same time, he decided the union had all the leaders it needed and closed the institute. It is still closed. The teamsters, of all people, opened a leadership training institute with great fanfare in Florida a few years ago. Early last year Frank Fitzsimmons, the union president, hailed the experiment as a great success. He announced that it would be expanded. A few months later it closed. That leaves the AFL-CIO almost alone in the field. Its Labor Studies Center is completing its fifth year in Washington, but the Federation has to keep nudging its affiliates to get up the money to subsidize scholarships and living expenses for second-line leaders in training.

POTENTIALS FOR UNION LEADERSHIP

The notion that young people have any great competence to straighten out labor or anything else does not rank high in George Meany's list of articles of faith. This is a sample of his thinking, as put forward at a news conference a couple of years ago:

> By what stretch of imagination can you say that a 20-year-old kid knows what is wrong with the world and what should be done about it to a greater extent than a person who has had years of experience? On what basis? Especially when you see the behavior of the kids. There is more venereal disease now among them than there was in my time, and it is going up all the time. There are more of them smoking pot and to say that because they have long beards and they look dirty and smell dirty that they are better qualified to run the world than the older generation, that to me is a lot of baloney.

When he was asked what role he felt young college graduates might play in organized labor, Meany's answer was pretty much the same as the one Samuel Gompers gave when he visited Harvard in 1919. When a law student asked the founder of the AFL what place there was for a college man in labor, Gompers' response was unhesitating. "We don't need any college men in the labor movement," he said. Meany was just a trifle less harsh. He said college men might come in as interns for a year or so. "But," he hastened to add, "there is no place for a great many of them in the trade union movement because we still get our people from the ranks." The place where people who didn't come up out of the shop could fit in, he suggested, was as staff technicians—lawyers, economists, etc.—provided they came from trade union families. That was about all the relaxation of the leadership closed shop he envisaged for men burdened with college degrees.

Unquestionably, Meany, for all his wilfulness, remains at seventy-eight the most astute as well as the most powerful of union leaders. Indeed, he has all but converted the federation into a one-man show. But a new breed of leaders is emerging in the affiliated unions. Among the latest to sweep to the top are Murray Finley of Chicago and Jack Sheinkman of New York, both lawyers, as president and secretary-general respectively of the prestigious Amalgamated Clothing Workers of America. Two lawyers have just been put in crown prince roles in the ILGWU: Sol C. Chaikin as secretary-treasurer and Wilbur Daniels as executive vice-president. In the United Mine Workers the tradition of dictatorial rule fostered by the majestic John L. Lewis has been swept into the slag heap by an astonishing rank-and-file revolution. The new slate headed by Arnold Miller represents living testament to the barnacle-encrusted leadership of other unions that the patience of the rank and file is not inexhaustible, even in the most authoritarian of organizations.

NEW IDEAS FOR WORKER SATISFACTION

When new leaders do take over, they may well elect to move along lines projected by the first of the multinational union leaders, Charles Levinson, secretary general of the International Federation of Chemical and General Workers Unions and a one-time protégé of Victor Reuther. Levinson is convinced that the emergence of multinationals, with their heavy reliance on cash flow for financing their own modernization and expansion, creates a new type of permanent inflation that calls for a changed approach by unions.

Instead of concentrating on higher wages alone, he feels they ought to

foster asset formation for the workers, or, to put it more clearly, the creation of equity and mandatory savings for employees to give them a stake in
the accumulated assets of the industry. As he sees it, the way to keep from
feeding the inflationary spiral by crowding more money into pay envelopes
and thus stimulating a faster leapfrog of wages and prices lies in giving
the worker a share of ownership in lieu of immediate wages.

The worker would build up a reserve of purchasing power as a but-
tress against future recessions or plant closings; there would be a lessened
threat to the democratic process from the enormous capital accumulation
in these private governments and, along with that, a positive gain for democratic process in giving the worker a share in industrial decision making.
When self-financing out of residual cash flow is replacing venture capital
in building up businesses that skip across national lines, there is little social
justice in denying workers a share of the increased equity created by this
trend.

While such a revised version of co-determination would fit in with the
need for giving labor a more active role in job redesign and enrichment,
it gets little encouragement from union leaders on this side of the Atlantic.
They are happier on the familiar merry-go-round of self-cancelling wage
increases, where everyone can keep running faster and faster with certainty
that he will wind up farther and farther behind.

The only innovative contribution to wage theory in major union
agreements was made fully a quarter-century ago by C. E. Wilson, then
president of General Motors, who spent six weeks in bed with a broken
leg and emerged with a "progress sharing" formula that still embodies
more good sense than anything that has come along since. It started with
the theory that automobile workers ought to be assured that their real
wages, in terms of purchasing power after allowance for higher prices and
taxes, would go up by 3 percent in line with the long-term growth in national productivity. So he combined a cost-of-living escalator with a fixed
annual improvement factor of 3 percent, and the United Auto Workers
accepted the principle—though in practice it loaded up the formula with
so many fringes that it became a jumping-off point much more than a
standard.

Yet, in one fashion or another, the Wilson formula remains the root
of most computations of basic wages, despite the frequency with which
strikes dislocate the economy, inflicting heavier damage on the community
than on the warring parties. At the beginning of this year, when Phase
Two wage-price controls were doing quite well at holding pay settlements
close to a Wilson-type guidepost of 5.5 percent (made up of 3 percent for
productivity and 2.5 percent to cover the President's inflation target),
George Meany did a skillful but hardly socially beneficial sales job of

persuading Treasury Secretary Shultz and the President that mandatory controls ought to be dropped because they were making a charade of collective bargaining—as if the leapfrog that preceded controls had not been an even more ludicrous charade.

At a series of summit meetings on the golf course at Augusta, Georgia, Meany kept hammering away at a single theme in his efforts to convert a not-too-reluctant Shultz. "You can't tell me that it's real bargaining when our people get across the table from management and the first thing they hear is, 'It's 5.5 percent; that's all you can get, no matter what arguments you put forward.' " After that pitch resulted in the premature demolition of Phase Two, Woodcock delivered the other half of the one-two punch inside the President's ten-man labor-management advisory committee, which was supposed to set some kind of meaningful rules for this never-never land of statutory jawboning. "The trouble with giving the number so much prominence," he said, never cracking a smile, "is that when we come back with 5.5 percent in wages—plus the extra seven-tenths of one percent in allowable fringe—which, in my book, is a damn good increase, our members say: 'What did you guys get for us? Nothing.' " All the moguls of industry seated around the table solemnly agree that it is a shame—the ceiling has now become the floor and a lot of people must be getting away with murder. No sooner had that "con job" been concluded than all the union leaders preparing for this year's heavy bargaining calendar announced that they would be expecting a lot more than 5.5 percent. What with food prices going wild, nobody even hinted at taking less. In fact, Meany himself led the parade in declaring that nothing short of 7.5 or 8 percent could give workers an adequate shield against the runaway cost of living.

Now the only thing wrong with that approach is that, in the end, the ones who get hurt most by the erosion and probable collapse of controls—even controls that leave out the most basic element in the family budget —are the workers, especially the sixty million or so who are not in unions and the millions of retired people living on fixed incomes. Under Phase One and Phase Two, for the first time in five years, workers were coming out ahead in terms of what their pay envelopes could buy. Secretary Shultz may be right in believing that Phase Two would have run out of steam any day now if the President had not stuck a pin in it first. Shultz told the members of the dismantled Pay Board at a jolly farewell party in Washington, "You guys wouldn't have been nearly this happy if we had kept your board alive and you were holding this party a year from now."

But the reality is that, once the clamps are taken off, especially with workers and their wives in a state of panic over the runaway cost of eating, each union leader has to outdo the one before, and we are all right back in the squirrel cage, wondering when we have to buy a wheelbarrow to hold all that worthless money. What I find incomprehensible is why, if unionists still see something evil in stock ownership, profit sharing, or other departures from the present empty procedure, they do not press instead for a change that would really make sense: a switch away from the present demeaning practice of paying production and maintenance employees by the hour. How much better to put them on the same kind of weekly salary basis that has long been standard for white-collar, professional, and supervisory employees.

The wall separating those with status from those without it went up at the start of the Industrial Revolution, when the hourly wage and the piece-rate system made explicit the concept of labor as a commodity to be sold by the clock. Even if Congress had not outlawed that concept in the Clayton Antitrust Act a half-century ago, it would be archaic at a time when millions of blue-collar workers are owners of suburban homes, cars, motorboats, even swimming pools.

Seven years have gone by since President Johnson's National Commission on Technology, Automation, and Economic Progress gave the drive for putting everyone on salary a powerful push by declaring that continuance of the present double standard reinforces a "status distinction and social stigma." The Commission's fourteen members—union heads, presidents of large companies, educators, and civil rights leaders—unanimously observed: "We see little justice in a system whereby a production worker is laid off or works 'short weeks' when the schedule so dictates, while office workers and clerks receive full salaries, whatever the flow of work."

For most workers in strongly unionized industries, the transformation of pay structures could be effected with no profound upheaval in practices that have been emerging since World War II. Collective bargaining already has erased collar color as a qualifying factor in access to pensions, vacations, company-financed insurance programs, and other perquisites once reserved for executives and office employes.

The trend toward leveling the divide between blue-collar and white-collar treatment has penetrated the pay envelope through supplemental unemployment benefits and related income guarantees. These now assure workers in most basic industries 85 to 95 percent of their normal weekly take-home pay for a full year after layoff. That type of security goes even further on the Atlantic and Gulf docks, where regular longshoremen draw at least two thousand hours pay a year, whether or not they ever unload a ship.

But for all the multiplicity of such full-pay assurances in periods of joblessness, the direct breakthroughs on the blue-collar salary front remain largely confined to companies that have no unions at all. The biggest is International Business Machines which decided as long ago as 1958 to abolish hourly wages for its factory employees and give them salaries just like everyone else at IBM. In the unionized plants the old sham battle for the buck continues its pointless and degrading whirl. The sense of being storm-tossed orphans in a polarized and dehumanized society that now drives so many workers into the arms of Governor Wallace and other demagogues might be greatly eased if the dual wage system went down the drain.

AN END TO STRIKES

Right alongside the slackness of the present union response to the meaningful aspects of worker attitude and wage determination, both crucial elements in a socially responsible economy, I would put the continued overdependence on strikes. Meany himself is the first to concede that strikes may be nearing the point of overkill, even though he remains as resolute as ever in his conviction that any legal deprivation of the right to strike is an abridgement on union freedom. "We find more and more," Meany has said, "that strikes don't settle a thing. Actually, we are getting more and more to the point where you have a well-established industry and a well-established union, you are getting more and more to the point where a strike doesn't make sense."

Incontestable as that estimate is in terms of the large number of strikes that degenerate into stylized kibuki dances, with the parties not really sore at one another and the public being toasted on the sacrificial pyre, the process of designing rational substitutes for the strike is proceeding with painful slowness. The American Arbitration Association launched a quiet effort four or five years ago, with Meany's blessing and with encouragement from many top industrialists, to get labor and management in some key industries to accept voluntary arbitration as a device for resolving disputes over the terms of new contracts. That is just what both sides have been doing in 90 percent of unionized industry ever since V-J Day on disputes arising out of the terms of existing contracts. But taking the next step is always reported just around the corner but never quite there.

Not surprisingly, the industries where the chances are considered brightest are both industries that have suffered through so many strikes and so many bouts of cost-push inflation that they are in shaky financial condition. The first is the merchant marine, just short of total shipwreck as a result of two decades of freebooting by operators and unions who felt subsidies for building ships and making up the differential between deep-sea wages and those of foreign crews would always keep them afloat. American-flag passenger ships are now virtually extinct, and container ships and tankers are the mainstays of the commercial fleet. Soviet grain shipments and an accompanying political deal to use American ships for about a third of it have helped bring a little flush of prosperity to the industry at heavy cost to the taxpayers. But the unions, with the longshoremen as the improbable whip cracker for a peace agreement, recognize that more strikes would be a disaster. The ship operators reached that conclusion long ago. Somehow, however, all the third-party efforts of the AAA have not quite brought both sides to an arbitration commitment.

The other prime prospect is steel, now worried over the fact that imports account for one-sixth of all current steel sales in this country. With its foreign competitors moving up in efficiency, the industry and the United Steelworkers of America have been cooperating on joint efforts to ease restrictive work rules and heighten productivity. They are also cooperating with the AAA on an arbitration approach for future contract disputes, but the union is skittish about sponsoring any specific idea with its membership. That is partly because the present union leadership, headed by I. W. Abel, came to office by discrediting the ambitious joint machinery the industry and the steelworkers had created after their disastrous 116-day strike in 1959. This so-called Human Relations Committee had been conceived as a device for joint solution of mutual problems, with the hope that it would become a vehicle for averting future tests of strength. Too much secrecy about what went on behind its closed doors made it a sitting duck for extinction in a palace revolution within the union.

Another deterrent to overexuberance by the present union leadership is that an even more widely touted mechanism for industrial peace created in steel after the 1959 strike is currently encountering heavy difficulties. This is the tripartite Long-Range Sharing Committee at Kaiser Steel's big mill in Fontana, California. With three of the country's best known neutrals as public members—David Cole, John Dunlop, and the late George Taylor—its goal was to eliminate unscientific incentive plans of the kind common in basic steel in favor of a plan that would give all the workers— production, maintenance, and clerical—a tangible cash stake in promoting automation at the plant. The plan was popular while the benefits were high, but emergency surgery had to be done every couple of years to keep rank-and-file dissidents from upsetting it. Last year, insurgents shut the mill down for six weeks in an effort to kill the plan and substitute a conventional incentive system. The international was loath to intervene, but the strike finally limped to a close with the sharing plan somewhat battered but still hanging by a hair. The probability is that it will be reconstituted as a

purely local effort, but hope that it would represent a brave new answer to
the elimination of strikes over technological change is gone.

One of the most durable of these plans for joint adjustment to new
technology is the Armour Automation Committee, established in 1959 by
Armour and the meat unions at a time when shifts in the technology of
meat packing were causing wholesale shifts in the location of packing
houses and in the skills required in them. Clark Kerr, whom you remember from his days at Berkeley, has been chairman from the outset. George
Shultz, now the Secretary of the Treasury and chief economic mogul for
the President, was co-chairman for a half-dozen years. It did some genuinely outstanding work in resettling workers, retraining them, and providing various cushions for those no longer needed in meat packing. An
initial grant of only $500,000 by the company took care of all the bills for
six or seven years. Since then, not more than $100,000 additional has
been put in by the employer. Rarely has so much been accomplished for
so little in maintaining human dignity and promoting harmonious relations.

Perhaps two other outstanding achievements in handling grievances in
a way that liquidated a vast accumulation of human discontent are worth
mentioning. David Cole played a leading role in both of them. One was at
International Harvester where 8,800 grievances had piled up awaiting arbitration, a backlog that would have taken Cole a half-century to dispose
of even if no new cases came in. Wildcat strikes were a daily occurrence
and production standards were plummeting. The UAW and the company
worked so well with Cole that the procedure was streamlined; the parties
cut down the backlog to virtually zero on the basis of information sugges-
tions from Cole, as distinct from written arbitration awards, and their relationship improved to a point where Harvester went for eighteen months
without a single new case going to arbitration. Strikes vanished; quality
zoomed.

The other big turnaround came at Inland Steel where Joseph Block,
then the company's chairman, and William Caples, its industrial relations
vice president, decided Cole ought to be called in to overhaul the grievance
machinery. Through constant meetings with two hundred union commit-
teemen and a comparable number of second-level supervisors, he got the
process squared away. Grievances and strikes went way down; efficiency
went up. A dozen years later the system is still working so well that a joint
survey committee set up by the union and the basic steel producers put Inland at the top in maintaining sound relations with its employees. The
whole experience may be one reason for Block's decision in 1962 to part
company with Roger Blough of U.S. Steel and the rest of the industry in
the companies' abortive price confrontation with President Kennedy.

OTHER UNION INTERESTS IN SOCIAL ISSUES

I mention all these things because I believe they have a direct bearing on corporate and union social responsibility, not just on the efficiency and profitability of the business. In those areas that are outside the immediate intraindustry relationship, the union record is mixed but generally weak. Again I except the legislative realm, where labor does consistently back programs not only in Congress but in state and local law-making bodies that do embody its idea of a better society—most of them lineal descendants of the original New Deal as updated by Harry Truman, Lyndon Johnson, and John Kennedy, but rarely containing any distinctive labor twists that are not narrowly concerned with wages, jobs, or labor laws. The killing of President Nixon's emergency strike law for arbitration of transportation disputes as part of a 1972 pre-election deal was one of the less salutary exhibitions of labor's political clout. The inclusion, through Meany's insistence, of the equal employment opportunities provisions in the Civil Rights Act of 1964 was a more wholesome one.

In the realm of industrial reform, Leonard Woodcock's first act after becoming president of the UAW to succeeding Walter Reuther, was to go to the General Motors annual meeting and support the proposal of the Project on Corporate Responsibility for expansion of the corporation's board to include a special review committee for corporate responsibility. He likened the idea to the UAW's own admirable Public Review Board, which has the right to overrule the union's international officers on matters relating to ethical practices and the democratic rights of members.

At the 1971 annual meeting of General Motors, Irving Bluestone, head of the union's General Motors department, spoke in favor of another Campaign G.M. proposal for full disclosure of the company's expenditures on antipollution and safety devices. His speech brought up echoes of Walter Reuther's famous call for a "look at the books" in the UAW's big postwar confrontation with G.M. in 1945–6. But Bluestone stressed that he was not interested in "tarnishing G.M.'s image in the eyes of the public." He added: "The workers we represent hold their jobs in G.M. and we want those workers to have security in those jobs. But full and frank and detailed disclosure as called for in this proposal would make sense for General Motors and it would make sense for the nation as a whole."

Ralph Nader, who is a bit interested in this kind of thing, finds that on environmental and consumer issues the unions have an inferiority complex as against management—something they rarely exhibit at the bargaining table, where they are accustomed to walk like lions. The unions don't have at the headquarters level in Washington anything like enough scientists or technicians to arm them with the necessary facts for governmental hearings or representations to the company.

Thus, in Nader's view, the paper mill unions swallow uncritically the industry line on the job-killing potentialities of wastes dumped in lakes and streams. The steelworkers fight state laws to put 5-cent deposits on tin or glass beverage containers as a means of discouraging disposable containers. Meany himself joins the fight by declaring that laws banning nonreturnable bottles ban jobs, not litter.

The giant Teamsters Union is among the worst in exhibiting unconcern about environmental or safety issues. Not only is it for paving all the countryside with superhighways, but it gives the back of the hand to pressure moves for tighter safety rules on trucks that would be of enormous benefit to its two million members. Nader says it leaves it up to a struggling little group called PROD, with three or four hundred Washington-area truck drivers as supporters and a single lawyer as staff, to press before the ICC and the Department of Transportation's Bureau of Motor Carrier Safety for better inspection of brakes and safer design of trucks and cabs. These lonely crusaders fight merciless schedules that call for as much as eighty hours a week on the road, with the official union attitude one of indifference, opposition, and often outright ridicule.

By contrast, the Oil, Chemical and Atomic Workers has formed a close working relationship with environmental groups on pipelines, oil dumping at sea, and pollution from refineries. When Union Carbide warned that it could comply with federal air pollution regulations only by laying off 625 workers at a Marietta, Ohio, plant, OCAW refused to join with the company in a plea for relaxation of the standards. In the end, the company backed down. That is one reason many of the major defenders of the environment backed the union when it called a strike against Shell Oil to protest against the company's refusal to agree to a joint committee to police occupational health and safety standards at Shell refineries. Eleven other companies had already agreed to such committees.

Even earlier on the scene in creating joint contractual machinery to advance occupational health and safety was the United Rubber Workers in its contract with Goodyear just about the time the tough new federal safety law was passed in 1970. Experts from the Harvard Medical School were brought in to survey health conditions in the fume-laden tire plants. The same kind of policing machinery is now general in rubber. In both the United Rubber Workers and the Oil, Chemical and Atomic Workers contracts, one of the ideas behind the joint committees is that, if toxic substances are present in oil refineries or rubber plants, they are likely to be spreading outside plant walls to neighboring communities. In any event, the plain right of workers to demand the safest and healthiest on-the-job conditions leaves no doubt that this is a perfect area for direct involvement in decision making.

The UAW dragged its feet in the early days of Nader's pressure for greater emphasis on automobile safety and only came up with supporting testimony in the closing days of the House committee hearings. However, its recent record in such matters has been exemplary. Nader himself was thrilled to get a transcript of a 1968 speech Walter Reuther delivered before the International Metalworkers Federation in Milan, Italy. "People tell me, 'You ought to be for more cars because it means more jobs for your members.' I'm not for more cars. We've got so many cars now that they're choking our cities and poisoning the lungs of our people."

The UAW under Woodcock did support the Big Three automobile makers in their petition for an exemption from the antitrust laws so that they could pool their research on emission pollutants in hope of meeting the 1975 standards set by the Clean Air Act. The Justice Department turned down the plea. Now Woodcock is saying that he doesn't know where hysteria ends and fact begins in some of the talk about pollution hazards. That leads to some expectation that he may support the automobile makers in their current attempts to postpone the Clean Air Act deadlines. However, the fact that the Wankel-powered Mazda has already qualified might make the union decide that the right thing for the industry is to try harder, not press the postponement button.

The Amalgamated Meat Cutters was in the forefront of the Congressional battle for a strict federal meat inspection law. It has also been doing the same for poultry. Paul Jennings of the International Union of Electrical Workers has told his members that it is not enough for them to be concerned about in-plant protection against the health hazards of radiation from the color television sets they manufacture. He says they have to be just as concerned about the effect of deadly X-rays on the consumer. That brings up a troublesome problem in industrial ethics posed by Nader. He wants plant workers and, particularly, industrial scientists to "blow the whistle" on health or safety flaws in the products their companies make. Most industrialists consider this a form of industrial espionage, not to say treason, that brings Big Brother right into the plant. But Jennings takes the Nader view that, as a matter of policy, union members should act forthrightly whenever they are aware that they are producing items that are unsafe.

Their first obligation, as the I.U.E. head sees it, is to go to management and inform it that the product is unsafe. But if no timely corrective action is taken their obligation is to tell the public that "we are making and selling an unsafe product." That goes, according to Jennings, even when the making of the product involves no direct risk to the worker. "The worker, through his union, has the right and responsibility to make sure that all products offered are always safe to the consumer," says this AFL-CIO vice president.

A thousand other aspects of union activity in running employer-financed day-care centers, financing legal aid services for members, and sponsoring consumer clinics deserve mention. Unions have become a driving force in the financing of community chests, once a Lady Bountiful pursuit of the rich. Roughly one-third of the money raised through United Fund drives for support of voluntary hospitals and other social agencies—an estimated $400 million a year—is contributed by union members. Labor has also played a useful role in helping to reorganize Better Business Bureaus to make them a more effective force for building consumer confidence in commercial enterprises. One might also identify some interesting and occasionally short-lived joint efforts at underwriting foundations in such fields as automation, manpower training, and collective bargaining and, most interesting of all, in the economics of distribution—a virtuous project that died stillborn as a result of the McClellan hearings into Teamster corruption.

Let me conclude, however, by getting back to the need for joint decision making to resolve not only the immediate discontents of the domestic workplace, but also to tackle the special problems created by the multinationals. Unfortunately, Meany seems to be going out of his way these days to sever the needed links between American and European labor in establishing some counterweight to these new quasi-governments. A principal founder of the International Confederation of Free Trade Unions in 1949, he has all but destroyed his own baby. The reasons are rooted in personality and politics, but it is melancholy to report that at the 1973 midwinter council meeting of the AFL-CIO in Florida he wrote off the ICFTU as useless and said that he saw no role for American labor in it. Just to make things worse, he declared himself "absolutely and completely" in disagreement with the British Trades Union Congress, a declaration he made while Victor Feather and other fraternal delegates from the TUC sat in the room open-mouthed. What irked Meany was a British decision to join what he chose to call a "Moscow-London axis." Their specific offense was a plan drawn up in anticipation of the expansion of the Common Market to its new nine-country membership, for a federation to link up all the major labor organizations in all nine countries. This would necessarily take in such left-wing movements as the CGT in France and the CGIL in Italy. Eventually, it might stretch out to take in labor from the Soviet Union and Eastern Europe, though that is still unsure. Meany rightly considers all these unions arms of the state; he not so rightly believes that it is a defamation of free trade union principles for Western unions even to talk to the Communist unions. "We don't buy it," was his farewell kick in the pants to the British. Many as are Meany's virtues, this arrogance in dealing with the rest of world labor is not among them. It is one of the reasons why I believe we are going to have to see a top-level change before labor exerts its enormous potential for effective and responsible social change.

Editor's Commentary

One additional aspect of labor's role in the socially responsible corporation needs to be identified. This is the relation of the union as a source of power and of the contracts it negotiates and helps to administer as a structure of rights and privileges, on one side, to the practice of full racial, sexual, and ethnic equality throughout the work experience in hiring, job assignment, promotion, and benefits, on the other side. While the primary social responsibility for initiating the policy commitment to equal opportunity is management's, union leaders have a related social responsibility to support the implementation of the policy. If they fail this responsibility—because of hostility grounded in prejudice, or because of indifference or political cowardice—the accomplishment of the essential social goal will be difficult and slow.

The performance of union leadership in this critical area to date is mixed. It ranges from full commitment and support, as in the case of the United Automobile Workers, to almost total opposition, as in the case of some building trades unions. Between these extremes, the record shows every variety of positive and negative response to one of the great current challenges to our society to convert the theory of American democracy into everyday practice. Imaginative and determined management can make progress toward the equal opportunity goal in the absence of cooperation across the bargaining table and in the administration of management-labor relations under an ongoing contract. Recalcitrant union leadership can create some very tough problems, however, and may also, possibly inadvertently, compel the entry of government in ways that are not in the long-run interest of either management or labor.

The problems created for the union leader by equal opportunity are not simple; in some ways, indeed, they are more difficult and resistant to solution than those confronting the corporate executive. In addition to the personal issues of individual social and moral values, which union leader and business executive share and must resolve for themselves, the union, unlike the corporation, is a political institution in concept and often in practice. A corporate chief executive can make a policy decision and insist on its execution. He may have to work hard and ingeniously at assuring that execution throughout a large, complex organization. But he has ultimate authority to compel obedience, however undesirable it may be for him to secure obedience by force.

The power of removal of the chief executive rests with the board of directors, not with the executive's subordinates. The union leader, in contrast, is an elected official and the power to bring about his removal is held ultimately by the union members. In many unions, of course, democracy is more praised than practiced, and the organization structure and operations are skillfully designed to protect the leadership against insurgencies from below. Even in these authoritarian structures, nevertheless, the leadership position is strengthened by assuring a continuing flow of economic and social benefits for the members and demonstrating sympathetic understanding of their needs, desires, and fears.

It is not easy, therefore, for a union leader to take up a policy position that many of his rank and file will view as contrary to their interests. By this action he may be inviting insurgent challengers who will seize the political opportunity to advance their own careers. To add to the complexity of the matter, in a number of industries, long-established management-labor practice, usually informally agreed to but sometimes incorporated by indirection in formal written contracts, has permitted and even endorsed racial, ethnic, or sexual discrimination. What is at stake, therefore, in creating full equal employment opportunity is more than an intrusion on folkways, although this can be a serious enough matter. It is a direct threat to vested economic interests, than which few issues are more serious for most people.

And yet there is another side to the issue that union leaders would be well advised to consider seriously. Just as American society is moving toward the development of ideas about the role and responsibility of business which may be described as a new social contract for business, in the same way and for the same reasons new ideas are pushing forward that bear on the role and responsibility of unions. The old social contract for business was, by indirection, also a social contract for unions. The reality of this proposition is fully documented by the overwhelming support of the capitalistic enterprise system by American union leadership and the absence from the American scene of radical unionism of the kind seen in Europe. If powerful forces in our society demand, as they are now doing with growing insistence, socially responsible performance by corporations, they will demand comparable performance by unions.

Partially hidden today because the spotlight is on business response to social needs, union performance will quickly command attention if evidence appears that obduracy on the union side stands in the way of equal employment opportunity, as it clearly does in a few industries. The business-oriented posture of union leadership will compel a common position with business in response to social pressure. Just as it can be argued persuasively that opposition by corporate leaders to the demands of a changing society can result only in increased social control by government and a corresponding reduction in corporate freedom, the case is equally strong that union opposition will lead to restriction of union independence. Our society will not accept one set of rules for business behavior and another set for union behavior. Business and labor have too many interests in common; they are viewed, in the last analysis, as possessing mutual, not adversary, concerns.

A particularly difficult problem is raised by demands that equal employment opportunity (not limited to the hiring desk, but extending through work assignments and promotion practices) be established retroactively. Business and labor are asked to do more than behave equitably from now on. The demand is to practice inequality of employment by discriminating in reverse until the ratios of racial, sexual, and ethnic origin of today's labor force are reflected in each corporate employee roster. This is going to be a hard standard for many of our citizens to accept. But it is probably going to be the practice they will have to accept, at least by discriminating in favor of the previously disadvantaged in every choice situation where candidates for hiring or promotion are otherwise equally qualified for selection. The population arithmetic demonstrates with compelling power that only in this way can we achieve fully equal employment within the working life of today's labor force. One may well conclude that this is about the limit of the peaceful patience of the presently disadvantaged among us. They are struggling not only to make a better world for their children. They want it for themselves.

Union leaders must face the same hard lesson that business leaders confront. Part of the responsibility of leadership, in some critical situations, is to lead their members by education and motivation. If they see the issue clearly, they will join management in this common task of working to make equal employment opportunity a reality in this generation. They have a credibility in this area—by virtue of their position—that management lacks. If they commit that credibility to the task, they will assist in preserving an enterprise system in which they and their members have as vital a stake as management.

There is an alternative. Together with laggard management in some organized industries, union leaders can try to resist the moving social tide and pander to their own worst instincts and those of a fraction of their more articulate members. Two results are likely to follow. The first is direct government intervention by the Department of Labor and the Equal Employment Opportunity Commission under present and supplemental legislation—and parallel actions at state and local levels. This is no chancy prediction. It is already happening. Some union leaders of limited vision might be inclined to welcome this development on the ground that a power greater than themselves has compelled a development they were unable to prevent.

Before they are totally seduced by the political attractions of this outcome, however, they would do well to consider the almost certain accompanying result: formation of competitive unions that will splinter the base of established labor organizations and erode the power of their leadership. Among senior labor leaders approaching retirement, the thought of "après moi le déluge" may have its attractions. Surely those in the "middle management" ranks of union leadership might entertain a different outlook.

Corporate management has an important stake in the decisions of union leadership in this area. Since they can execute the socially responsible policy of equal employment opportunity much more easily and quickly with the cooperation of union leadership than in its absence, and surely than in the presence of its open opposition, corporate management should openly solicit that cooperation. Together they can help to preserve a set of institutions by accommodation to a changing society. The alternative is not attractive to either.[1]

---

[1] The significance of these observations is emphasized by an agreement concluded early in 1973 by the American Telephone and Telegraph Company, the United States Department of Labor, and the Equal Employment Opportunity Commission. Under the agreement, AT&T and its subsidiaries are committed to make total lump-sum payments of $15 million to 13,000 women and 2,000 male members of minority groups who suffered alleged job discrimination. Immediate pay increases aggregating $23 million are being made to some 36,000 workers whose advancement may have been constrained by discrimination. The Bell System is also committed to further corrective wage increases costing $25 million to $35 million annually for the next five years. Beyond this, the company has agreed to alter its practices for hiring, promoting, and transferring employees; to establish goals and schedules within each of seven hundred geographic areas for upgrading female and minority employees; and to end sex stereotypes associated with specific jobs, such as operators and maintenance workers. The EEOC has also filed discrimination suits against a number of other major corporations and trade unions.

The Public Relations Function in the Socially Responsible Corporation

Harold Burson

The role of the public relations officer in the socially responsible corporation will be radically transformed from his traditional function. From serving as reporter and interpreter of corporate policies and actions to selected external audiences, this officer must enlarge his responsibilities to include an even more important function; interpreter of the social environment to the corporation's leaders. In fulfilling this responsibility, he will contribute to and participate in the formulation of major corporate policies and programs. These new demands will call for knowledge and skills that have been minor, even negligible, requisites for effective execution of traditional public relations assignments.

Chapter 12 examines the new public relations responsibilities and opportunities and proposes ways and means for their effective implementation.

Harold Burson, the author of this chapter, is Chairman of Burson-Marsteller, one of the world's largest public relations organizations, and Treasurer of its parent company, Marsteller Inc., an international advertising and public relations agency.–EDITOR

D OES ANYBODY remember Mrs. Jellyby?
  She is one of Charles Dickens' most memorable characters. She
ives—and that is the right word for it—in Dickens' novel *Bleak House.*
Today, someone might describe Mrs. Jellyby as a "do-gooder." There
wasn't a worthy cause anywhere that she didn't espouse. And the farther
he injustice from home, the greater her concern.

  When Mrs. Jellyby first appears in the novel, we find her totally ab-
sorbed in the plight of the natives of Boorie-goola-Gha, who, Dickens tells
us, lived on the left bank of the Niger River. Mrs. Jellyby called her concern with the natives' problems her "African project"—and it occupied all
her time.

  Then Dickens shows us the state of Mrs. Jellyby's personal affairs.
Her house is strewn with rubbish, the furniture is covered with dust. Her
children are totally neglected. Her son has got his head stuck between the
banisters of the stairs. She doesn't seem to notice. Because, you see, Mrs.
Jellyby is worrying about the Boorie-goola-Gha!

  More than a hundred years ago Dickens was putting at least one
aspect of social responsibility into proper—and satiric—perspective. He
was poking fun at a kind of social responsibility he called "telescopic
philanthropy." Mrs. Jellyby (and, perhaps, Dickens was saying, Victorian
England also) could see only the problems that were far away, not the
ones close to home.

  Dickens' portrait of Mrs. Jellyby was, of course, greatly overdrawn.
But it makes a point that applies to the relationship between public relations and corporate responsibility. I do not by any means suggest that the
lesson of Mrs. Jellyby applies to modern social critics and reformers, self-
appointed or otherwise. But it might apply to *some* of them. And I do
not suggest, either, that Mrs. Jellyby is related to any modern corporate
executives, although there may be just a bit of kinship there—especially as
it involves some types of corporate response to social problems and issues.

PRIMARY CORPORATE RESPONSIBILITIES

  A corporation's first duty, as I see it, is to manage its own affairs
properly and profitably. That is the greatest service it can perform. A
corporation has a duty to compensate its employees and reward its investors to the best of its ability. It has a duty to create favorable working
conditions, and to produce goods and services that meet the highest tests of
safety and reliability.

  This is not an assertion that good management is the answer to all our social woes. Simply, it puts the proposition that a poorly managed company can't make up for its inadequacies with good deeds that have no bearing upon its daily operations. It is socially useful for a corporation to support educational institutions or cultural activities ranging from symphony to ballet. A company ought to be congratulated for making a sizable contribution to the local hospital or the United Way. It deserves accolades for putting Shakespeare on television, either on public broadcasting or on a commercial network. All these good works demonstrate a concern that goes over and beyond what is often derogatorily described as "merely making a profit."

Not one of these activities, however, identifies the truly socially responsible corporation. Moreover, not one of these activities faces up to current issues of broad-based social concern. No demonstrations have been mounted (so far) against corporations that have decided *not* to support the opera or build playgrounds. But there have been innumerable demonstrations against corporations that have not moved quickly enough in hiring members of minority groups, promoting women to managerial positions, or installing pollution abatement equipment.

The point is this: a company that engages in visible good works may not be any more socially responsible than Mrs. Jellyby. A corporation isn't socially responsible because it supports artists by hanging their paintings in its lobby or displaying their sculptures on its lawn. To be truly responsible, a corporation must do something more than practice "telescopic philanthropy."

THE PUBLIC RELATIONS FUNCTION

There are a lot of misconceptions about public relations. One of the most prominent is the notion that public relations is the substitution of imagery for substantive acts. Another is that public relations people try to create a climate that will enable corporations to do whatever they damn well please. These views, of course, are quite wrong. One of the prime functions of the professional public relations practitioner is to act as mediator between the corporation and the society.

The public relations executive provides a qualitative evaluation of social trends. He helps formulate policies that will enable a corporation to adapt to these trends. And he communicates—both internally and externally —the reasons for those policies. Public relations is involved in all the steps —from analysis through action to communications—a corporation must take to meet its obligations to the public. And those obligations are numerous and constantly changing.

Since trends and change are so closely involved, trying to define a socially responsible corporation is like trying to define a socially responsible citizen. Although we find it hard to come up with a dictionary definition ahead of time, we know one when we see one. In any case, definitions are not important. What is important is the in-depth relationship between public relations and social responsibility.

I plan, first, to discuss the nature of the corporation: what it is and what we can rightfully expect from it. We don't, after all, condemn the automobile because it doesn't fly. And so we shouldn't condemn the corporation if it doesn't do everything we might want it to. But the corporation, like the automobile, is still quite a flexible entity. We can modify it and add extras so that it will work for us in many ways.

Then I will discuss some of the new pressures that are being applied to the corporation to make it change. In this respect, I plan to emphasize two aspects of our contemporary society: the profound and growing conflict between individual and institutional rights, and the compression of time.

Finally, I will indicate how these social phenomena affect the role of the public relations executive as he tries to mediate between the corporation and the total society.

THE CORPORATION AS AN INSTITUTION

The first and perhaps most obvious point to be made is that the corporation is a conservative institution. It isn't to be found at the head of reform movements, and indeed it shouldn't be. It wasn't created to reshape society. It was created to produce the goods and services people want and need. That, traditionally, has been its mandate. Until recently, the public did not look to the corporation for much more.

The corporation is not a moralist by nature; it is an activist. The people who work for it and manage it are usually governed by one overriding impulse; they like to get things done. Consequently, it would be silly to condemn the corporation for not taking a leadership position in reforming society. It is difficult, if not impossible, to be a dedicated salesman one minute and a dedicated social reformer the next. They are not the same kind of men at all.

The pressure for change, then, must come from outside the corporation. Indeed, in a pluralistic society such as ours, there are institutions far better equipped than corporations to serve as social critics. Churches, universities, government agencies, even protest groups formed by the people themselves are far more suited to make value judgments about social goals —and to seek to implement them.

Institutions that help maintain the status quo have their place, too. They provide for stability and continuity and conservancy. Corporations, no matter how ponderous, must adapt to both types of pressure. They need built-in sensing devices that can detect changes in the social winds. The job of detecting those changes and charting a new course belongs to the public relations professional. The real measure of a corporation is not whether it has organized itself to lead, but whether it has organized itself to *respond* to social change.

Corporations are diverse in capability and background. They have a wide range of attributes. Indeed, the wider the range, the greater the enrichment of our society. Where diversity exists, so must tolerance. No corporation has a monopoly on virtue. No corporation has a monopoly on sin. This being the case, an examination of their performance ought to avoid absolute judgments.

We cannot, and probably should not, try to develop a list of "Thou shalt nots!" applicable to all companies in all situations. Judgments must be made in context. It is very easy to say, for example: "Thou shalt not pollute!" But such an all-encompassing dictum may be damaging. It is much more difficult to say: "We find, in your case, that we can tolerate x amount of emissions, provided you do thus and so." Such a relative standard may be beneficial to both the corporation and its plant community.

We can say that corporations have the capacity for responsible and irresponsible acts, and sometimes they can behave both ways at the same time. There are companies that have excellent pollution abatement programs, but have done little about minority employment. There are companies that are strong on product purity and weak on occupational health. There are companies that are responsive to a broad spectrum of current social needs, and others that have to be dragged screaming into contemporary society.

In short, corporations have the same capacity for contradiction and paradox as people. We might carry the analogy even further and say that the corporation, contrary to popular conception, is a collection of flesh-and-blood people. The corporation can't feel, think, or act, even though you can sue it or hale it into court. Only people can be sentient. Only people can be responsible. A corporation run by responsible managers will be a responsible corporation. A corporation run by irresponsible managers will be an irresponsible corporation.

Henry David Thoreau summed it up simply and pointedly in his essay on Civil Disobedience: "It is truly enough said that a corporation has no conscience; but a corporation of conscientious men is a corporation with a conscience."

Thoreau's essay has had a powerful influence on history—from Gandhi to Martin Luther King. Many of the social reformers of our own day have seized upon Thoreau as their hero and have done things in his name that he would surely deplore. But Thoreau himself was typically American in that the individual and not the institution (or corporation) was at the center of his cosmos. He would be among the first to note that executives can no more hide behind their corporate charter than professors behind their tenure or officials behind City Hall. Ultimately, individuals must accept full responsibility for what their institutions do.

Among the values that define the American society, the idea of "individual responsibility" is central. Our cultural heritage focuses attention on the individual. We believe the individual is unique. It is in this context that we must recognize that the conflict between large institutions and individuals is the cause of much social unrest. The idea of large institutions moves against the American grain. This is not a matter of political orientation of the Right or Left. Rather it is a deep element in the American character. We have traditionally celebrated the individual and traditionally suspected the large corporation. The larger it is, the greater the suspicion.

This is one of the realities that public relations practitioners must face up to in the years ahead. We must find ways to reconcile the individual with the corporation and the corporation with the individual.

We cannot dispense with large corporations. Advanced technology and large corporations go hand in hand. There is still room for a variety of size and shape in corporate structures. Nor do I mean that large corporations and individual rights are in conflict. Large corporations often seem to represent vast accretions of power which can be dangerous. But large corporations also represent vast resources which can enrich the life of employees, to say nothing of shareholders and consumers. And that can be advantageous.

The healthy society is the society that offers its citizens the greatest number of options, including an intermix of large and small business institutions. Just as the founding fathers through the creation of a bicameral legislature attempted to distribute power equitably, so in our time we must find ways to encourage and protect the coexistence of large and small institutions.

PUBLIC RELATIONS AND
SOCIAL RESPONSIBILITY

One obvious objective for the public relations practitioner in the corporate environment is to make sure that business institutions perform as servants of people. Our tradition of individuality must be preserved within the context of a society that is no longer rural or agricultural, but technological and urban; in short, the kind of society in which the individual increasingly functions as part of social and economic groups without sacrificing his personal identity.

The major issues of the day identify the sources of conflict between individuals and institutions. There was a time when a corporation could hire, according to its needs, whomever it wanted and whenever it wanted. The criteria for employment were closely related to the efficient operation of the corporation. Today that is not acceptable. The corporation is expected to hire, train, and even educate members of all minority groups so that they can experience fulfillment in the mainstream of the economy.

There was a time when corporations made managers out of male employees and secretaries and clerks out of female employees. They did this in passive acceptance of the folklore that the male was the breadwinner and had a right to the higher-paying job.

Today the basic view about the roles of the sexes has altered dramatically and corporate practice is expected to reflect that fact. We are asked to respect women as individuals in the business environment and give them the same chance to advance as men.

There was a time when *caveat emptor* was the prime rule of the day. The corporation was expected to produce goods that it could market profitably and that was the limit of its obligation to the public. Today, the corporation is expected to recognize the "rights" of the buyer not only as a consumer but as a person. The corporation is expected to provide information that may affect the buyer's ultimate decision to purchase or reject a product.

The social pressure is not new. Corporations have *always* been subjected to pressures of one kind or another, political, social, economic. Today, however, there is an element that corporations have never had to confront before. The catch phrase is "future shock." Time has become compressed. The public demands not only that corporations be responsive, but that they respond immediately.

Public opinion seems to develop and coalesce more quickly today than ever before. Yesterday's stirrings become today's demands. The social analysts give several reasons for this change. The population is generally younger and young people tend to be action-oriented. The population is also better educated, and educated people tend to be more impatient. Perhaps the main reason for the contraction of time is the rapid transmission of information. News travels faster than ever and in much more vivid ways. A comparison of the information aspects of the Korean war with those of the Vietnam war will illustrate the social impact of the acceleration.

The Korean war, just twenty years ago, was a distant encounter half-way around the globe. The American public was no closer to it than the printed descriptions in daily newspapers or the words of the radio news report. Pictorial displays consisted largely of coverage in *Life* magazine. Ironically, *Life* is now defunct because it ceased to be as vivid or as fast as its principal competitor: television network news.

The Vietnam war, by way of contrast, took place before our very eyes. Those of us who thought the nation was protected from the ravages of war were wrong. The war invaded our living rooms. We literally watched it while it was going on. The impact was tremendous. How could it be otherwise? You actually saw the Vietnamese police chief put a bullet in his captive's head. You actually saw the planes dropping bombs. You actually saw your own soldiers shot in action. Mothers and wives sometimes saw their own sons or husbands. Rapid and visual communications thus became the overpowering factor, and time was compressed. More than anything else, this generated demands for instant action and increased the tension between hawks and doves.

Other examples are at hand. Compare the woman's suffrage movement in the nineteenth century with the woman's liberation movement of today. Susan B. Anthony and all the "Bloomer Girls" first started to insist on extending the right to vote to women in the 1850s. But it was not until 1920 that Congress ratified the Nineteenth Amendment to the Constitution.

In contrast, consider the instant impact of the woman's liberation movement. Indeed, one of the more activist groups calls itself the National Organization of Women, mainly, I suppose, so it can parade its demands under the acronym NOW. Moreover, social pressure groups like NOW have become adroit at using communications media to transmit their ideas and marshall public opinion in their favor.

This time compression between formulation of idea and expectation of response puts a special burden on the corporation. It means that what is opinion today may very well be legislation tomorrow. The time element between communication and law is of critical importance.

If we assume that all significant social demands will eventually be enacted into law, as has certainly been the case in such instances as truth-in-lending, pollution abatement, and equal employment opportunity, the critical question becomes: when should the corporation react to rising social pressures and start its own reforms? It has been observed that some companies appear regularly to anticipate social changes while others usually lag. Companies that anticipate change are far less vulnerable to criticism, and frequently derive economic benefits from their social responsiveness.

When to react to social change is a critical decision in which public relations can play a crucial role. Those corporations which have reacted promptly and voluntarily to social change are, by and large, those which are generally regarded as socially responsible—or, at the very least, responsive to social change. Those which are visibly laggard are usually identified and stigmatized as unresponsive to social needs and requirements.

Timing is important. The corporation that reacts too quickly may find itself penalized in relation to its competition, since a response to social change usually involves an added cost. On the other hand, the corporation that responds too slowly may also be penalized, since failure to act may carry economic penalties. Beyond this, the company that waits for legislation—waits, that is, for government to force it into compliance with public opinion—may suffer loss of reputation. And reputation is not just an abstraction; it affects sales.

In my own company we publish a quarterly report which, in one issue, examined the relationship between economic penalties and corporate social responsibility. The title of the report was "Ecology and Economics: the Joining of Issues." We said:

> The boundary between what's good for the environment and what's good for business is no longer quite so clear. An enterprise can no longer make sound economic decisions without taking into account the environmental consequences of its acts.
>
> The way a company copes with its pollution abatement problems affects its balance sheet, its profit and loss statement, its price-earnings ratio, its ability to raise capital at competitive rates, and maybe even its ability to sell its wares. In short, environmental protection is now a business reality, and environmental decisions have become economic ones, too.

Almost everything said in our report about pollution can also be applied to other issues of social discontent. Timing, therefore, is critical. At what point in time should the corporation start to react to anticipated social change? The public relations professional must enter this decision-making process. It is his responsibility to sensitize management to a ground swell of public opinion sufficiently significant to lead to social change. It is also his responsibility to participate in the policy determinations that will lead to an effective response.

The public relations executive is not the only officer in this critical position. Certainly, he is not the only executive who must relate to the public. The marketing vice president must relate to the customer; the financial vice president must relate to the financial community and the shareholders; the personnel officer must relate to employees. And the chief executive officer must relate to everyone. And woe be to any one of them who fails to recognize his multiple responsibilities!

DUTIES OF THE PUBLIC
RELATIONS OFFICER

But the duties of the public relations executive are more explicit and quite different. First, the public relations executive must, drawing on training and experience, understand the role of communications and know how to assess and respond to pressures for change. Second, the public relations executive is the one corporate officer charged with responsibility for maintaining contact with all the corporation's publics. The financial vice president focuses, almost exclusively, on the financial community and the shareholders. The marketing vice president focuses, almost exclusively, on the consumer. The personnel vice president focuses on employees. And the chief executive officer—while fundamentally interested in all these publics—has other important matters on his mind, which always seem more pressing than public relations.

So it comes down to the chief public relations officer. He sees it all. If he is competent, he sees the interrelationships. He sees that the consumer is also a shareholder. He sees that the shareholder may also be an employee. He sees that any one of these constituents of the corporation may also be a member of the local Izaak Walton league and the first to report that an effluent from the local plant is damaging his favorite fishing stream.

The public relations professional doing his job for the modern corporation fulfills a role that may be divided into four parts. First, he serves as the sensor of social change. He perceives those rumblings at the heart of the society that augur good or ill for his organization. In a way, he is like a radar operator. He gives the early warning. And, after detecting the yearnings and stirrings, he interprets the signals for the management team.

His perceptions, of course, cannot be founded on intuitive judgments and guesswork. He must be objective and analytical; he can bring the insights of the social sciences to bear upon his conclusions. In analyzing change, he must have a strong sense of reality. He must identify the situation as it really is, not as he imagines it to be. He must be able to separate enduring social changes from current fads.

The significance of this function can be illustrated from recent history. When the subject of automation first gained prominence, it was taken very seriously. Yet the social consequences of automation have not really shaken up the corporation. On the other hand, when Women's Liberation first became prime news, it was not really taken very seriously. Yet the consequences of the Women's Liberation movement have substantially affected many companies, and will soon affect all. It is the job of the public relations executive to make distinctions of this kind, so that he can advise his management: "You may think this stuff is nonsense, but it is a potentially powerful development. So let's start to make plans."

It is the job of the public relations executive, in his capacity as corporate sensor, to keep the attention of his management focused on the problem. How often have we heard businessmen who should know better claim that the critics of business are trying to "tear the system down." There are revolutionaries in the society, to be sure, but the current mood is more one of reform than of insurrection. Corporate managers have enough to do without going through the enervating motions of setting up straw men so they can knock them down.

Consider Ralph Nader, who hardly qualifies as the businessman's best friend. Even Nader declares that his objectives are not to destroy the system, but to make it work within the context of a free market economy. Nader is widely perceived as a populist and reformer, not launching a fundamental attack on capitalism or democracy.

The second role which the public relations man must fulfill is that of corporate conscience. One should not infer from this that a person must be a public relations professional to be sensitive, or that public relations people behave in ways that are either more moral or more in the public interest than executives with other responsibilities. But the assignment of serving as professional corporate conscience is not part of the job description of other executives. It *is* part of the job description of the chief public relations officer.

The third major role of the public relations professional is that of communicator. The tendency is to think that communication is his only role. That is hardly the case, although it is an important function.

Communications related to social issues have two aspects: internal and external. The emphasis is usually placed on external communications. Although the external communication function is important, it is, in many respects, secondary to and dependent upon an effective internal communication program. The lesson of Mrs. Jellyby reminds us not to focus on the distant problem before we resolve the one at hand.

What happens when a corporation responds to a social issue? Take minority employment, as an example, since it is a problem faced by almost every corporation in the United States. Suppose that a company adopts a policy of representational employment, founded on the proposition that a minority group should have representation in the company's work force equal to its share of the community population. Moreover, members of the minority group should be found in equitable numbers at all levels from the assembly line to the executive suite.

It is one thing to adopt a policy of that nature—and a number of companies have. But it is quite another thing to make it work, especially in a corporation doing business at several locations. The first task is to convince employees that the policy is not cosmetic. The people who must make an equal opportunity policy work are not at corporate headquarters. Most of them are in the field offices, in the divisions, and in the boondocks. If they don't believe the corporation means business, nothing will happen.

Then there is the matter of informing present employees that, as a result of the corporation's new policies, on a certain Monday morning they will be working alongside a newly eligible group of employees.

Internal communications must do more than tell or inform. Its primary function is to bring about understanding. The greater the sensitivity of an issue, the more important the need to communicate effectively. The internal communication program must make available to all affected employees the information that will enable them to understand not only what is happening and what they are expected to do about it, but why the new policies have been adopted. The initial message must be followed by ample continuing communication to indicate how the program is progressing.

The success of any new policy, no matter how well-intentioned, will depend to some considerable degree upon how well the corporation has handled its internal communication program. Indeed, it is not advisable to communicate any information about the new policy to the external community until the policy has taken root and is operating effectively.

Communicating with the public outside the corporation is an equally difficult undertaking. The problem for the public relations manager is to convince the public that the corporation is, indeed, being responsive. Critics on the outside looking in tend to question a corporation's sincerity. All too often they mistake a genuine response for a cosmetic response. When a corporation asks for time to make an adjustment, critics charge that management is stalling in the hope that it can somehow escape the need to act.

The fact is that the corporation is often slow to react. It is easy for the chief executive officer to issue a public statement that literally reverses a long-standing policy overnight. But it is just as difficult for the corporate executive to cause change by fiat as it is for the President of the United States, on certain matters, to mandate change. Policy statements are not enough.

If the corporation informs the public that it has a new policy, the response (unspoken, but not unreal) may very well be: "We're not interested in knowing about policy changes! We're interested in substantive acts. What have you really done?"

On the other hand, if the corporation neglects to inform the public that it has, in fact, changed an important policy, the public may accuse it of failing to take action. The function of external communication, there-fore, calls for a complex and subtle combination of description of policy commitment with supporting rationale, indication of implementation strat-egy, identification of targets to be accomplished, timing of action pro-grams, and persuasive portrayal of progress to date and promise of further progress ahead.

The fourth function of the public relations professional is to serve as corporate monitor—a function to be implemented in the spirit of an om-budsman. Obviously, he cannot serve as an ombudsman in the strict sense of the word. But since public relations is involved with public issues, there is a need for constant monitoring of corporate policies and programs to assure that they match public expectations. If the programs are not func-tioning, or if they fall short of expectations, it is his job to agitate for new programs and new policies.

Perhaps what we are saying is that social accountability is just an-other management art that corporations are going to have to learn. In the long run, the corporation which does the best job of managing its oper-ations will also do the best job of adapting to social needs.

CONCLUSIONS

In presenting my views I have developed certain fundamental ideas under eight main points:

1. A corporation cannot compensate for its inadequacies with good deeds. Its first responsibility is to manage its own affairs profitably.
2. Corporate social responsibility defies precise definition because no two corporations are exactly the same. We know a socially responsible company when we see one, but we can't completely describe it ahead of time.
3. We should not expect a corporation to adopt a leadership role in chang-ing the direction of a society. The corporation was simply not designated for that role.
4. Most of the pressures on corporations stem from two developments: the growing conflict between individuals and large institutions, and the compression of time.
5. The public relations function must separate issues from fads and work out a timetable for the corporation's response and adjustment.
6. In planning for social change, the role of the public relations executive is critical. He must judge which issues are real and which are merely fads, and he must help decide when the corporation should start to make reforms in policy.
7. The public relations executive has four main roles. He must be the

corporate sensor, the corporate conscience, the corporate communicator, and the corporate monitor.

8. The corporation must communicate to, and convince, the public that it is indeed being responsive to the changing expectations of society and that it is not merely stalling for time.

EDITOR'S COMMENTARY

The public relations function in the socially responsible corporation must undergo an important and difficult expansion. This will require knowledge and skills beyond those needed for the traditional corporate public relations assignment. In addition, a new organizational relationship must be established between the public relations function, specifically the chief public relations officer, and top-level executives responsible for policy decisions that affect all aspects of a corporation's public performance and posture, long-term as well as short-term.

The traditional public relations function has been largely concerned with transmitting two types of communications to selected external publics. One, large in volume and on occasion technically demanding, is product publicity, concerned with the preparation and media placement of news about company products and services. The other, growing in scale in recent years, is corporate publicity—the preparation and media placement of statements describing corporate policies, actions, and people. The former is closely related to advertising, part of the communication component of marketing programs. The latter is related to that often-maligned, though often useful, activity termed "image building." Depending on circumstances, the approach may be offensive in character—designed to transmit favorable news—or defensive—designed to portray inherently unfavorable news in a favorable manner. On occasion, the defensive objective may be to minimize all the way to total silence the reporting in news media of corporate activities or events about which management judgment is "the less said, the better."

Both of the traditional functions essentially put the director of public relations in a passive role. Here, he is told, is a new product or process or service: get a story out that will bring it to the attention of the appropriate audience. Here is a new corporate policy or action that should be publicized: prepare and place the appropriate story. Here is an action taken by the corporation, or not taken, about which the less said the better: take the necessary steps to ensure minimum exposure in the media. In all these familiar situations the initial news-generating decision is made by corporate and operating officials with, typically, little or no advance consultation with a public relations officer. The public policy and public posture aspects of corporate behavior have not, again typically, been the source of, or even a significant input to, management decisions. The national press reported, for example, that the General Motors decision to try to defuse Ralph Nader's first attack on GM product safety by finding a chink in his personal armor was made by a corporate lawyer; the devastatingly adverse publicity fallout was grossly embarrassing to top management, as well as costly in cash damages. Many other examples could be cited from the experience of other corporations, equally painful though less dramatic on the national scene.

The effective design and execution of socially responsible policies and programs by a growing number of companies in the years ahead will be greatly aided by opening up three new areas of activity for the public relations function. Two of these will require the public relations officer and his staff (and outside counsel, if employed) to take initiatives in communicating information to corporate management, interpreting the immediate and potential significance of the information, and offering counsel on the formulation of relevant policies and programs. This will involve a radical transformation of the public relations function, moving it from a passive to an active posture in relation to many aspects of corporate policy making, and, more than incidentally, calling for professional talent not previously required in the passive mode.

The first of the new areas is identified by Mr. Burson as the "sensor" role, the function of creating and operating an early warning system for identifying social changes and interpreting their meaning for corporate management. It is at least curious that while business leaders widely acknowledge that social changes can be as full of opportunity or threat as economic changes, very few corporations appear to have competent counsel on the fact and meaning of social change, while most corporations use both captive and outside professional help for economic forecasting and interpreting. As only one example of the danger inherent in this situation, many corporations directly within the field of influence of today's broad-based consumerism appear not to have grasped its power or significance for the way they will be compelled to operate in the future. Alert managements are becoming sensitive to this deficiency. The corporate public relations director must prepare to expand his operating scope from interpreter of the corporation to the public to interpreter of the public to the corporation. The more effective he becomes in performing this service at the leading edge of social change, anticipating rather than simply reporting, the greater will be his value to his chief executive officer.

The second of the new areas evolves directly from the first. As reporter and interpreter of social change, the public relations officer must participate from the outset in the formulation of fundamental corporate policies and programs. Beyond this, he must take responsibility for proposing policies and programs which, if adopted, will create effective responses to observed or anticipated social changes. It can be predicted with considerable confidence that in the years ahead a growing share of top-level policy decisions will take off from social considerations rather than from the familiar complex of marketing, technological, competitive, and financial considerations.

To make this kind of input to policy formation possible, it will be necessary to give the public relations function an organizational position within the top management group, with direct access to the chief executive officer. The public relations director cannot in the future, as so commonly in the past, wait outside the door while the top corporate staff determines policy for which, when reported to him after the meeting, he will be instructed to create appropriate expression and communicate to selected publics through the appropriate media. He should be in a position to say, "This is what we should do," not, as hitherto, "This is how to report to the public what you gentlemen have already decided to do." To play this role, the public relations officer needs recognition by his peers of the policy significance of his counsel, direct personal participation in policy formation, and the confidence and respect of his associates in the quality of his professional knowledge and skill.

The third new area is a simple extension of a familiar public relations activity: external communication. As pointed out in Chapter 3 (Creating a Management Environment for Socially Responsible Performance), the most difficult problems in implementing socially responsible policies and programs will be met in lower management ranks. Here a combination of ignorance, prejudice, hostility, and conflict between individual and corporate goals is likely to fuel an inherent skepticism about the sincerity of top management's commitment to social objectives. A carefully planned program of internal communications can be a valuable instrument for top management use in informing and motivating its subordinates. For certain types of socially responsible programs, such as those involving equitable treatment of members of minority groups in hiring, job assignment, and promotion, public relations professionals can also make an important contribution in communicating the facts about the new practices, together with the reasons for their adoption and their expected effects, and in developing educational materials and instruction in their use for supervisors who will meet the first shock of possible blue- and white-collar opposition.

Only a few in-house corporate public relations staffs—and probably equally few outside public relations professionals—are prepared by training and experience to execute the enlarged scope of responsibility described here. Traditional knowledge and skill in communication, the kind required to write a good story and place it in the right media, will need to be supplemented by sensitivity to social thrust and change that are transforming the interface between business and its surrounding world. Even more demanding will be the requirement to participate constructively in the formulation of corporate policy in a setting in which initiatives come from what many officers will regard as noneconomic considerations.

The educational implications of this new public relations responsibility are loaded with challenge. Schools of journalism and business, probably working together and drawing on other faculty resources as well, will have to design curricula giving heavy emphasis to social psychology, economics, the process of public opinion formation and influence, and political and governmental processes, in addition to the traditional content of journalism and business programs. This will require judicious pruning and, more important, creative reconstruction of traditional content to make room for the new materials.

If imaginative administrators and faculties of even a few schools move in this direction, we can anticipate over the decade ahead a growing attraction of careers in public relations for talented young men and women who, until now, have looked on this field with skepticism if not contempt.

A Program for Management: Imperatives and Options

Melvin Anshen

This concluding chapter summarizes the prospects for corporate social responsibility in terms of management choices between business options and public imperatives. Unless appropriate initiatives are forthcoming from the business side, in response to the expectations and demands of a society in transition to a new set of relationships with business, the available number and range of options will diminish and the imperatives will increase until they dominate the scene. Evidence is mounting that this outcome would be disadvantageous for both business and the society as a whole.–EDITOR

AMERICAN society is at a stage in its development when it needs, expects, and is beginning to demand a range of business behavior radically different from the previously accepted and approved pattern of business performance. The evolutionary process can be described as the creation of a new social contract between society and business. The initial expression of the contract is in perceived public needs and expectations; the ultimate expression of the contract is in legislative, administrative, and judicial acts. The causes of this fundamental social transformation are complex and their relative influence is far from completely clear. But the power of their thrust is beyond debate, as every corporate chief executive officer knows.

Business responses to the requirements of the new social contract present difficult, often new, management problems for corporate executives. The problems range from goals and values to operating details. The traditional profit-seeking enterprise system is being challenged and criticized in ways that cannot fail to concern all managers who know at first hand its vigor, dynamism, and creative power, and who respect, as even its severe critics do, its capacity for generating economic wealth. Concerning part of the business response to society's expectations and demands, there is no choice. Concerning another part, there are options which need careful analysis. With respect to both the imperatives and the options there are complex, if familiar, management problems of what to do and when and how.

Much of the debate about the nature of these problems and strategies of response is reflected in the pages of this book. The contributors are not in agreement about how to handle the problems, although they are in full agreement about the existence and character of the social change and the necessity for corporate executives to think through and implement effective responses. The contributors have reported their views in the chapters under their names; the views in this final chapter are those of the editor.

THE CASE AGAINST
CORPORATE SOCIAL RESPONSIBILITY

The magnitude of the change in the business role in our society that is implicit in the emerging social contract is probably most clearly seen by reviewing the case against the concept of corporate social responsibility. This case was set forth with clarity and vigor in *Fortune* for June, 1973 ("The Hazards of Corporate Responsibility" by Gilbert Burck):

1. The social performance of business is a hazy concept at best. It can't be measured in any useful fashion. Advocates of a "social audit" tool of socioeconomic accounting are playing meaningless games with subjectively-determined data.

2. To the extent that corporate executives are led by voluntary initiatives or governmental action to invest in such things as cleaner air and water, training of members of minority groups, and other desired programs, they are curtailing the investments that will underwrite rising productivity. And rising productivity is the only source of real social gains. If the productivity trend line flattens, the average living standard will re-

main constant or decline, unless, of course, people are willing to work longer hours.

3. Rising productivity is generated by investment in successful innovation and cost reduction. Since the drive for profitability is identical with the drive for lower costs, profit is a valid measure of business contribution to social welfare. One anonymous critic of the pressure for corporate social responsibility quoted by *Fortune* observed: "If the responsibility buffs really want to promote national welfare, they should be complaining that companies aren't making *enough* money."

Concern with social welfare, quite aside from its diversion of investment funds from productive uses, also threatens to divert the attention of corporate leaders from what should be their prime objective of aggressively pursuing higher profits. Here Milton Friedman is cited to the effect that this substitution of political or social considerations for market considerations interferes with rational allocation of resources and in the long run reduces economic efficiency.

4. If society is determined to compel business to perform noneconomic activities, such as setting up day-care centers for employees' children, it should enact legislation to force the burden equally on all companies. Social responsibility advocates have not recognized that corporations are not equally profitable, not equally in a position to carry nonproductive costs.

5. Even those companies that have the resources to support socially responsible programs may lack the skills required to decide what to do and how to do it. Managers are trained and experienced in responding to market mechanisms, not to social needs or political pressures.

6. Even the argument that business response to social needs enhances long-run profits and strengthens the possibility of survival of some kind of qualified free market is specious. Professor Henry Manne is cited to the effect that voluntary corporate altruism has never made a significant contribution to solving serious social problems: "Corporate social responsibility, a doctrine offered by many as a scheme to popularize and protect free enterprise, can succeed only if the free market is abandoned in favor of government controls."

7. Socially responsible behavior may even handicap business operations, whatever the cost. Operating managers in the middle ranks of corporate organizations often find their energies dissipated on unfamiliar assignments, even on efforts to execute responsibilities that directly challenge their sense of appropriate priorities in profit-oriented tasks. Inefficiencies tend to creep in as bewilderment spreads and morale erodes.

The case against corporate social responsibility has weight and seriousness and the issues it raises are central to the performance of the economic system. It deserves careful consideration and a reasoned response.

THE CASE FOR
CORPORATE SOCIAL RESPONSIBILITY

A central issue—probably the single most critical issue—in the debate is a judgment about the inevitability of the social thrust for a new contract with business. If the demand for business contributions to the removal or amelioration of various social ills is viewed as a temporary aberration, stimulated by a few unusually talented activists and sustained by certain passing social and political conditions that will not long endure, forthright opposition by corporate leadership can be persuasively presented as a rational strategy. At least some of the criticism cited above has relevance in such a setting. There can be no doubt, for example, that a large-scale corporate commitment to socially responsible programs is likely over the long pull to be accompanied by a somewhat slower growth in GNP than would otherwise be experienced.

On the other hand, if the contrary judgment is made that today's social pressures are indications of a society in transition to a new period with a broad commitment to values and goals previously cherished by only a few radicals, utopians, and other seekers of heaven on earth, a strategy of forthright opposition by the business community is a ticket to disaster for the private enterprise system. One thing we know for sure: what the majority of members of a democratic society want, they will ultimately get—sometimes at a price they would not have been willing to pay had they been aware of its magnitude. Neil H. Jacoby, former dean of the Graduate School of Management at UCLA and member of the Council of Economic Advisers under President Eisenhower, argues in his new book, *Corporate Power and Social Responsibility,* that business has no choice in the matter.[1] Political forces are just as real as market forces, and business must respond to them. Against this standard, commitments to support socially responsive programs must be assessed as profitable in the long run because they help to maintain an environment in which business can continue to function, even if at the cost of some curtailment in profits and, for society, some possible curtailment of the supply of traditional economic goods and services. Lurking beneath the surface of this point of view is the proposition that there is more to the good life than high and rising GNP, however equitably shared, and vital needs other than those served by advancing productivity created by unending innovation and gains in traditional input-output efficiency.

Those who share this view will conclude that the question addressed

[1] Neil H. Jacoby, *Corporate Power and Social Responsibility* (New York: Macmillan Publishing Co., Inc., 1973), pp. 194–196.

by the critics of corporate social responsibility is an empty issue. It is not a matter of whether business should accept any responsibilities to society other than its classic one to enhance the general welfare by driving for maximum profits within the law. Rather, the critical issues are identifying those socially responsible programs that are feasible for a specific corporation to undertake, those that are feasible only for some type of cooperative effort among the firms in a single industry or location, and those that require some kind of government intervention to which business can give valuable guidance, in its own and society's interest, if corporate leaders understand how to handle their relationships with governmental institutions and with the general public. Following these decisions of policy and strategy are many management problems related to the tactics and procedures of implementation.

In the context of this general conclusion, responses to the specific critical points included in the case against corporate social responsibility can be developed along the following lines:

1. The concept of the social performance of business is in most cases quite poorly defined; it must be defined in terms specific to an individual company. The notion of a generalized responsibility is not an operational concept, any more than is the idea of profit maximization. A company's goals, policies, and strategies must be uniquely determined in light of opportunities and threats sighted in its external environment, its internal resource strengths and weaknesses, and the values held by its principal managers. This is the foundation of all realistic planning in the traditional scope of corporate administration. In the same way and for the same reasons it must be the foundation of realistic planning in the sphere of corporate social responsibility. What is feasible should be uniquely determined within each business organization.

Some type of measurement system—using techniques drawn from managerial economics, cost/benefit analysis, and financial accounting—must be developed to support this decision process, and also to provide continuing audit of inputs and outputs to meet the requirements of realistic control and for internal and public reporting of accomplishments. Specific social audit techniques must be created. It is not an impossible task and some interesting beginnings are already on record. Inevitably, gross estimating will be incorporated in the audit process, particularly in the early stages. But financial and cost accounting, after many years of development and application (decades, even centuries, in the case of financial accounting), still rely in part on estimates and are not regarded as worthless tools of management because of the inclusion of estimates.

2. It cannot be denied that investment in environmental hygiene and many other socially responsible programs will, to some degree, curtail in-

vestment in new production technology and heightened production efficiency. This will mean some restraint on gains in productivity as traditionally measured. But part of the concept of a new social contract is a
commitment to innovative ideas about efficiency and productivity. When
critics of GNP as the absolute measure of social welfare urge improvement
in the quality of life along multiple parameters, they are in effect arguing
the case for new concepts of efficiency and productivity.

And, indeed, economic efficiency is not the only kind of efficiency we
have learned to value. It should not stretch our imaginations unduly to
consider the possibility of developing a national measure of social wealth
and welfare parallel to GNP, with the ultimate goal of accomplishing a
reasonable balance between the two. Reinforcement for this notion can
be found in the observation that reduction of some of the traditional economic costs of business accomplished by transferring costs to the general
public—by environmental contamination, underemployment of human
talent, and other familiar means—is not an acceptable strategy for increasing the economic efficiency of business operations.

3. Broadening the measure of business performance does not diminish
the necessity for earning profits. An unprofitable business is not a social
asset by any measure. Only a profitable business can generate the resources and provide the management skills to undertake socially responsible programs beyond the traditional contributions of employment and the
production of goods and services to meet market demand. However, new
criteria of profitability will evolve that encompass both economic return
and social return.

This is a less revolutionary concept than the critics of corporate social
responsibility want us to believe. Throughout the corporate world for
many years there has been a widespread, if unpublicized, acceptance of
standards of satisfactory earnings, rather than profit maximization. In a
new economic environment, this view will find broad support. But the real
issue is not all that dramatic. No socially responsible management should
undertake programs that put its operation at a significant cost disadvantage
relative to its competitors. Further, at least some socially desirable programs will also turn out to be profitable (as isolated examples even now
attest). Finally, added costs, when distributed equitably among competitors, will ultimately, like all other costs, be at least partially reflected in
prices and paid by customers.

4. The critics' point on equitable sharing of nonproductive costs is
well taken, as noted above. Legislation has already been enacted aimed at
this objective in product safety, environmental protection, and other areas,
and we can anticipate more. Contrary to past corporate practice, however,
managers should recognize the importance to their companies as well as

to the society of participating constructively in the design of legislation and related administrative procedures. The end in view should be not simply legislation equitably applicable to all competitors, but legislation that uses technology and business systems in the interest of effective and efficient accommodation of business and social goals. The danger inherent in business assumption of an adversary posture when government intervention is both desirable and inevitable has been commented on at several points in this book.

5. The critics' observation is correct that few managers now possess the training, experience, and skill required to develop and administer socially responsible programs. Effective implementation of responsibilities imposed on business under the emerging social contract will extend the demands placed on managers. This is not an unusual development, however. The moving edge of technology in industry, including information and decision technology, has repeatedly extended requirements for management knowledge and competence in recent years. As might have been expected, the challenge was met successfully by many executives, and not by some. There appears no reason to anticipate a significantly different response to this new challenge. Probably more critical will be the development of a motivational structure for operating managers that will reorient their attitudes and their priorities. This may well be the most important contribution a chief executive officer can make to the full implementation of corporate social responsibility.

6. The charge that corporate social responsibility can be implemented only if the free market is abandoned in favor of government control recalls the fears of some business leaders in the early 1930s that the enactment of legislation providing for collective bargaining, social security, unemployment compensation, and other measures would translate private capitalism into an American socialism devoid of energy and capacity for creative innovation, while also shrinking profits and destroying incentives to invest.

The changes collectively labeled "New Deal" certainly brought about a dramatic transformation in many business practices, but it would be hard to find support in the record of the following decades for the dire predictions of pessimistic critics. There is certainly a different capitalism today than in the time of Calvin Coolidge and Herbert Hoover. There is a different society, too. But for whom is it a less desirable system?—or one less open to business success based on the effective deployment of superior technology, management skill, and service of customer needs and wants? Has it not always been the case that those who understand and operate effectively in the status quo prefer its continuance to any substantial changes that may challenge their ability to continue their successful per-

formance? The preference is understandable. We need to remind ourselves, however, that the profits are always being eroded out of steady-state
situations and that the greatest business successes have been recorded by
those managers who have been the first to predict and exploit change. We
also need to grasp the constant shift of social values and priorities, including those that affect society's economic engine. And finally, if there is
indeed in process of formation a new social will concerning business performance, a positive response by corporate leaders would appear preferable
to blunt negativism. Indeed, it is only through such a response by those
who thoroughly understand and cherish the advantages of the free market
that most of its values are likely to be retained while other social needs
and wants are also met.

7. The last point in the critics' case, as noted in paragraph 5 above, is
valid and important. The values, attitudes, and skills of operating managers, especially in middle and junior levels, will be critical factors throughout the implementation process. This area is likely to be the real testing
ground of top management's sincerity in accepting the concept of corporate
social responsibility. It is worth observing, on the other side of the issue,
that an increasing proportion of college and business school graduates
entering management ranks bring with them attitudes toward corporate
social performance that are critical of a concentration solely on traditional
economic outputs regardless of social costs. Given the opportunity and the
incentive to apply their beliefs, training, and growing skill to a broader and
more balanced corporate performance, they are likely to respond constructively. A changed business image will in time also help in recruiting some
of the talented young men and women who have been turned toward other
careers in recent years by their perception of a business system that was
heedlessly destructive of its environment, disinterested in the problem of
minorities suffering from gross inequities in employment and opportunities
for advancement, and indifferent to the problems of an industrialized urban
society.

IMPERATIVES INCREASE—OPTIONS DECREASE

The imperatives acting on business management will increase in the
years ahead and the available options will decrease. The new social contract for business will be fulfilled, at least in general terms, during the coming decade or two. To the extent that initiatives are not forthcoming on
the business side, they will almost certainly be generated on the government side by social pressures acting through the political process to create
legislative and administrative responses. This is not a prediction with a

low order of probability. Precisely this transfer from business options to government imperatives has occurred or is presently occurring in a number of familiar areas of social concern, including environmental pollution, product safety, and equal employment opportunity. The trend is clear and there is no reason to anticipate its reversal, if business continues to be unresponsive to society's needs.

From both the business and the social viewpoint this would be an unfortunate development. With some confidence we can predict that changing the rules of the game in the absence of business initiatives and participation is likely to result in gross inefficiencies in resource utilization accompanied by high economic and social costs, frictions among social groups, and mounting hostility toward a business system that has lost general public confidence. None of this is necessary. Most of it can be prevented by appropriate initiatives on the business side to exercise options before they are displaced by imperatives.

The options available to business are not limited to those identified as feasible for individual corporations within resource and profit constraints, or to those available through cooperative or coordinated actions with industry or geographic business consortiums to the extent permitted by law. They also include timely and constructive initiatives by business to propose governmental intervention where private action is not feasible or effective, and to participate in its design. A positive approach by business leaders who understand the truly revolutionary character of this period of social change in which we are immersed and who see the value to business and society of exercising private options before they convert to public imperatives will go far to assist society in accomplishing its goals effectively and efficiently. It will also help to preserve the dynamism and the economic, social, and political freedom of the private enterprise system.

Index

Budget (*cont.*)
  See also Cost-benefit analysis; Measurement and control; Social audit
Burck, Gilbert, 240–41
Burton, John C., 125
Business behavior, *see* Corporation and corporate existence
Business-government relations, *see* Government actions and programs
Business and Society Review, 5–6, 77
Business organizations
  accountability of, 131–32, 137–40, 234
  function and structure, 24–29, 31–36
  global, 28–29, 61–62
  and politics, 27, 29, 62, 70, 183–88, 190–94
  social demands on, 3, 15, 19–20, 29–30, 36, 42–43, 59–64, 130–31, 134, 229–30
  social expectations of, 42–43, 131
  See also Corporation and corporate existence
Business Week, 59

Cahill, William T., 67
Cantril, Hadley, 122
Caples, William, 213
Casey, William J., 131
CGIL, 217
CGT, 217
Chaikin, Sol C., 207
Chamber of Commerce of U.S., 36, 71
  Education Committee of, 188
Chaplin, Charlie, 204
Childhood Immunizations, Action Committee for, 52–53
China, 129, 162
CIO, *see* AFL-CIO
Citibank, 140, 141
Civil Rights Act of 1964, 214
Clayton Antitrust Act, 210
Clean Air Act, 216
Cleary, Catherine, 9, 10
Cole, David, 212, 213
Collective bargaining, *see* Labor, organized
College Retirement Equities Fund (CREF), 146
Commodity Credit Corporation, 34

Common Market and Common Market Commission, 202, 217
Communist Manifesto, 185
Communist unions, 218
Competition and competitive enterprise, 3, 6, 7, 31, 63, 76, 154
  and coordinated social programs, 19–21, 31, 73, 157–59
  and direct controls, 65, 66, 70, 94, 241, 244–45
Conference Board, 133
Congress, U.S., 129, 200
  General Accounting Office of, 119, 122
Connecticut, State of, 143–44
Conservation, *see* Environment and environment problems
Consumers and consumerism, 3, 25, 63*n*, 67, 94, 106, 107, 236
Control, *see* Measurement and control
Converse, Philip, 122
Coolidge, Calvin, 185, 245
Corcoran, Thomas G., 68
Corporate Power and Social Responsibility, 242
Corporate Social Audit, The, 100
Corporation and corporate existence
  behavior standard for, 5–8, 9–12, 15–16, 133–35, 169, 239–40
  charitable giving of, 76, 136, 154, 164
  as conservative institution, 225–27
  dual function and responsibility of, 42–43, 178–79
  as economic instrument, 59–60, 61
  and foreign policy, 61–62
  morality of, 10, 134
  organizational changes in, 37–38, 136
  and political process, 183–98
  social intelligence system of, 142–43
  social responsibility of, defined, 2, 95–100, 225, 234
  survival of, 93–94, 180
  and time element, 228–30
  See also Business organizations; Public relations
Cosmetic effect, *see* Tokenism
Cost-benefit analysis, 13–15, 20, 75–91
  business application of, 82–84
  and cost overruns, 79–80
  decision-making and, 76–77

STUDIES OF THE MODERN CORPORATION

Columbia University Graduate School of Business